15-99

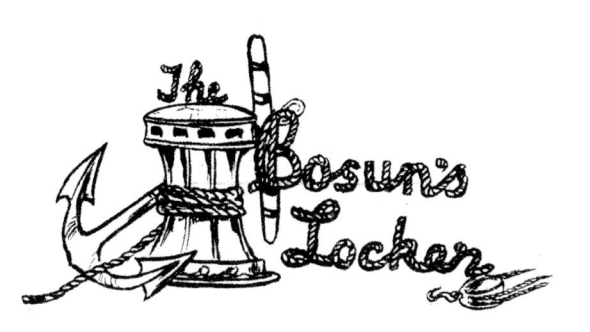

The Bosun's Locker Stan Hugill

Published by David Herron Publishing, Wellington Road, Todmorden, Yorkshire OL14 5DY
in conjunction with The Chantey Cabin, Ribble Avenue, Freckleton, Lancashire PR4 1RH

This paperback first edition published 2006
Copyright © The Estate of Stan Hugill and Spin Magazine

All rights reserved. No part of this publication, including text, music and illustrations, may be reproduced or stored in a retrieval system. No part may be transmitted in any form, or by any means electrical including the internet, digital and electronic media, mechanical, photocopying, recording or otherwise without prior written permission of the publisher.

ISBN: 9780954068240
0954068240

Designed and typeset by Bryan Ledgard   www.bryanledgard.com
Printed in Great Britan by Henry Ling Limited, The Dorset Press, Dorchester DT1 1HD

The Bosun's Locker

by
Stan Hugill

The Bosun's Locker Stan Hugill

Dedication

I would like to take this opportunity to thank all those people who have made possible the publication of this book in honour of Stan's memory.

Bronwen Hugill-Gowers

Editorial

When we embarked on this journey nothing could prepare us for the myriad ways in which Stan Hugill affected the lives of so many.

Stan carried on the family tradition of going to sea as a young man at the start of a rich and fascinating life.

He was the last working shantyman to sail the high seas under sail, an artist, fluent in Japanese and other languages, a POW during the war, Bosun at the Outward Bound School in Aberdovey, and had a pub named after him in France! Above all a husband and father and friend to all who knew him.

Once things were underway the stories came flooding in – everyone was keen to tell us of the time they spent with him and what they learned from him about ships, sailing and maritime music.

From English folk clubs and pubs, to festivals in Seattle, San Francisco and Maine in the United States, to appearing before thousands of cheering students in Poland during the '80s, he left many vivid memories and an enduring legacy.

We truly believe that without this man so much of this music would now be lost in the mists of time – so we all owe him a great deal.

Our thanks to Ali Cran for polishing our efforts at proofreading and editing, to Bryan Ledgard for his meticulous and imaginative layout and design, and to everyone else who has helped to get Stan's work published.

Above all, our thanks to Stan's widow Bronwen Hugill-Gowers, and to Beryl and Tony Davis and Eunice Williamson of *Spin* magazine for their kind permission to publish the material in this book.

**Ken and Jan Lardner
and David Herron**

The Bosun's Locker Stan Hugill

Contents

	page			page
Foreword by Beryl Davis	6	Vol 4 No 1	Another Folk Process	86
Introduction by Stan Hugill	8	Vol 4 No 2	Folk Song Festival in Hawaii	89
Vol 1 No 4 A Bosun's Locker	12	Vol 4 No 3	Shanghaied!	92
Vol 1 No 5	14	Vol 4 No 4	The Press Gang	95
Vol 1 No 6	16	Vol 4 No 5	Shanty and Seasongs Discs	99
Vol 1 No 7	19	Vol 4 No 6		102
Vol 1 No 8	20			
Vol 1 No 9 Forebitters	22	Vol 5 No 1	Yo Ho 'n' a Bottle of Rum	107
Vol 2 No 1	26	Vol 5 No 2	Songs of the Wooden Walls	112
Vol 2 No 2 The Speed of the Shanty	30	Vol 5 No 3		119
Vol 2 No 3	33	Vol 5 No 4	Women at Sea	123
Vol 2 No 4 Pumping Ship Songs	37	Vol 5 No 5	Humour at Sea	128
Vol 2 No 5 Give us a Sea Shanty	40	Vol 5 No 6	"Thar She Blows" Leviathan!	132
Vol 2 No 6	42			
Vol 2 No 7	45	Vol 6 No 1		136
Vol 2 No 8 The Repertoire of the Singing Sailor	48	Vol 6 No 2		140
Vol 2 No 9	50	Vol 6 No 3	Songs of the Ratcliffe Highway	142
Vol 2 No 10	52	Vol 6 No 4	Songs of the Ratcliffe Highway 2	150
Vol 3 No 1 Sailors Called a Spade a Spade	54	Vol 6 No 5	Songs of the Ratcliffe Highway 3	155
Vol 3 No 2	57	Vol 6 No 6	Songs of the Ratcliffe Highway 4	160
Vol 3 No 3	61			
Vol 3 No 4	63	Vol 7 No 2	Some More Songs of Jack Ashore	167
Vol 3 No 5 Songs of American Sailormen	67	Vol 7 No 1	Songs of the Ratcliffe Highway	172
Vol 3 No.6 Liverpool Sailor Songs	69			
Vol 3 No 7	73	Vol 7 No 3	Shipboard Music and Dancing	177
Vol 3 No 8 Reflections on Refrains	77			
Vol 3 No 9 A Shanty Without a Chorus is Like an Egg Without Salt	81			
Vol 3 No 10	84			

		page			page
Vol 7 No 4		181	Vol 9 No 1		202
Vol 7 No 5/6		185	Vol 9 No 2	Fresh Finds in Shanty Research	205
Vol 8 No 1	Blood Red Roses	187	Vol 9 No 3	Fag-ends	211
Vol 8 No 2	The Limejuice Act	188	Vol 9 No 4	Were Shanties Ever Sung Aboard Whalers?	216
Vol 8 No 3		192			
Vol 8 No 4		196	Rolling Down to Old Maui		221

The Bosun's Locker Stan Hugill

Foreword

In October 1961, the first (duplicated) edition of *Spin*, all 300 copies of it, was launched upon the world by a handful of enthusiasts from the Spinners Folksong Club. This all happened at my address and following their burst of hectic activity they disappeared never again to return. The post brought some subscriptions and the pricking of my conscience at nothing happening caused me to take on the production of the second and some following issues but not using my name, in the hope the original members would reappear. Finally, I accepted the situation and with the assistance of my friend Eunice Williamson, who was my next-door neighbour, took over the editorship of *Spin* myself.

Then followed some of the most interesting years of our lives, taking the magazine from ancient typewriter and duplicator to offset litho and computer. At the time the printer himself was just going into 'offset' and we learned together – the hard way – Polycell is definitely not the thing to use for pasting up! We were also lucky enough to have some most interesting people writing for us. Leslie Haworth, Paul Oliver, Leslie Shepard, Johnny Handle among others all offered vibrant material and of course Stan Hugill whose *Bosun's Locker* appeared in the fourth (still duplicated) issue and stayed with us over the years until the end. A friendship of which we treasure the memory.

Stan Hugill was born in the old coastguard station at Hoylake, Cheshire early in the 1900s. He came from a seagoing family, both his father and grandfather having served their time at sea sang sea songs, some of which were written down in a book which later came into Stan's possession. Stan was about four years old when he first went aboard a sailing ship with his father, while the family was based for a while at the coastguard station at Anstruther West in Scotland. It was a Norwegian barque loaded with pit props and his father was investigating an allegation of cruelty regarding the flogging of a cabin boy.

Later the Hugill family returned and remained in the Liverpool area and it was from that port that Stan joined his first ship. It was a steamer and ended up shipwrecked off the coast of New Zealand – so much for his first trip – Stan thereupon moved into the world of sail and shanty on the 'Saucy Kate' coasting by sail around New Zealand.

The 1920s and '30s brought many ships and adventures trading by sail around the Pacific; sailing around Cape Horn for the first time in the world's largest sailing ship the 'Gustav', shipwrecked for a second time when the last British square-rigged, four masted barque the 'Garthpool' struck the African coast; sailing on a Bluenose ship in the West Indies and seeking the treasure of Caprtain Morgan, the famous buccaneer, aboard a ship chartered by the National Geographic Society of America. It was in those early years that Stan heard and learned so many shanties and sea songs just when sail seemed to be coming to a close. Supplemented by the notebook in which his father and grandfather had written down their songs he became interested in the many forms and variations of this music.

After spells ashore building roads in New

Zealand, hoboeing in Australia and working on a sugar plantation in Trinidad, Stan finally went back into steam in about 1936. After a number of trips he settled with the Blue Funnel Line. It was aboard the Blue Funnel ship 'Automedon' off Sumatra, one day's run from Penang, that Stan was taken prisoner of war by the German raider 'Atlantis' on 11th November 1940. This event has at least one book and a couple of television programmes about it and is an adventure in itself, as are Stan's tales about life in a Prisoner of War camp where he remained until released by the Armoured Division in 1945.

After the war, Stan became bosun at the Outward Bound School at Aberdovey, North Wales, where he married Bronwen and together they brought up a couple of sons, Philip and Martin, who continue singing the songs their father collected. The book "Shanties from the Seven Seas" published in 1961 was the first of several books which caused quite a stir and opened many eyes regarding sea shanties.

When writing for *Spin*, Stan often sent us material he had not been able to fit into his book or something which had turned up later. He once said he though of *Spin* as a sort of supplement where he could keep adding his latest discoveries or explain something he thought may not have been made clear and we at *Spin* are proud to have printed his words. It is sad to think that this whole world of knowledge, this whole way of life could become lost as time passes. Most of all, Stan said that songs which are not sung, die! So sing them!

Beryl Davis
Spin Publications
August 2006

The Bosun's Locker Stan Hugill

Introduction

Stan Hugill was born in the old coastguard station, Hoylake, and spent his school days in Bootle. He went to sea in steam, was shipwrecked in New Zealand, and there joined a small wooden sailing ship, which was the start of his interest in sail and shanties. After an adventurous life, which included four years as a prisoner of war, he ended his seafaring life with the Blue Funnel Line of Liverpool. Stan is now giving the benefit of his experience at the Outward Bound School.

At the close of the sailing ship era the shanty – that rousing work song of the deepwater sailor – was in danger of following the webbed feet of the Dodo. Octogenarian Jack Tars had fragmentary bits to offer; and the J.F.S.S. (Journal of the English Folk Song Society) was a museum-like repository of these work songs. Everywhere it was cold print and bits and pieces. Then came the period of bold basso-profundos and baritones in dickey bows and boiled shirts with full orchestras endeavouring to resuscitate them. They did their best, but they failed to understand the fact that the shanty had nothing in common with the robust pirate and Dibdinian sea-songs of the Victorian parlours. Too much striving to put an operatic quality into the notes and not emphasis on the words; no breaking of the voice, no free time in the solos, and last but not least too much camouflage. All this helped to prevent the shanty returning to its pristine glory.

Then came the modern 'folk song revival' – a true stimulant to say the least. Even the adopted rig of the singers, jerseys and dungarees, or, if you prefer it, sweaters and jeans, brought atmosphere. The 'beat' generation too was one which could readily adapt itself to the singing of shanties, for the simple reason that a good 50% of these sailor work songs emanated from Negro singing and are full of beat.

"'Tis impossible to sing a shanty without the feel of a rope or a capstan bar in one's mit" was a cry of old shellbacks, but although it *is* impossible to recapture the full atmosphere of shantying without having the background of canvas and hemp, the effort being made nowadays is, in my opinion, the finest ever achieved, and many landlubbers and landlubber groups are now producing shanties almost as good and true as they were in their native salt – all praise to ye.

So long as these young folk singers carry on as they are, remembering

- A strident voice is preferable to a gentle one.
- Free time in the solos is a true part of shantying.
- Strict time in the refrains is essential, and
- Let's hear the words

– and what words! Then I'm sure thousands of shellbacks from Fiddlers Green will in ghostly voices echo these sentiments of mine!

Stan Hugill

The Bosun's Locker Stan Hugill

Vol. 1 No. 4A
The Bosun's Locker

A bosun's locker is a place aboard ship where all sorts of nautical paraphenalia is stowed.
I am a bosun and in my locker I have all sorts of bits and pieces which may be of interest to folk song enthusiasts. I doubt very much whether my locker is Davy Jones' unfathomless, but I do aim to supply this with shanty, forebitter and general sea-song, tidbits for the next few issues of *'SPIN'* at least. If I fail in the attempt please don't hang me from the yardarm!

My book *'Shanties from the Seven Seas'* has been called by reviewers 'definitive' meaning 'there ain't no need for further shanty books this one tells all'. Strangely enough I disagree. I've been gathering fresh material ever since the publishing of the book. Naturally I will make much use of the material already made public through the book, but I also hope by means of this corner to put into print items as yet unprinted.

First I would like to give you the gen on the differences between the Shanty and other classes of sea-song.

A shanty was without exception a **work song,** used for heaving and hauling; seamen would **heave** at the capstan and the pumps, and **haul** on the innumerable ropes. It was divided into two main categories:

The capstan song, and
b) The halyard song.
The capstan song was subdivided into: -
a) The windlass, or anchor capstan shanty,
b) The capstan song, sung when doing a job-o-work other than heaving the anchor.

The former song was usually of a slower tempo than the latter. *Shenandoah*, *Santiana* and *Rio* were typical anchor songs, with *Sally Brown* and *Johnny Come Down to Hilo* for general capstan work such as setting sail with a small crew or one watch, sheeting home the sails, or warping the ship alongside the pier. The halyard shanty, used for hoisting sails, was sub-divided into:
a) Long pulls
b) Foresheeters
c) Bunt-stowers
An example of a) is *Ranzo*, of b) *Hanging Johnny* and of c) *Paddy Doyle's Boots*. Yanks called a) long drags and b) short drags.

For pumping it was considered that any old sea-song would do, so long as it had a good grand chorus. This, however, only applied to the latter day Downton Pump, which was worked by heaving on two large wheels. With the earlier brake-pumps the songs had to be more *functional* – timed to the upward and downward jerk of the long levers or brakes. This also applied to the old-

Most ancient form of windlass (15th century) and still used abouard Chinese junks.

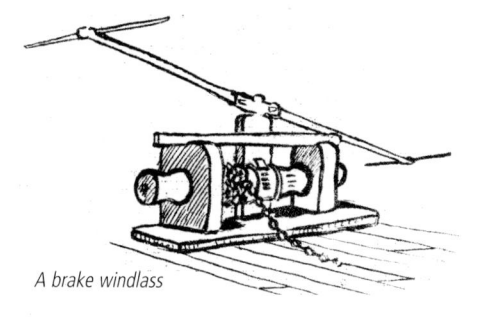

A brake windlass

The Bosun's Locker Stan Hugill

time brake-windlass used for anchor work. In the case of the capstan, since it was only a steady walk-around any song – even one from shore side could be used as long as it had a good grand chorus.

This brings me to a point of interest that I haven't mentioned in my book, something which dawned on me after a study of Scandinavian shanty books.

The *shape* of shanties such as *Sally Brown*, *Heave Away Me Johnnies*, and the Yankee version of *Leave Her, Johnny, Leave Her* (the version popular with folk singers), i.e. two solos and two intermittent refrains, is strictly speaking a *hauling song shape*. This has worried many collectors, including myself. In other words, the songs mentioned don't look like capstan shanties; if we didn't know for certain we would be inclined to class these with *Blow The Man Down* and other halyard shanties.

Perhaps the Scandinavian classification of heaving and pumping shanties will help to clarify this?

Heaving Shanties
   a) Bradspil (brake-windlass) shanties
   b) Gangspil (capstan) shanties

Pumping Shanties
   a) Nikkepumps (brake or nodding pump) shanties
   b) Hjulpumps (wheel or Downton pump) shanties

It is obvious that the Scandinavians divide both their heaving and pumping songs into
a) Those with a *jerky* motion, and
b) Those with a *rolling* motion.

The jerkiness of brake pushing at the

A capstan

brake-windlass (bradspil) and brake-pumps (nikkepumps) necessitates a word to *push* on, as in the halyard shanty a word is needed to *pull* on. Take *Sally Brown*, originally a brake-windlass shanty:

<u>Sal</u>ly Brown she's a <u>bright</u> mu<u>la</u>tter
Chorus: <u>Way</u>-ay, <u>Hay</u>-ay, <u>Roll</u> an' <u>go</u>!
 <u>She</u> drinks <u>rum</u>, an' <u>chews</u> ter<u>bak</u>ker
Chorus: <u>Spend</u> my <u>mon</u>ey on <u>Sally</u> <u>Brown</u>!

The up and down movements of the brakes come on the accented words. When the capstan came into being this jerkiness was jettisoned, because, instead of standing in one position pushing long levers up and down, the men now marched round an upright barrel merely pushing the bars steadily in front of them. The older form of *Santiana* is another brake-windlass song; once the capstan arrived a grand chorus was added.

In the case of the pumps this also occurred. The early brake-pump needed jerky four-liner shanties like *Leave Her, Johnny, Leave Her*. When the Downton pump came on the scene with its rotary, instead of jerky, movement a grand chorus was added, and its jerkiness rounded off to suit wheel turning.

Before the days of the capstan and wheel pump songs like *John Brown's Body* with its grand chorus could not have been used by sailormen, hence I feel certain that the four-liner form of the heaving shanty is by far older. This is something which until now has never been explained in print. If we take this reasoning as true it means that the four-line heaving songs like *Shenandoah*, *Lowlands* and *Stormalong* have fair antiquity, whereas *Rio Grande*, *Sacramento* and *Johnny Come Down to Hilo* are of quite modern growth. And heaving shanties with two forms such as *Leave Her Johnny* and *Santiana* are old in the short form, and newer when the grand chorus is added. If this theory is correct, then a doubt will be thrown on the antiquity of the tune, if not the words of *A-Rovin'*. But perhaps the grand chorus of 'A-rovin', a-rovin' since rovin's been my r-u-i-n' is a later accretion.

The Bosun's Locker Stan Hugill
Vol. 1 No. 5

I have suggested that the four-line solo, refrain, solo, refrain, shanty is the true and original shanty-form, in the heaving as well as the hauling song, the grand chorus being a fairly modern addition, and that this theory upsets somewhat the well established belief that *A-Rovin'* in the form we now have is a shanty having great age. Of course it may have been sung *ashore* in this form, but certainly not as a work song at the brake-windlass or pump.

In the case of the text however the word 'antiquity' perhaps <u>can</u> be applied. All shanty and folk song books declare that the bawdy words of the shanty – 'I put my arm around her waist, on her knee, thigh,' and so on, are to be found in the play the *'Rape of Lucrece'* by Thomas Heywood in the form of a song, common in the Elizabethan period, known as a 'catch'. However, the song in question is not the accepted form of catch – the 'Oh, Hell, oh, Hell oh Helen I love you' sort of thing. Although all collectors refer to this song when speaking or writing of *A-Rovin'* not one has had the audacity to put it in print – so here it is and I have kept the punctuation and vague spelling of the original text.

Two of the cast – Valerius and Horatius – wish to know from the clown what happened to the fair Lucrece when assaulted by Sextus, but the clown is bashful and will not say a thing, so they persuade him to sing about the incident.

Valerius: Did he take the fair Lucrece by the toe man?
Clown: Toe man.
Valerius: I man.
Horatius: And further did he strive to go man?
Clown: Go man.
Horatius: I man.
Clown: Ha, ha, ha, man, Fa ferry, derry, derry, downe ha fa derry dino.
Valerius: Did he take the fair Lucrece by the heel man?
Clown: Heel man.
Valerius: I man.
Clown: Ha, ha, ha, ha, ha, man.
Horatius: And further did he striue to feele man?
Clown: Feele man.
Horatius: I man.
Clown: Ha, ha, ha, ran ha fa derry etc.
Horatius: Did he take the lady by the shin man?
Clown: Shin man.
Valerius: I man.
Clown: Ha, ha, ha, ha man.
Horatius: Further than that would he be man?
Clown: Be man.
Horatius: I man.
Clown: Ha, ha, ha, ha man hey fa derry etc.
Valerius: Did he take the lady by the thigh man?
Clown: Thigh man.
Valerius: I man.
Clown: Ha, ha, ha, ha man.
Horatius: And now he came it somewhat nigh man.
Clown: Nie man.
Valerius: But did he do the tother thing man?
Clown: Thing man?
Valerius: I man.
Clown: Ha, ha, ha, ha man.
Horatius: And at the same time had he a fling man?
Clown: Fling man.

The Bosun's Locker Stan Hugill

Horatius: I man.
Clown: Ha, ha, ha, ha man hey fa derry etc.

A friend of mine called this type of folk song 'anatomical progression' and apparently not only did the sailor pinch the idea to fit it to *A-Rovin'*, but the same theme is to be found in *Gently Johnny my Jingalo*:

> I put my hand upon her toe
> The fair maid is a lily-o
> I put my hand all on her toe
> Says she to me do you want to go?

And other folk songs, not to mention the modern song *Roll me over in the clover* popular during the last war. It would seem to me that the catch in *'The Rape of Lucrece'* is the sire of a great family of songs stretching from 1640 until today.

Next month I would like to show tunes and variants of that ever-popular windlass song *Santiana*, from several aged four-line versions to the more modern type.

The Bosun's Locker Stan Hugill
Vol. 1 No. 6

The four-liner brake-windlass and brake-pump shanty *Santiana* is thought to have come into being shortly after the war between Mexico and the United States, most versions being more or less unhistorical accounts of the battle of Molina del Rey (Buena Vista) in 1847 between the American general Zachary Taylor and the Mexican general Santa Ana. Although the shantyman sang of General Taylor running away, and Santa Ana gaining the day, in fact the reverse ocurred; the fight being the first success the Yankees had in revenge for the terrible blow they received at the hands of Santa Ana at the Alamo. This halting of the so-far victorious Mexicans in a mountain pass spelt the finish of the Mexican War and Santa Ana shortly went into exile. Taylor later became president of the United States.

Most of the tunes of *Santiana* seem to be of mixed Irish and Nego origin, and the usual opening bars and the first refrain ars similar to the opening bars of *Whip Jamboree*, and the final refrain bears close resemblance to the last bars of *Clear the track Let the Bulgine Run* which in turn is almost identical in entirety with the ancient Irish folk song *Shule Agra*. Now if, as has been suggested, the tune of *Santiana* was composed of bits and pieces of *Jamboree* and *Clear the Track* obviously these two grand chorus songs are the older. And we do know that *Clear the Track* is almost 100% *Shule Agra* – a shore song of great age, all of which upsets my theory of four-liners being the oldest form of shanty – or does it? Well perhaps I can wangle out of this!

There were of course many alternate solo-refrain shanties which ran to more than four lines – six, eight and even more alternating solos and refrains are to be found in such shanties as *John Cherokee*, *Bunch of Roses*, *Ekidumah* etc. Taking this for granted then, and noting that the grand choruses of both *Jamboree* and *Clear the Track* have the same staccato-ness as their verses, it is quite possible that early shantymen sang the whole shanty in the solo-refrain type manner viz.

Solo: Oh, the smartest packet ye can find
Chorus: Ah, ho way ho, are ye mos' done?
Solo: Is the ol' Wildcat of the Swallowtail Line,
Chorus: So clear the track let the bulgine run!
Solo: Timme high rig-a-jig in a jauntin'car.
Chorus: Ah, ho way ho, are ye mos' done?
Solo: Wid Liza Lee all on my knee,
Chorus: So clear the track let the bulgine run!

The Bosun's Locker Stan Hugill

[Musical notation with lyrics:]

Oh, San-ti-a-na gained the day, A-way San-ti-a-na! San-ti-a-na gained the day, All a-cross the plains of Mex-i-co!

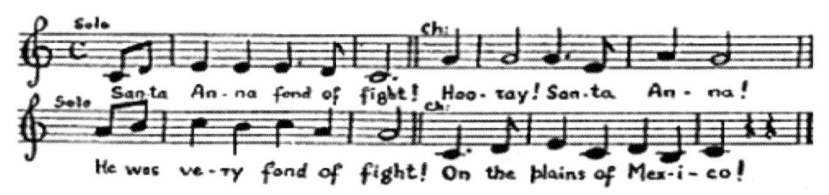

Santa An-na fond of fight! Hoo-ray! San-ta An-na! He was ve-ry fond of fight! On the plains of Mex-i-co!

In Mex-i-co where the land lies low, Hoo-raw, boys, hoo-raw ho! Where there ain't no snow on' the whale fishes blow. Heave a-way for the plains of Mex-i-co!

This theory naturally excludes these shanties from being called 'grand chorus' ones and gives them all fair antiquity. Miss Gilchrist (collector and contributor to the Folk Song Journal) seems to think that the tunes of *Santiana* and *Clear the Track* are both forms of *High Barbaree*, a sea-song of great age. However, the texts of the following tunes of *Santiana* fail to place the birth of the shanty much before the 1850s.

In my book *'Shanties from the Seven Seas'* two more tunes are to be found, and then of course is the *grand chorus* one sung by the Spinners, originally, I think, collected by Lomax, all of these coming into being from the mid-nineteenth century onwards.

Couplets sung to all these tunes are as follows:

Santiana gained the day,
General Taylor ran away

Santiana was a dammed fine man
Till he fouled the house with Uncle Sam.

'Twas on the field of Molly del Rey,
Santiana lost a leg that day.

Santiana marched along
With his army proud and strong.

[Musical notation with lyrics:]

San-ta An-na was a man-o-war! Hoo-ray! San-ta An-na! She hun-ted ev'-ry bad cor-sair! Heave 'n' weigh we're bound to Mex-i-co!

The Bosun's Locker Stan Hugill

Santiana did attack
General Taylor shoved him back.
Them gals is fine, wid their long black hair,
They'll rob ye blind and skin ye bare.

The Dago gals ain't got no combs
They comb their hair with whalefish bones.

Although Bone seems to think that Santiana may have been the Breton fisherman's saint, Saint Anne, we have no such proof, and no pre-Mexican war versions seem to exist, at least that is how things were until, from a Danish source, I came across the following. This tune has a Latin touch, the words having nothing to do with the Mexican Santiana, but are about a corsair chasing man-o'-war called *'Santa Anna'*. It was collected by a Captain Jensen; a friend of mine, Capt. J Lyman USNR, has discovered in an old copy of the *'Mariner's Mirror'* a reference to a sixteenth-century Mediterranean vessel called *'Santa Anna'*. Both he and I are wondering whether this version is the most venerable one, prior to it becoming associated with the Mexican War. If so, this is quite a find!

Of course the variant of *Santiana – Round the Bay of Mexico* (a version of which I have in my book, my informant telling me it was a cotton-stower's song), was collected and presented to the American Library of Congress many years ago. This came from the Bahama Islands. Belafonte took it and adding the name of Susiana made a pop hit out of it. Whether this variant is older than the others is difficult to say. It is quite a Herculean task to fit these songs into their proper relationship in this salty jigsaw puzzle, and I doubt if we will ever succeed – however we can but try.

Vol. 1 No. 7

As well as the four-liner windlass song *Santiana* being fitted with an all-hands-in chorus – the Yankee version, as is often sung:

We wuz sailin' down the river from Liverpool
Chorus: Heave away Santiana!
The wind wuz fair and the hatches full
Chorus: All across the plains of Mexico.
Full Chorus:
So we'll heave her up an' away we'll go,
Heave away! Santiana!
We'll heave her up an' away we go
All across the plains of Mexico.

Many other shanties were given this improvement(?) in the latter days of sail. *Blow the Man Down* is a halyard song but was sometimes sung with one of its verses doing duty as a grand chorus:

As I was a-walkin' down Paradise Street
Chorus: Timme way, hay, blow the man down!
A flash lookin' packet I chanct foe ter meet,
Chorus: Oh gimme some time ter blow the man down.
Full Chorus:
Blow the man down bullies, blow the man down,
Timme way, hay, blow the man down!
Blow him right down ter Liverpool town
Oh gimme some time ter blow the man down.

Thus it became a capstan shanty.
Another halyard shanty having a similar face-lift was *A Long Time Ago*; the using of one of its verses as a grand chorus transformed it into a capstan song.

Three ships they lay in 'Frisco Bay
Chorus: Timme way. Hay, oh, high, oh
Three ships they lay in 'Frisco Bay
Chorus: A long time ago!
Full Chorus:
Oh, a long long time, an' a very long time
Timme way. Hay, oh, high, oh
Oh, a long long time, an' a very long time
A long time ago!

Haul Away Joe and *Haul on the Bowline*, both foresheet shanties, i.e. ones used so as to get an extra drag on the sheets of the lower sails, the pull coming on the final word of the chorus, met the grand chorus in both cases. A capstan version of the halyard shanty *Roll the Cotton Down* appears in my book with a grand chorus of:

Roll the cotton,
Roll the cotton, Moses!
Roll the cotton,
Oh, roll the cotton down!

And of course *Leave Her Johnny, Leave Her*, originally a four-liner used at brake pump and halyards, followed this pattern by having a grand chorus tacked on,

Leave her Johnny, leave her
Oh, leave her Johnny, leave her etc.

This applied to the British version only; the Yankee version remained a four-liner right to the end of sail. I understand that this transformation is known in folk magazines as the 'folk process'.

Topical mentioning of the shore songs *St James' Infirmary* (*The Unfortunate Rake* etc.) and *John Reilly, Bleacher Lassie* etc. gave me the idea that a few words on such alterations and variations in the shanty and sea-song

The Bosun's Locker Stan Hugill

now I t'ought I heard the Ol' Man say, Leave 'er, Johnny leave 'er! Ter-morrer ye will git yer pay, Time for us ter leave 'er!

field would not be amiss. Although I have endeavoured to include in my book as many versions and variations of tunes as space permitted, it is still highly probable, that in the near future some Old Geordie sailor, say, may glance at a certain shanty, *Rio Grande*, perhaps and adamantly declare "Ah diva na yon version. In the old *'Tamar'* out o' Shields, we used t' sing so-an-so."

It would be a Herculean task to record every version of text and every difference of melody within the pages of one book. From Liverpool, the Tyne, Sunderland, London, the Bristol Channel ports, Glasgow and so on, dozens of different local versions of each shanty were to be found. Very often aboard each ship or line of ships from these different areas the folk process would be at work,

producing still further versions. American and Bluenose (Nova Scotian) seamen sang versions different again to the British ones, their songs having differences too depending on whether they were sung by seamen hailing from the Down East ports, New York, 'Frisco or the Gulf ports. And of course, many English worded shanties would be altered and twisted again in the mouths of German, Scandinavian or French shantymen – very often with continental words and phrases mingled with the original English ones. A Swedish version of Reuben Ranzo illustrates this:

Så franå en bond Street Sailor,
Chorus: Ranzo, boys, Ranzo!
Han shipped on board a whaler,
Chorus: Ranzo, boys Ranzo!

Vol. 1 No. 8

Of course the ever-recurring metamorphosis of the shanty from its very inception, often a shore song, produced a mass of what the folkniks call 'related' songs. One of the best examples of this process is to be found in the *Cheerily Man* family. Probably originating from some as yet undiscovered old English naval ditty of Shakespeare's day – the word 'cheerily' having a naval background with sense of rousing one to better efforts – with at some time a spot of illicit intercourse with the Jamaican folk song *Missa Ramgoat*, some of its widely different forms as used aboard

sailing ships are illustrated here (fig. 1).

This version (fig. 2) is probably the oldest version in print, since it is to be found in *'Incidents of a Whaling Voyage'* by Olmstead (1841). Olmstead, however, gives 'Heave her away, heave her away' as the refrain.

This one is obviously related to the West Indian song (fig. 3). It is a very old form; in more recent years it was sung in the fashion of fig.4.

Forebitters too – the type of song sailors sang for relaxation as opposed to work – suffered many changes. Of some of these I may write next time.

The Bosun's Locker Stan Hugill

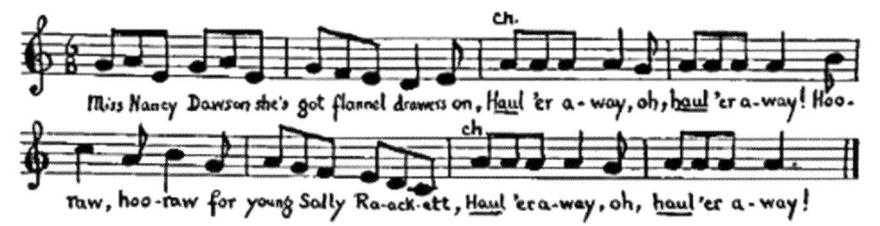

Figure 1

Miss Nancy Dawson she's got flannel drawers on, Haul 'er a-way, oh, haul 'er a-way! Hoo-raw, hoo-raw for young Sally Ra-ack-ett, Haul 'er a-way, oh, haul 'er a-way!

Figure 2

Lit-tle Nancy Dawson, Haul 'er a-way! She's got flannel drawers on, Haul 'er a-way! So sez our ol' Bosun, Haul 'er a-way! Wid a hauley high-O! Haul 'er a-way!

Figure 3

Missy Ramgoat O! Bar-ba deh yah! Missy Ramgoat O! Barba deh yah! Can you len' me yo' rāz ăr? Barba deh ya! For to shave off me long beard, Barba deh yah!

Oh, Nancy Dawson, aye yeo, Cheerily man! So sez the Bosun, aye yeo-o, Cheerily man! Has flannel drawers on, aye yeo-o, Cheerily man! Oh, hauley, aye-yeo-o, Cheerily man!

Figure 4

Oh, Nancy Dawson, aye o-o, Cheer-ly man—! She's got no drawers on, oye oh, Cheer'ly man —! So sez the Bosun, aye o-o, Cheer'y man O, hauley high ho - Chee-ee-ry man—!

21

The Bosun's Locker Stan Hugill

Vol. 1 No. 9
Forebitters

Forebitters, or as the Yankees called them 'mainhatch songs', were sung by the sailing-ship Johns in their leisure time. Leisure time, in actual fact, hardly existed in the days of sail. At sea sailors worked 'watch and watch', that is four hours on and four hours off, continuously throughout the outward and homeward passages. In port 'daywork' was the rule – roughly 6am to 6pm. The sea watches from 8pm one day to 4pm the next were of four hours' duration, but the watch from 4pm to 8pm was divided into two, and these sections were known as the 'dog-watches'. In the first of the two some work was done; it was also a period for eating, but the second dog-watch was, apart from some occasional pulley-hauley, one of leisure. Running the easting down – that is sailing with square yards, running before the 'brave west wind' down in the high latitudes between the Cape of Good Hope and Leeuwin in Australia – was a good time for the singing of forebitters, in the dark, damp, smelly fo'c'sle lit solely by swinging oil lamps, with the creaking of the timbers, and the swishing of wet oilskins hanging from their pegs on the bulkheads, along with a squeezebox, fiddle or concertina, forming a dramatic background music.

In the warmer weather of the trade winds, when hardly a rope would be touched, the crowd would squat around the fore or main hatch, or else sit on the iron bitts on the fo'c'sle head (the bitts, which gave the songs their name). Here dog-watch concerts would be held, with sometimes a 'fufu band' presiding. The latter consisted of home-made triangles, fiddles made from cigar boxes, and pig bladder drums extracted by bribery from some sea-cook.

Forebitters were of all types. Love songs, drinking songs, shore songs and ballads of the time were sung by the sailor, but the true forebitter was something apart – a salty folk song created by the sea-folk.

Some were humorous, like *Married to a Mermaid* and *Paddy and the Whale*, others were dramatic and reeked with cruelty such as *Andrew Rose* and *The Cruel Ship's Captain*. A fine example of the long rambling type, beloved by Sailor John, is *The 'Flying Cloud'*. Whaling songs such as *The Dundee Whalers*, *The Greenland Whale* and *The Coast of Peru* were heard in every ship's fo'c'sle. There were pirate songs such as *Captain Kidd*, *Henry Martin* and *High Barbaree*. Sealing songs and fisherman's ditties were also heard – *John Martin*, *The*

Bitts (iron)

Typical wooden bitts or Knightheads at the heel of a bowsprit

The Bosun's Locker Stan Hugill

'Nimrod' and *The Fishes*, when such men formed part of a deep-sea crew. *Maggie May*, *Jack-al-Alone* and *Ratcliffe Highway* told of Jack being bilked, then songs like *Doo Me Ama* and *Cawsand Bay* pleased Jack because in these the sailor gained his objective! Others like *The Fire-ship* and *The Young Sailor Cut Down in His Prime* sang of the sticky end he came to thanks to the syphilitic harpies of the ports. Some like *First Came The Bosun's Wife* were straightforwardly obscene — even Joyce camouflaged it in his *'Ulysses'*!

Sentimental songs such as *The Barque was far from the Land* or ones based on a named ship like *The 'Dom Pedero'* or ones dealing with nautical manoeuvres, *All Hands on Deck*, were rarer. Also rare were songs singing of sailor beliefs and superstitions such as *The 'Flying Dutchman'*. A few naval songs e.g. *The Ponwell Frigate* and *Spanish Ladies* would be heard, particularly if an old man-o'-war's man had shipped among the crowd. Forebitters telling of shanghaiing like *Off to Sea Once More* were common enough, and those telling of girls who shipped as sailors such as *The Female Cabin Boy* were also plentiful. Transportation ballads like *Botany Bay*, historical themes like *The 'Shannon' and the 'Chesapeake'* and *The 'Stately Southerner'*, drinking songs such as *When Jones' Ale Was New* and narrations of voyages, e.g. *From Liverpool to 'Frisco* were also popular with the foremast hand. In fact Jack being a versatile sort of a chap created forebitters about most things.

As in the shanty the 'folk process' is to be

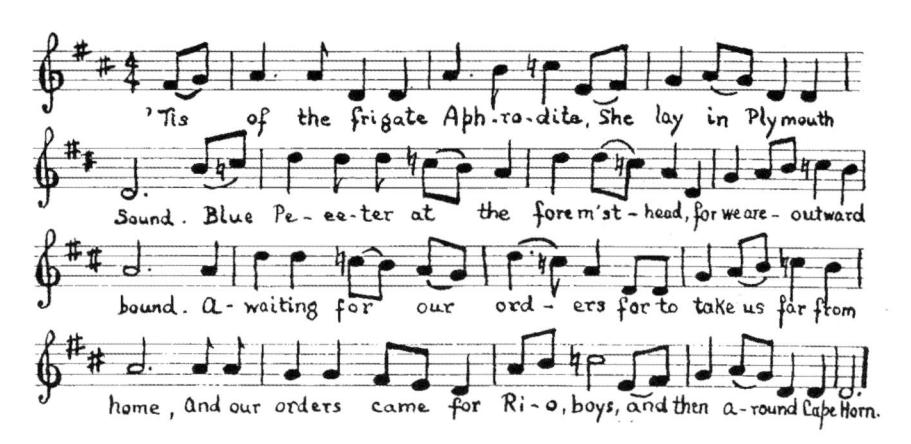

The Bosun's Locker Stan Hugill

Oh, 'tis of the Ponwell frigate, boys, In Portsmouth she did lay, A-waiting there for orders, boys, for to take us far away, A-waiting there for orders, boys, for to take us far from home, And our orders came for Ri-o, boys, And then a-round Cape Horn.

found in the forebitter as well. A large percentage of them, in particular those in the narrative type, took on new tunes so that some forebitters may have as many as five tunes each, and the words varied according to the singer or the environment.

The *Girls Around Cape Horn* is one good example. The most usual tune with English seamen is as follows. This is what my father used to sing. He said that, although there were both naval and Jack variations the song was undoubtedly one of the old Sailing Navy.

The next tune I had from a shipmate, and I have learnt since that this was also sung to a Bluenose (Nova Scotian) or Down Easter (Maine) ditty about Portland rum!

Finally there was the *'Flying Cloud'* tune (or shall I say one of the *'Flying Cloud'* tunes).

The remaining verses were common to all, but sometimes two extra verses were to be heard – after the first verse, and between the second and third verses.

Not only in the tune, the name of the ship and the number of verses but other differences also occur, such as 'Chileno' or 'Peruvian' girls instead of 'Spanish Girls', 'Liverpool Girls' instead of 'English Girls', and the final line is sometimes sung as 'God bless them little Dago girls that live around Cape Horn'.

But one of the most unusual passages in the singing of this old forebitter is that as sung by Mr Bolton to Miss Gilchrist in which 'the coast of Chile' is made to rhyme with 'while'!

Next month I hope to show a process which is even more diverse.

The Bosun's Locker Stan Hugill

THE GIRLS AROUND CAPE HORN

'Tis the famed ship Gari-bald-i-O, a ship of high renown, There she lay in old Liverpool Bay, just close to old Liverpool town, A-waiting there for orders, boys, to take us far from home, Our orders came for Rio, boys, and then a-round Cape Horn.

Oh, we beat our way, across the Bay, with a fair wind in the line,
The royals all set and the stays all taut, the Trades they blew so fine;
Our Johns they all were fighting fit, good seamen all were we,
For to hand and reef and steer, myboys we all worked bravely.

When we arrived in Rio, boys, we anchored there a while,
We set up all our rigging, and we bent all our new sail;
From ship to ship they cheered us, as we did pass along,
And they wished us pleasant weather in a-rounding of the Horn.

When beating off Magellan Straits, the wind blew stong and hard,
While shortening sail two gallant tars fell from the tops'l yard;
By angry seas the lines we threw from their weak hans was torn,
We had to leave 'em to the sharks that prowl around Cape Horn.

In the rounding of the Horn me lads, fine nights and pleasant days,
And the very nexy place we anchored was in Valpariso Bay;
Where al them pretty girls come down, I solemnly do swear,
Oh, they're far above them English girls with their dark and wavy hair.

They like a jolly sailor when he is on the spree,
They'll dance with you and sing withyou, and spend your money free;
And when your money is all gone, they'll not on you impose,
Oh, they're far above them Yankee girls who'll stael and pawn your clothes.

Farewell to Valpariso, boys along the Chile main,
And likewise all those Spanish girls, they treated me just fine;
And if I live to get paid off I'll sit and drink all morn,
A health to them dashing Spanish girls that live around Cape Horn.

The Bosun's Locker Stan Hugill

Vol. 2 No. 1

On our last voyage we ploughed through the, as yet, mainly uncharted seas of the so called 'folk process' of forebitters, showing how many, as time advanced, rigged themselves in one or two, if not more, entirely different tunes.
Now we give an example of the true folk process, the slow altering, step by step, ship by ship, of both the *tunes and the words* of a certain forebitter until almost a new song or series of songs comes into being.
The forebitter, often used as a shanty, called *The Fishes* is this apt example. The chorus of the drawing room version

'Then blaw the wind southerly, southerly, southerly
Blaw bonnie breeze, blaw my lover to me ....'

is of course widely known. But the sailor versions which have, in the main, stemmed from fishermen's versions, fishermen's songs from both above and below the border, from the East Coast and from sou'west England, and from the fishermen of Gloucester and so on in America and Nova Scotia, are in themselves widely different.

Blow ye winds westerly, gentle south westerly.
Blow ye winds westerly! Steady she goes.
(Whall)

So blow the wind wester, blow the wind blow!
Our ship she's in full sail, how steady she goes. (Cecil Sharp)

Windy weather, stormy weather,
When the wind blows we're all together.
(Whall)

Note that the first three are concerned with the wind blowing, in a certain direction, finishing with the ship going steadily along, while the last chorus refers to the weather.

The tunes and full versions of the above are given in my *'Shanties from the Seven Seas'* for anyone wanting to trace the full process, and here I will just give one representing the first group and one representing the last item.

This one was once popular with Bristol Channel seamen:

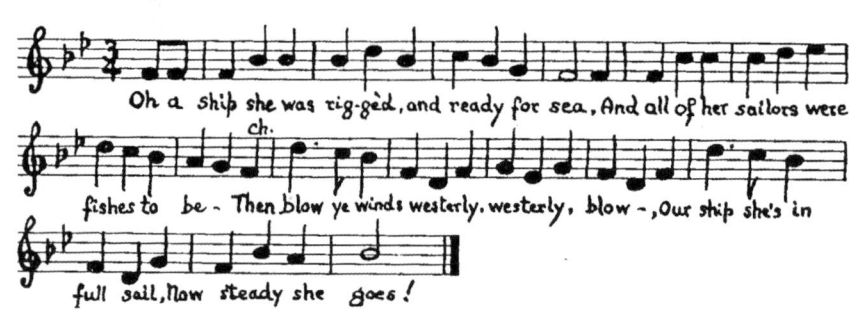

Oh a ship she was rig-ged, and ready for sea. And all of her sailors were fishes to be - Then blow ye winds westerly, westerly, blow -, Our ship she's in full sail, now steady she goes!

And here is a South or East Coast version, the fisherman's version of which has been popularised by Bob Roberts:

I'll sing ye a song of the fish of the sea, An' I'll trust that ye'll join in this chorus wi' me, Wi' a windy ol' weather! Stormy ol' weather! When the wind blows, well all heave together.

Now if we take the chorus of the latter example and place it first and then take the chorus of the first item and tack it onto the latter we would have a full chorus very similar to the next version. This is from Nova Scotia and Newfoundland and is obviously a combination of the two equally popular refrains of the British types. Did this combination come about unconsciously or was it done deliberately? 'Tis hard to say, but the results we know to be a fact.

to mind, and then another of the crowd would crash in with another fish and so on until the job was done. A further usage of these stanzas was the latter-day linking of them to the tune of *Blow the man down*:

First came the herring sayin' I'm King o' the Seas
Way ay. Blow the man down!
I'll show ye the best way to get a fine breeze,
Gimme some time to blow the man down.

There was once an old skipper, I don't know his name. Although he once play'd a remarkable game. And its wind-y weather, boys, Stormy weather, boys, When the wind blows, we're all together, boys, Blow ye winds wester-ly, Blow, ye winds, blow— Bul-ly sou'wester boys, Stead-y she goes.

And here are some of the verses, which can be fitted to all of the tunes. The common trick amongst seamen was, after the shantyman started the song one of the haulers would roar out a verse about the fish he could call

Dozens more fish would be included in a long heave or haul but the following stanzas are sufficient to show how the song went.

The Bosun's Locker Stan Hugill

There wuz once an ol' skipper, I don't know his name,
But I know that he once played a bloody fine game.
When his ship lay becalmed in a tropical sea,
He whistled all day but he could get no breeze.

But a seal heard his whistle and loudly did call,
Just stow yer light canvas, jib, spanker and all.

As well as a certain shanty or forebitter being sung differently aboard each ship, or from out of each port or maritime region, or by different shantymen, there was also the possibility of a certain seaman singing a certain shanty in a slightly different manner, both words and tune, each time he sang it. This is a common phenomenon known to most transcribers of folk songs.

If several of the shanties in Runciman Terry's *'The Shanty Book'* are compared with their counterparts in Cecil Sharp's *'English Folk Chanteys'* it will be found that they differ in many ways, yet both collectors obtained their items from the same shantyman – John Short of Watchet in Somerset. Perhaps John Short was not the hero of the old forebitter but he was essentially a real deepwater man and a true shantyman of the Era of Sail. Thanks to a pen friend, Mr Michael Bouquet, who was shipmates with Mr Short's son I am able to give a list of sailing ships aboard which Mr Short learnt and sang his shanties, shanties which have since become world famous. (see opposite)

From thence onward Mr Short was mate aboard coastwise vessels out of Watchet, Somerset. Last reference 30th May 1904. He was for three years mate of the schooner *'Annie Christian'*.

Obviously a well travelled seafaring man, whose shanties have travelled even furter than he did!

Ships of Mr John Short – b. 1839 d. 1933
Brig: '*Promise*' of London (Cadiz and Quebec)
Ship: '*Earl of Balcarres*' of London (Bombay and Karachi)
Brig: '*Hugh Block*' of Southampton (Valparaiso)
Schooner: '*Zecimpra*' (to Malta and Catania)
Barque: '*Jane Grey*' of Blyth (Rio de Janeiro)
Ship: '*Mary Ann*' of St Johns (to New Brunswick)
Ship: '*George Washington*' of London (to China and Japan in 1861)
Ship: '*Woodcote*' of Swansea (Australia, discharged Swansea 5/12/1862)
Aux: SS '*Queen of the South*' (East Indies, discharged London 4/5/1864)
Ship '*Levant*' of Liverpool (foreign, discharged Liverpool 14/9/1866)
(This was an American ship under British registry – at the time of the American Civil War – and service in this ship gave Short his nickname of 'Yankee Jack', which stuck to him for the rest of his life.)
Barque: '*Benjamin Buck Greene*' of London (Mauritius discharged London 8/8/1863)
Barque: '*Benjamin Buck Greene*' (Mauritius again discharged London 14/1/1867)
Ship: '*Conference*' of Bristol (Callao, discharged Plymouth 20/4/1868)

The Speed of the Shanty

"These songs are normally sung slower than we sing them on this disc."

"The singing of the shanties, I feel, was far too fast."

Such notes and criticisms are common in reference to the present-day singing of shanties. With the sale of a record in view, or, in order to give the impression that all sailor songs are members of the hornpipe family, many shanty singers step on the throttle and give each and every song a rattling, hell-bent-for-election speed-up. On the other hand we have the ethnic sycophants who, having heard or read somewhere that all shanties in their heyday, when used for hauling and heaving were sung legato, voice these virile songs in such a painfully slow fashion that if the ghost of an ancient shellback was handy he would be bound to sing out an old-time nautical expression:

"Don't drag it, sonny! Take it to the windlass!"

In actual fact this slowness has been overdone in print, and orally – sailor John sang both fast and slow, but rarely *too* slow. The slow and belaboured singing of a pride of octogenarian shellbacks trying to recapture, in some sailor snug harbour or seaman's home, the hectic days of their youth is hardly the yardstick to go by.

The same men in their prime, in all probability, would have sung at a much faster rate, and obviously in a more virile fashion, than when thrilling field-collectors in the winter of their days.

Probably the only shanty sung with any real degree of slowness was the mate's anathema *Tom's gone to Hilo.*

"If yer must sing for Gawd's sake strike up sumpin' a bit more lively, will yiz? Sounds more like a bloody dirge than a haulin' song!" would have been a mate's normal reaction to the singing of this halyard song. *Stormalong* – a pump shanty – perhaps falls into this category – the mate's anathema, but even this would have been speeded up a bit at times.

Go through some of the foreign shanty books, books such as the German *'Knurrhahn'*, a collection put together by a bunch of Kiel Canal pilots, all sailing ship men but not windbag ancients but, seeing that Germany has had windjammers until quite recently, late middle aged men with salt still damp on 'em, and one finds that *Blow the Man Down* for instance bears the legend 'Schnell' (fast) crowning the first bar. But *Blow the Man Down* in most English and Yankee collections is indicated as being sung slow or in a leisurely fashion.

With most of the editors of English and American collections there has been a gap of years spanning the period when they actually sang the songs or heard them sung at WORK and when they put them down in print. Not so with the German, French and Scandanavian editors – their working day is not so distant. Hence, perhaps, the truer translation …..

Taking more or less any hauling song we find that whereas the refrain always carried the same speed, in the solos free time was the thing and certain phrases were sung slower than others. This slow singing of certain passages – not the whole shanty – was common in both shanties and forebitters. A hauling song with two pulls in the refrain was slower than a song which had only one pull in the refrain. Actually this latter type of hauling song was normally sung quite fast, but what really governed the speed of the shantey was the work itself.

When setting a sail after a few 'dry pulls' when the shanty was raised — as the wet folds of the sail collapsed outwards from the petrified position in which the gaskets had held them for some time — the first few verses would be sung fairly fast, but as the wind bellied the creases out the shantyman would automatically slow the song a little. Then as the parrel of the yard slid higher up the mast and extended the weight of the wind-filled sail, the weight of the yard and the tiring of the haulers had to be taken into account — particularly so if the men were hoisting up the mizzen tops'l after having hoisted the fore and main — and the speed of the whole shanty would automatically slow down, with the shantyman changing, perhaps to a rather quick chant with one pull at the end of the refrain in order to sweat up the final foot or two.

So as to the question: Was a shanty sung fast or slow? The obvious answer is that it all depends on the job position or the amount of work already executed, whether the mate was a bucko or not and many other seemingly irrelevant, but actually most important influences.

For instance, if the watch below had been roused out of their bunks to help the watch on deck to hoist a tops'l, naturally they would hurry the job up so they could get below again for a few more moments of hard-earned sleep. Just as the watch on deck came down from aloft in a leisurely fashion by means of the laddered rigging, the watch below would slide down the backstays, getting to the deck and their bunks as quickly as possible. In a similar fashion the watch on deck would tend to sing the shanty slowly — the watch below roused out from their rest trying to turn it into a hornpipe as would be expected.

Capstan songs, of course, were rather faster at the beginning of the anchor-heaving operation, being changed to slower ones as the ship drew over her anchor. For instance, the 'beef' would start with *Sally Brown* and finish up with *Shenandoah*, the final few heaves to 'break the anchor out' from its bed being accompanied by shouts such as "HEAVE and she must come!" "HEAVE and bust 'er!"

So when you sing these songs, sonny, use your discretion; sing some fast: sing some slow — but never TOO SLOW, because you know you ain't working aboard a windjammer — and I reckon you never will now. 'Tis too late!

Rolling Home was one of the slower capstan songs. Versions of words and tunes vary but little, but here is an unusual form from a Scandinavian source which is entirely new, both in words and tune, to print. The interpolated refrains 'Heave away, my bullies' and 'Heave away, and sing' in the verses are not to be found in any other version. Patterson, a seaman and collector of shanties, as noted in my book, *'Shanties from the Seven Seas'* gives several popular shanties with unusual interposed refrains in the verses not found elsewhere, but as he doesn't give the tunes we are at a loss to know whether these are really authentic or not. However, the version of *Rolling Home* presented here is. We can vouch for that.

The Bosun's Locker Stan Hugill

Rolling Home

Heave away me bully boys
Chorus: Heave away me bullies!
Can't you hear the calling voice?
Chorus: Heave away and sing
Rolling home, rolling home etc.

Listen now ye'll hear it all
What a fine and hearty call

That voice is calling you and me
Oh, bully boys, come home from sea

Then heave, me boys, the cape'n round
Me bully boys, we're homeward bound

Our ship is loaded down with corn
We'll drive her homeward, round Cape Horn

We'll drive her home thro' calm and gale
We'll row her when we cannot sail

Then heave for you and heave for me
We'll heave the hooker in from sea

* The expression *for-bee* seems to mean *passing by* or *near*

32

The Bosun's Locker Stan Hugill

Some time ago I explained by drawings the different types of capstan and windlasses used to heave up a sailing ship anchor; the pushing around or jerking up and down of which would be accompanied by the singing of a capstan or windlass song. Also I drew the different types of forebitts from which sprang the word 'forebitter', meaning a sailor song of recreation.

In this issue I give a plan of a typical sailing ship mast showing which sails were hoisted to a shanty and which were not.

Both the lower topsail and the lower topgallantsail – after being released from their confining ties called 'gaskets' and having their clewlines or tackles which haul up the corners of the sails thrown off their belayin'-pins and left slack – would be set by hauling on the sheets – wire ropes or chains which haul out the corners of a sail to the yard beneath it.

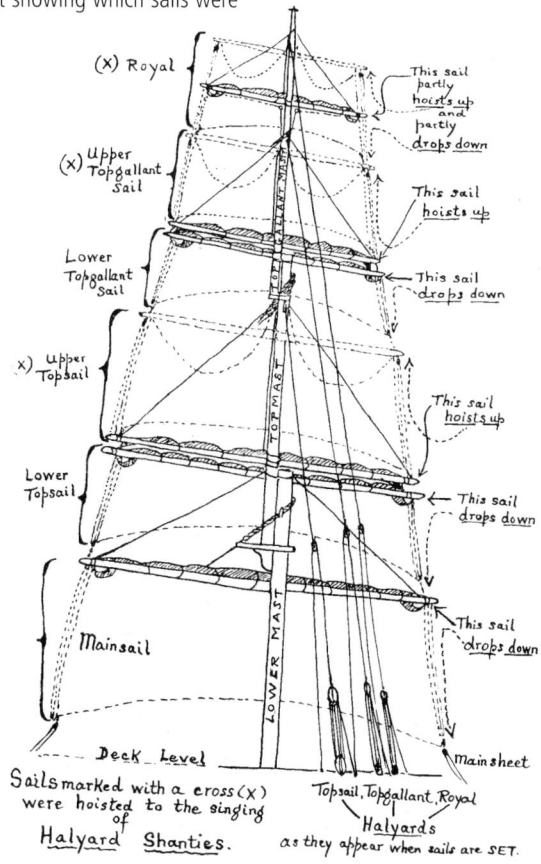

No shanties were needed for this job, nor for the setting of the lower sails of course, although in the case of the latter a song such as *Haul Away Joe* would be used to get the last few pulls on the sheets.

But the upper topsail and upper topgallantsail and sometimes the royal were sails in which the yards moved up and down the mast – the lower topsail and the topgallant sail yards being fixed – and when setting them a 'Halyard Shanty' would be just the job.

The longest job was the setting of the upper topsail – more rope would have to be hauled through the blocks than in other cases – and this would always be accompanied by a long, rambling song such as *Blow the Man Down*.

My plan of how some sails were hoisted and some 'dropped' is, I believe, the first in print, and I hope it will explain some of the mysteries and the details of an old windbag job-o-work. Some other time I will explain the type of pump at which pumping songs were sung.

Halyard Shanties were also used when bending sail. This means sending the sails up aloft from the sail-locker by means of ropes known as 'gantlines', so as to clothe the naked yards – after a ship has lain in port a while or when the fine weather sails are changed for storm ones prior to reaching Cape Horn. By means of the gantline tied to its middle the sail is hauled up higher than the yard to which it is to be tied, and then it is gently lowered, its two dangling ends are hauled out to the two ends of the yard and the sailors then tie its upper edge to the jackstay of the yard. Many halyard shanties were used for this job. A well-remembered incident is when, after a rowdy night ashore, I awoke with a fat head to hear the old Cornish bosun bawling forth a raucous *Reuben Ranzo* at the gantline while those of the mob who were nearly sober swayed the main topsail aloft. The shanty roused me to my senses and vaulting from my upper bunk, half clothed I dashed up the fo'c'sle ladder, intending to join in the hauling and singing, but, unfortunately, on reaching the deck and heading straight for the crowd swaying on the rope, I disappeared with a yell down the open trap-hatch of the sail-locker, landing in a heap on the hard canvas stowed in the hold.

The singing of shanties when bending sail has not previously been mentioned in print and another job-o-song similarly omitted from the written word is the operation in which the ship's bottom was scraped **at sea**. Each skipper had his own torturous device, sometimes made of boards, sometimes of metal, or of canvas and ropeyarns, but in each case the operation was the same. The instrument of torture was lowered over the sides and held directly under the ship by means of ropes coming up port and starboard to the deck. The men manned the ropes and the devil's instrument was hauled from for'ard to aft and from aft to for'ard, hour after hour, under the blazing tropical sun, in a near useless attempt to rid the ship's bottom of barnacles, weeds and shellfish. And to lighten his labour 'stamp-an'-go' songs such as *Drunken Sailor*, *Roll the Old Chariot* and *Hieland Laddie* would be sung.

The Bosun's Locker Stan Hugill

Bonnie Hieland laddie-o British version

O, was ye ever in Que-bec? Hieland laddie, Bonnie laddie! Launchin' timber on the deck, Me bon-nie hie-land lad-die O! Way-ay an'away we go! Hieland lad-die, bonnie laddie! Way-ay, an'a-way we go! me bonnie hieland lad-die O!

Where have you been all the day?
Chorus: Hieland laddie, bonny laddie
Where have you been all the day?
Chorus: Me bonnie Hieland laddie o!

Was ye ever in Quebec,
Launching timber on the deck?

Was ye ever in Mobile Bay.
Screwin' cotton on a summer's day?

Was ye ever off Cape Horn,
Where the weather's never warm?

Was ye ever in Mirramashee,
Where ye tied up to a tree?

Was ye ever in Bombay,

The Bosun's Locker Stan Hugill

Bonnie Hieland laddie-o American version

Was ye ever in Quebec, Hie-land laddie, Bonnie laddie!
Launching timber on the deck, Me bonnie hie-land laddie O!
'Way-ay, an' a-way we go, Hie-land laddie, Bonnie laddie! Way-ay,
heels 'n' toes, Me bonnie hie-land laddie O!

Was ye ever in London Town,
Where them gals they do come down?

Was ye ever in Bombay,
Drinkin' coffee an' bohay?

Was ye ever in Vallipo,
Where the gals put up a show?

Was ye ever in 'Frisco Bay,
Where the gals all shout 'Hooray!'

Drinkin' coffee and bohay?

Vol. 2 No. 4
Pumping Ship Songs

This time I want to talk about the piece of sailing-ship machinery which gave rise to the expression 'All hands to the pump'.

In early wooden ships pumping ship was a daily, almost hourly task. Wooden ships leaked to every stress and strain of wind, sea and weather in general. When ships leaked they smelt clean below decks; that is the bilges or ships 'sewers' were 'sweet' thanks to the clean water running in and out continuously. When wooden ships were sound their bilges stank to high heaven, and it used to be said that men on joining the ship would stand over the open hatch sniffing. If the smell was vile then she was a 'good' ship and they would carry on to the fo'c'sle with their traps. If, however, the smell coming up from below was sweet the potential hands would do an about turn and get ashore as quickly as they could. She was, in Jack's mind, a packet that would come to a sticky end probably by foundering a thousand miles from anywhere. Whether this was true or not, thousands of seamen did sail in veritable coffin ships, where pumping was the rule not the exception. Hence the number of pumping songs in shanty collections.

As well as the well-known pumping shanties like *A-Rovin'* and *Lowlands*, many shore songs were roped in and salted for sailor use. As the job often lasted hours and was a steady one – sometimes 'watch 'n watch' for days on end – songs with good choruses and many verses were preferable. *Fire Down Below* of course was one used at the pumps in relation to the hold being on fire. Many cargoes were highly combustible and therefore far more dangerous in wooden ships than in the later iron ones. Some iron ships made long passages with fire down below in the hold all the way and reached port aglow like a red-hot cinder, but with the possibility of being saved even if the cargo was lost. Wooden ships rarely stood such a chance, once on fire their end was pretty certain.

Wooden ships were often lost by virtually bursting apart at the seams. Ships loading cotton down in the Gulf ports of the Southern States had the bales forced into the holds by great jack-screws. When the ship got to sea the cotton would swell with the damp and something had to give; it is a known fact that many ships foundered in this way.

The oldest type of pump was the 'Brake-pump' or jiggitty-jig, with which long brakes were used and the motion jerky; in the later Downton Pump the motion was rotary, hence a greater number of suitable songs came to be used at this job. In Norwegian and other 'Scandahoovian' or 'Scowegian' ships between the main and mizzen masts would be found a great windmill just like one sees in Norfolk or along the dykes of Holland. This contrivance pumped the ship continuously as long as there was wind, an improvement indeed on the Armstrong Patent of British and

The Downton Pump

The Bosun's Locker Stan Hugill

American vessels. Here is a rather curious offering apropos the word 'sailor'. In very olden times the words used to describe a seafaring man were 'mariner', 'shipman' or 'shypman', 'seaman' and so on, the word 'sailor' being unknown. In fact, one of the earliest dictionaries gives 'SAILOR: a man who looks after the sails on a windmill'!

I give a drawing of the more modern Downton pump. The brake-pump was similar to the brake-windlass given earlier.

Strike the Bell

The song this time is a pump shanty called Strike the Bell. Its tune has wandered all around the world. My father has a version Ring the Bell, Watchman. There is a Welsh version without a chorus, and everyone by now has heard the version from Down Under, from the shearing sheds of Australia. Such is the way of a popular tune – you can't kill it! Here are two versions of the tune with verses to go with both.

Aft on the quarter deck, walkin' a-bout, There is the starboard watch, so steady an' so stout. Thinkin' of their sweethearts,an' we hope that they are well. An' I wish that you would hurry up an' strike, strike, the bell. Strike th' bell. Second mate! Let us go be-low. Look well to wind'ard, Ye'll see it's gonna blow, Look at the glass ye will see it as well. An' I wish that you would hurry up an', Strike, strike the bell!

Aft on the maindeck working on the pumps,
There is the larboard watch a-longing for their bunks,
Lookin' to wind'ard they see a great swell (squall)
They're wishing that the second mate would strike,
strike the bell. *Chorus*

Aft at the wheel there poor Anderson stands,
Grasping at the spokes with his cold mittened hands,
Looking at the compass, the course clear to tell,
He's wishing that the second mate would strike,
strike the bell. *Chorus*

The Bosun's Locker Stan Hugill

Aft on the poop there is walking a-bout — Our bully second mate so able and stout, What he is thinking' of he doesn't know himself, It seems to us, he's quite forgot to strike, strike the bell!

Ch. Strike the bell, second mate, let us go below, If you look to wind'ard you will see its goin' to blow — Look at the glass, you will see how it's fell. I wish that you would hurry up and strike, strike the bell.

For'ard on the fo'c'slehead keeping sharp lookout,
There is Johnny standing, he's ready for to shout,
'Lights burnin' bright sir! and everything is well!'
He's wishing that the second mate would strike, strike the bell.
Chorus

Aft on the quarterdeck our cap'n there he stands,
Lookin' to the wind'ard with his glasses in his hands,
What he is thinkin' of we know very well,
He's thinking more of shortening sail than strike, strike the bell.
Chorus

The Bosun's Locker Stan Hugill
Vol. 2 No. 5
"Give Us A Shanty"

Once an 'ologist' puts his findings on paper, classification is the thing. All he collects must go down under this heading or that.

Although hardly an 'ologist' of any kind, nevertheless, I too have been guilty of this methodical itemisation and classification. For the record in my book *'Shanties of the Seven Seas'*, I *did* point out that the up-till-now lumping together of sailor work songs under capstan, halyard, pump or other headings with further sub-classification into bowline, bunt and so on groups was a rather erroneous method since many of the songs put by various collectors under certain headings were placed by other 'experts' into entirely different work categories. I tried to get round this by grouping the shanties into families, giving each song as many jobs as cited by all the various well-known collectors. Also I have been guilty of roping in forebitters – the songs that sailors sang of an evening with the fiddle or squeeze-box seated on the forebitts or forehatch – placing them under capstan and pump headings; a great crime according to the 'ologists'. Yet I too, in line with the latter, have many times declared the well-worn, part-truism that sailors never sang a forebitter at work. However in actual fact in the heyday of sail I feel certain that all this pigeon-holing and strait-jacketing didn't exist – at least not to the extent that modern writers would have us believe. Neither do I believe that seamen used the word 'shanty' as often as one finds it in print. "Give us a shanty" or "Give us a halyard shanty" may be printed in nautical yarns but I doubt if many seamen heard it under sail. As for "Let's have a <u>sea</u> shanty?" ... well this would have turned a shellback green! The usual cry when a song was needed would run something like this:

"Are ye deaf, or are ye dumb? C'm'on ye bloody Port Mahon baboons, cain't one of yeez raise the song? Strike a light there one of yiz, will yeez!"

or

"Give it lip ye bloody cawpses – who's the bloody nightingale in yer watch? Blow 'er down ye parish-rigged barstards and let's 'ear some noise!"

or

"Bend yer backs an' break yer spare-ribs an' let's 'ave some noise. Don't stand there up 'n' down like fathoms of pump water .... Give us the song Paddy!... an' heave!"

In fact the word 'shanty' was rarely used – wade through Dana's *'Two Years Before the Mast'* if you don't believe me! – and as for clear-cut designations such as capstan shanty or halyard shanty, well the men at the halyards instinctively knew what song to raise, and as I've pointed out in my book, some shantymen would start a halyard song at the capstan or a capstan song at the halyards. No, I am sure that in the balmy days of sail these strong definitions did not exist – literature brought them about.

And again in regard to the forebitter, seamen in the fo'c'sle in heavy weather seated on the long wooden benches or on their sea-chests or the edges of their bunks, or in the Trade Winds spread all over the forehatch, or hunched on the forebitts and fore-peak hatch on the fo'c'sle head, would start a sea-song going, by one of them saying quite normally "C'm'on, Paddy me broth ov a bhoy, what about givin' us *Maggie May*." The

The Bosun's Locker Stan Hugill

word forebitter would not be heard once in a blue moon. And forebitters too – not the long ballad type of thing 'sans chorus' like *The 'Flying Cloud'*, but ones with lusty choruses such as *Ratcliffe Highway* – would often be used at work, in particular at the pumps, where, as an oldtimer once informed me "any old song 'ud do as long as she be a good'un with an all hands-in-chorus."

No! Sailors weren't such purists as our literature tends to prove. We can feel this in the songs themselves. Individual shantymen often sang texts which modern authorities deplore as being historically wrong, but the sailor was always a cheerfully inconsistent individual, happily ignorant and orally taught. No book-learnin' for him. And if he wanted to make Napoleon cross the Rockies, the Andes or the Himalayas, or General Taylor get beaten at Monterey, or a Blackball sail to Timbuctoo, well that was his prerogative. If the song went right, the gang worked right and the ship was right. And after all is said and done he was his own critic.

My song this time is a whaling one, which I feel, has several markings, sufficiently colloquial in a salty sense, pointing to a sailor and not a shore origin. Some of the verses when sang by old timers had a number of bawdy lines.

Eight Bells

Oh, me husband's a saucy fore-top man —, Oh a chum of th' cooks don't ye kno-ow —, He put his head down the cook's fu-un-nel —, An' he shouted come up from be-low —. Eight bells — Eight bells — Rouse out there the watch from be-low —, Eight bells —, Eight bells —, Rouse out there the watch from be - low!

When up in the hoops he wuz dandy,
At sighting a whale when she blowed;
An' when out in a whaleboat was handy,
A smarter young tar never rowed.
Chorus: Eight bells, eight bells etc.

At the end of his watch, oh, his fancy,
Wuz to git to his bunk quickly O!
For he wanted to dream of his Nancy,
So he shouted, 'Come up from below!'
Chorus: Eight bells, eight bells etc.

An' now he's no longer a sailor,
He often wakes up in the night,
Thinkin' he's still on that whaler,
Shouts out with the greatest delight.
Chorus: Eight bells, eight bells etc.

The Bosun's Locker Stan Hugill
Vol. 2 No. 6

The recent shanty-singing evening aboard the *'Cutty Sark'* reminded me that on this vessel, and aboard many more of her type and time, certain devices, neither capstans or windlasses, were used for hoisting and working cargo.

On *'Cutty Sark'* at the foot of the mainmast (and fore, if I remember rightly) is to be found a winch. This is not mechanical in the steam or electrical sense, but merely an apparatus of wooden rollers and cogs worked by metal handles. It was possible to raise a shanty – a capstan or pump song – at such a device, particularly during a long job of working cargo. Such a winch would handle the main runners which would run from the winch, through a 'gin block' hung halfway down the main or forestay, and down the hatch. The 'yard-arm runner' which would be shackled to the main runner, the cargo hook being shackled to the 'eyes' of both runners, would run through an iron 'gin block' slung from the arm of a cock-billed yard.

The yard-arm runner would most likely be worked from a 'dolly winch' standing (bolted) either near the scuppers or on the rail itself. This runner worked the cargo from and to the quayside; the main runner working in and out of the hatch. Incidentally the phrase 'yard-arm runner' is still used at docksides nowadays for that part of the derrick which swings over the wharfside.

A year or so ago I corresponded with a naval sea-faring man from 'the days of transition' (the 'Down funnel, up screw, make sail' period) when naval vessels were fully rigged with sails as ships, barques or barquentines, but also had sails to drive them. They were 'Ironclads', (they mostly had 'ram-bows'), and in such ironclads my correspondent told me, chipping the rusty iron over the side was a constant occupation for the matlows. And he said that they sang 'Paint Chippers'. Now this was something new to me, and I am sure new to print. He couldn't remember all the 'Chippers' and some anyhow were not fit to print, but he sent me the following specimens …
I have left them un-barred as he sent them; they are only fragments, perhaps maybe a reader will be able to add further verses. This musical activity is worth perhaps further investigation. Another activity, 'longshore' rather than sea-faring, at which a song was raised was the art of ropemaking. In the days before rope was made by machine, and prior to the usage of chain, in all the major seaports of the world would be found long, usually narrow, streets or alleys, adjacent to the waterfront, along the length of which men and women tramped back and forth

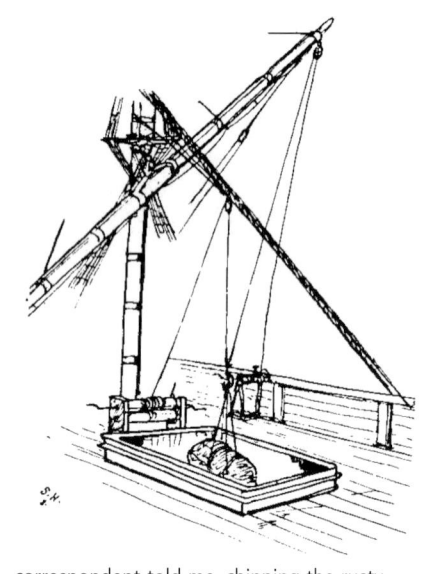

The Bosun's Locker Stan Hugill

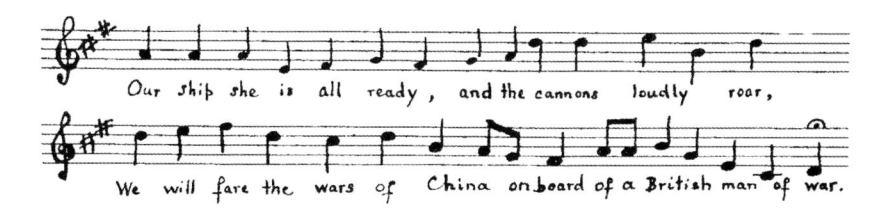

Sheet music with lyrics:

1. Our ship she is all ready, and the cannons loudly roar,
We will fare the wars of China on board of a British man of war.

2. She dress'd as a gallant young sailor, In trousers and jacket of blue,
Her father he fell quite motionless, When first she appear'd to his view.

3. Why sailors, why sailors, got no money to spend? The white man took my silver, and the black man took my brass, The white man kiss'd my ruby lips and the black man kissed — WHY SAILORS
(repeat from start)

twisting and making rope. These roperies were usually called 'rope-walks'. The famous Cannebière in Marseilles has the same meaning, as also has the notorious district in Hamburg called the Reeperbahn. In London we have Cable Street.

Now as these ropemakers trudged backwards and forwards songs would be sung to while away the tedious job, but unfortunately of these we know but little.

The only other as yet unmentioned nautical job in which songs were used to lighten the labour was that of rowing. Boatmen songs used by inshore fishermen, merchant seamen (particularly when carrying cargo to and from anchored ships), and whalemen (when chasing the Sperm or other whales), are unfortunately a type of song no-one has collected. Now I am afraid that it is too late.

We have a handful of Hebridean rowing songs, one or two English fishermen's boat songs, the reference to rowing songs in Dana's *'Two Years Before The Mast'*, and that's about all. Years ago the intelligentsia thought such rude and coarse songs unworthy of collecting — hence the deficiency, and something we, however desirous, at this late stage cannot accomplish.

Collectors have done their best to get into the eighteenth century, and earlier, with the earliest printed shanty, but although they have tried hard, I doubt if they have proved anything.

It has been suggested by C.H. Firth (*'Naval Songs and Ballads'*) that

'Captain Chilvers gone to sea,
I, boys, O boys!'

may have been an early shanty. I doubt this. It does not mean that every sea-song with a 'High ho! Boys!' or 'Yeo heave ho, my lads!' refrain can be called a shanty or was used for work; such songs were extremely common in the Navy, where shantying was taboo, from time immemorial.

My friend G. Legman pointed out to me that a song used in Shakespeare's *'Tempest'* may be some sort of genuine shanty. Shakespeare, it is thought took existing songs of his day and used them in his works instead of composing them himself. The song to which he refers is also found in *'The New Academy of Complements'* 1669 (London) Song number 110. The song, of course, is:

The Master, the Swabber, the Boatswain, and I
The Gunner and his mate,
Lov'd Mall, Meg, and Marina and Margery
But none of us cared for Kate,
For, she has a tongue with a tang,
Would cry to a Saylor go hang,
She loved not the savor of Tar, nor of Pitch,
Yet a Saylor might scratch here where e're she did itch,
Then to sea boys and let her go hang.

Shakespeare's version had, I believe, Marion for the third girl, Tailor for the Saylor in the penultimate line, and 'her' instead of 'here' in the same line.

It has been pointed out to me that in the Massachusetts Archive of a trial in 1665 of the captain of the *'Mary Galley'*, who was accused of putting his ship ashore on purpose on a ledge of rock outside Gloucester harbour, mention is made of the crew as they worked the ship out of harbour on a Sunday morning, being encouraged to sing *The British Grenadiers* while a drum was being beaten. But even this evidence does not prove that a shanty was being sung in 1665.

Harlow, a competent Yankee seaman of the sail, has included in his own collection of shanties, many songs sung as shanties. I, too, have done this in my book, but whereas it is permissible in a book of working songs of the sea, it is hardly evidence of an 'early shanty' to offer such a truly shore and sailor song as *The British Grenadiers* as proof.

Harlow, incidentally, has many shore-songs and sea-songs which he declares were used as shanties. Here are some with the job he gives for them in brackets;

Christopher Columbus	(pumps)
I Love the Blue Mountains	(halliards)
The Bosun's Story	(walkaway)
Boston Harbour	(capstan)
Nancy Lee	(capstan)
Adieu to Mamuna	(capstan)
Married to a Mermaid	(capstan)
The Darkies Sunday School	(hand-over-hand)
Dixie's Isle	(capstan)
Do Me Ama	(pumps)

The earliest genuine shanty I have found in print is given in my book *'Shanties from the Seven Seas'* with the date 1811, but recently I discovered what I think is an even earlier one, and one which I intend to give *'SPIN'* magazine readers at some later date.

Naval ship of the Transitional Period.

The Bosun's Locker Stan Hugill

Vol. 2 No. 7

Did shanties or any sort of work song exist before the nineteenth century? This is a query many people have tried to answer. In modern times ships, barques, and 'four-posters' were manned by small crews – small crews in big ships, ships much bigger than the ships of the early nineteenth century, and of the eighteenth and seventeenth centuries.

The round-sleeked, pot-bellied craft of the privateersmen, buccaneers, circumnavigators, and early whalers and merchant traders were small in burden compared with the ships of the second half of the nineteenth century and the beginning of the twentieth, but as regards personnel, they had more men than space. They were crowded with men to such an extent that 'dry-pulling' and arduous hauling to shanties (the shanty being worth ten men on a rope) so necessary to a later generation of shellbacks were both unknown and NOT NEEDED. Of this I feel certain. One would have thought that big single topsails would need more shantying than the double topsails of a later date, but the big crews and capstans obviously eliminated the need of hauling songs. The amount of 'beef' in each of these old-time ships would be able to 'walkaway' with any sail, and a rhythmic song to ease hauling was absolutely unwarranted.

The Clipper ships of the mid-nineteenth century too, were so heavily manned – many carrying double crews when tea racing – that it is rather doutful whether they bothered with shanties to the extent of latter day seamen and they certainly didn't invent any. The East Indiamen and the Blackwall Frigates were both run on naval lines, and here the accomplishing of work to a bosun's pipe or to the ship's drum and fife band was commoner than to shanties.

It was aboard the soul-grinding, heavily-geared rigs with small crews of later days that shantying grew. In fact it was the cutting down of the crews and enlarging of the tonnage that developed shantying to its perfection. This of course is mainly true in regard to HAULING. In the matter of heaving at the capstan, songs were probably used in earlier times but there is no proof that these were TRUE SHANTIES.

So those who strain themselves in trying to discover shanties (such as we know them) extant before 1800 are, I feel, seeking for needles in haystacks. I doubt if many, if any, existed. After research and cogitation this is the conclusion to which I have come.

Around our coasts many years ago the often semi-literate or even illiterate seamen and skippers of coasting craft invented 'songlets' or rhymes which were sometimes referred to as 'pilot verses'!

By means of these ditties longshore pilotage was committed to memory and probably saved many a good ship from finding a hard bottom. Very few of these have been saved but here are one or two to show the type of thing they were – and perhaps to arouse the interest of someone in saving such 'briefs' from extinction.

When it's high tide at London Bridge, it's half-ebb in the Swin.
It's low water at Yarmouth Roads and half-flood at Lynn.

First at Dudgeon, then the Spurn,
Flamboro' Light comes next in turn.

The Bosun's Locker Stan Hugill

Flamboro' Light you do pass by,
Scarboro' Castle you do draw nigh,
Scarboro' Castle runs out to sea
And Whitby light bears northerly.
Huntley Foot, point o' land,
Twenty-one miles from Sunderland.

After the first two lines of the latter verse many variants were to be found:

> Flamboro' Head as you pass by,
> Filey Brigg is drawing nigh;
> Scarboro' Castle stands out to sea
> And Whitby Light bears northerly.
> Huntley Foot, that damned high land,
> Is five and twenty from Sunderland,
> And our Ol' Man says: "If things go right,
> We'll be in the Tyne by tomorrow night."
> There 't' will be handle the spade,
> Damn and bugger the coal trade.

or

> Flamboro' Head comes next in sight,
> Whitby now lies in the bight,
> Then Hartlepool a dull red light,
> And we'll be in, if all goes right,
> Canny auld Shields tomorrow night.

These latter are guides to north-bound ships on the East Coast. The southern-bound had this ditty:

> Roker, Whitby, Flamboro', Spurn,
> Outer Dowser next in turn,
> East Dudgeon and Cromer bold,
> Look out for Haisboro' and the Wold,
> Then Kentish Knock, the Goodwins Three,
> North, east and south in turn, you'll see,
> And Dover with the cliffs so white,
> Dungeness and Sovereign now in sight.
> Beachy and Owers, stream the log,
> Down the Channel clear of fog,
> Point to point and light to light,
> We'll sail along both day and night.

Probably dozens of these little chants existed once sung to various melodies but where are they now?

Dundee Whalers

[Musical notation with lyrics:]

There's a mighty fleet of whalers, a-sailing from Dundee. They're mann'd by British sailors — for to take 'em o'er the sea, On a western o-cean passage — there's none that can compare, An' th' smartest ship to-o make the trip is Balena I declare.

Chorus
And th' wind is on the quarter —*, An' th' sails are full and free* There's not another whaler, a-sailing th' Arctic sea, Can beat the old Balen-a, An' she need not try it on, For we challenge all, both great an' small, From Dundee to St. Johns!

(* This sometimes ran — "An' th' engines working free")

There's the new-built Terra Nova, she's a model without doubt,
The Arctic an' Aurora, ye've heard so much about;
There's Jackson's model mailboat, the terror of the sea,
But she couldn't beat Balena on the passage from Dundee.

Bold Jackson carries canvas an' fairly raises steam,
An' Cap'n Gay the Erin Boy goes ploughin' thro' the stream;
An' Mullen says the Eskimo will beat the bloody lot,
To beat the ol' Balena oh, she'll find it rather hot.

And now that we are landed where the rum is mighty cheap,
We'll drink success to the Cap'n for guidin' us o'er the deep;
A health to all our sweethearts, an' to our wives so fair,
Not another ship could make that trip but Balena I declare.
Chorus

The Greenland Whale Fishery in which these whalers were engaged came to a finish by the end of the nineteenth century. It wound up in Hull (1870) and Greenock (1870) a little earlier. I learnt this song from an old Dundee whalerman, who told me that when heaving up the anchor it was often *played* by a *piper* – most Scottish whalers having a pair of bagpipes aboard.

The Bosun's Locker Stan Hugill

Vol. 2 No. 8
The Repertoire of the Singing Sailor

The repertoire of the Singing Sailor was vast. From all countries we have already learned that sailing ship man cribbed bits of this song and that, hymns, grand opera, musical-hall ditties, and so on, all being fish to the shantyman's net and many of which he altered, shortened or lengthened to suit the job of hauling on a rope or heaving at a capstan. Sometimes he kept many of the original words of a foreign song, or rather mangled forms of the words, other times he jettisoned the lot and made up a new set. In my shanty book I have given an example of how he took the *Huntsman's Chorus* from *'Die Fledermaus'*, how it is possible *Blow the Man Down* may have some musical connections with the carol *Stille Nacht Heilige Nacht* and how *The Princess Royal* in one of its music versions may be the hymn *Immortal, Invisible* of John Bunyan, and how *Reuben Ranzo* is definitely the Sicilian fisherman's song *Sciacamunnista Lampa*.

For his forebitters too many Irish shore tunes have been pinched and even sometimes much of the shore text.

Shore-composed sea-songs such as *Hearts of Oak* and *Tom Bowling* he wasn't very partial to; in regard to the former probably because of its insincerity – it sings that 'to honour we call you, not press you like slaves', just at the time when impress men and press-gangs were a feature in every seaport and often in inland towns. As to the latter, well this was a song normally tabooed aboard ship, sailors believing that anyone singing it would be courting death from drowning or falling from aloft during the voyage in question.

But in fact no shore sea-songs, even Dibdin's, were popular with Jack Salt.

Although from superstition, fear banned *Tom Bowling*, on the other hand that famous song *The 'Flying Dutchman'* was always popular at fo'c'sle 'banyans'. I have given a version of it here – a version I learnt from my father.

Sentiment was rarely to be found in a sailor shanty or forebitter, but occasionally a song would be heard aboard ship, chock-a-block with sentiment, which tradition for some unknown reason would deem permissible. Of such a category is the tear-pulling *Sailor's Grave*. The German seamen too had a *Sailor's Grave (Seemann's Begrabnis)* sung to the tune of *John Brown's Body*.

As he called at the ports of the Seven Seas, Sailor John naturally picked up many shore songs popular at the time, and many a fo'c'sle has rung to the strains of some Argentine *ranchero* as a ship left Buenos Aires, or a Bengali dance-tune as another ship left Calcutta. Pidgin English songs too were popular with the sailing-ship man, ditties like *Me have got a flower boat*, *Sixteen Annas One Rupee*, *From Canton to Macau*, and the Japanese ditty *Jonkina* were once heard wherever a covey of matlows got together for a sing-song.

Many people have asked how obscene Jack Tar was in his songs and shanties. Well to put it bluntly pretty nigh every one of his shanties were lewd, or partly so, and some of his songs too. But although he usually called a spade a spade, there were times when his *double entendre* out-Frenched the French. His nautical idiom was just the job for this sort of thing, where sailor words meaningless to the landlubber would have the sailorman in fits. On this tricky subject I hope to write at a future date.

From what I have written it would appear the sailing-ship man was what journalists would call 'catholic in his tastes of song', but with the advent of steam much of this catholicity disappeared, and the steamboat-man, with his quick turn-round and short stays in port, relied almost entirely on landsmen's songs of his own homeland.

The Flying Dutchman

It was a wild and stormy night far southward of the Cape, When from a stiff nor'wester we had just made our escape, Like a baby in its cradle, oh, the waves were hush'd to sleep, and peacefully we sailed along the bosom of the deep, and peacefully we sailed along the bosom of the deep.

When suddenly the helmsman, gave a shout of danger and of fear,
As if he had seen some sudden danger near:
He looked around the horizon and there upon our lee,
We saw the Flying Dutchmen come bounding o'er the sea.   *(repeat last line of chorus)*

'Take in yer flyin' canvas!' our watchful captain cried,
'To you find your ship's company, great peril doth betide!
The billows crested high with foam, all angry doth appear,
The wind springs up a hurricane, now Vanderdecken's near.

He sails too well, he goes too quick, to mark his eagle flight
And lightering like the Dutchman's stern, will soon pass out of sight
And distant ships they shudder at the breeze,
That sends the Flying Dutchman in fury o'er the seas

Now mourn for Vanderdecken, for terrible is his doom,
The oceans round the stormy Cape, shall be his living tomb,
The Dutchman beats about the Cape, night and day,
In vain he tried his oath to keep, by entering Table Bay.

The Bosun's Locker Stan Hugill

Vol. 2 No. 9

In sailing ships what type of singer did the crowd prefer?
Although it was usual to hear far more baritone voices, with the lone piping treble of the ship's boy, than tenors when work was being carried out aboard a windbag, the kind of soloist – the shantyman – preferred by all was one with a high-pitched, strident voice. The baritone chorus would be strong enough to be heard miles away, but the lone voice of the shantyman carrying the solo lines had to be high-pitched so that, above the wind strumming in the rigging and the roar of the sea, the words could be distinctly heard.

Classed in the main, Geordie, Scots and Welsh sailors were deep singers, but those of Ireland, Liverpool and London often tended to have high-pitched, strident voices of the kind sailormen preferred to lead at halyard and capstan. Of course this was typically true of shore folk singers of a past age. Street ballad 'chaunters' of murder, marriage, war, suicide, crime and scandal all used a 'false' high-pitched voice when singing, in order to sell their broadsheets. Even in deep-voiced (generally speaking) Wales the wandering old ballad-mongers of Victoria's age would sing falsetto. Negroes, too, although they usually sang deeply, could affect falsetto when needed, hence they made good shantymen, especially when it came to singing the 'hitches' or break-the-voice notes heard in true shanty singing.

In the singing of the old forebitters too, a high-pitched voice was preferred by the crowd. German and Scandinavian singers usually were of the deep-throated kind, although they also, in particular the Germans, could affect a falsetto when leading a 'sing-out' or 'hand-over-hand' on brace, clew line or jib halyard. In fact I've always felt that Germans were the best sailors, when it came to a 'sing-out', of all the maritime races. Shore singers of shanties rarely manage to get the right 'atmosphere' into their offerings; they are not raucous or strident enough.

Elizabeth Linklater in her *'Child Under Sail'* writes about shanties:

> 'There has, of course, been a great revival of interest in them, but I do not care for their modern setting and the refined way in which they are sung on the wireless. I think of the bronzed, weather-beaten faces of the men who sang the songs; of their huge, tarry hands, into which they always spat before grasping a brace; of their tattooed and brawny arms with the muscles standing out like ropes when the braces were hauled. I think of the high nasal voice of the shantyman, and the roar of the chorus, regardless of the tune – but all I hear, when I turn on my wireless, is refinement and nicely balanced parts, and with relief I turn instead to something where there is no make believe.'

We have had the *Shenandoah*s of Paul Robeson and Flint MacCulloch, and the one with the 'bath-tub' effect: these all having a hothouse beauty – the polite beauty of the concert hall, but they'll never compare with the wild vigorous beauty of *Shenandoah* as voiced, raucously perhaps, but compellingly, by the strong salty-voiced sons of Neptune in the forceful days of sail, in some rainless, sunburnt saltpetre harbour tucked away on the Flaming Coast of Western South America, as a three-month slimed mudhook was hove 'up'n'down' from its erstwhile doss-house by these 'Sons of forty sea-ports roaring yo, heave, ho!' (Bill Adams)

But, although I am averse to full-throated baritone radio treatment of shanties, I am all for the making of 'new' sea-songs, especially if they reach the standard of Hughie Jones' *Marco Polo*. Here is a marvellous sea-song indeed with all the *sound* and the right words of the genuine article. But I am averse to the origins of such songs being kept secret. It is troublesome enough these days for the collector to separate the wheat from the chaff, but if songs invented nowadays are not always given their composer and a note saying that they are not genuine, then God help the harassed collector of the future.

Here is the song I mentioned but omitted in the last issue of *'SPIN'*. It is called *The Sailor's Grave* and was very popular at fo'c'sle singsongs.

The Sailor's Grave

Our barque was far, far from the land, when the bravest of our gallant band, Went deadly pale, and pined away, Like the twilight of an autumn day.

We watched him through long hours of pain,
Our hopes were great, our task in vain,
His end was near, we felt sad qualms,
But he smiles and died in his shipmates' arms.
He had no costly winding sheet,
We placed two round shot at his feet,
And we sewed him up, he was canvas-bound.
Like a king he lay in his hammock sound.

We proudly decked his broken chest
With the *Blood'n'Guts across his chest

The flag we gave as a mark o' the brave,
And he was ready for a sailor's grave.
Our voices broke, our hearts were weak
And wet was seen on the toughest cheek,
We lowered him down o'er the ship's dark side,
And he was received by the rolling tied.

With a splash and a plunge and our task was o'er
And the billows rolled as they rolled before,
And many a wild prayer hallowed the wave,
As he sank deep to a sailor's grave.

* *Sailor name for the Red Ensign.*

The Bosun's Locker Stan Hugill
Vol. 2 No. 10

This issue, unfortunately, I am rather tied up with demanding work, so apart from giving you the old sailor song, *All Hands On Deck* or *Unmooring,* I won't have much to say. By the way, the only other printed version of this song is to be found in Captain Whall's *'Sea-songs and Shanties',* and his version is somewhat different in tune and words to mine.

Regarding the demanding 'work' I am engaged on. I may as well tell you that it is my new book *'Sailortown'*. Perhaps I may be allowed to blow my own trumpet a little and give it some advance publicity by stating that, although not a songbook, it has some interest to folk singers interested in sailor songs and shanties. In actual fact it has stemmed from what the several reviewers of my book *'Shanties from the Seven Seas'* said when pointing out the fact that shore composers of sea-songs sang of 'bounding billows', 'wet sheets' and 'raging gales', whereas Sailor John in his self-composed ditties sang rather of the 'beach'; of how he was 'rolling down Paradise Street' and so on, his eyes always directed towards the delights of the land. So on this theme I got together all I knew of the Sailortowns of the world, from Liverpool to 'Frisco, and from London to Shanghai, describing in the book the streets, pubs, crimps, boarding-houses, brothels, prostitutes, famous characters and shanghaiing and so on, and when a song existed connected with such things, a verse or two of such a song has been inserted. Hence the book could help those who are interested in the background of shanties and sea-songs. It will be going to the printer within the next month.

On the shanty research front it is most unusual nowadays to come across anything new. In my *'Shanty Book'* I stated, with other authorities agreeing, that Holland has never had any shanties of her own, preferring to use those of Britain and Germany. However, I am delighted to report that the Dutch Cape Horn Association, who until now have agreed with my findings, have at last run to earth the first, and only, Dutch shanty known. It is called *The Iron Man,* and as they have sent me its origin, Dutch text, English translation and music, I will, at a later date, allow *'SPIN'* to print it.

Sorry to be so brief this time, but may do better next issue.

The Bosun's Locker Stan Hugill

All Hands On Deck

All hands on deck, the bosun cried, in a voice like thunder roaring, All hands on deck his mates replied. 'Tis the signal for unmooring — Then your messenger bring to, heave the anchor to the bow, And we'll think on them girls when we're far, far away, And we'll think on them girls when we're far, far away.

The anchor's up!' our bosun cried, 'Vast heavin' boys, vast heavin',
Yer cat and fish take nimbly to, haul out yer bars, me boys,
Then obey yer bosun's call, walk away with the catfall,
And we'll think on them gals when we're far, far away.

Chorus: Oh, we'll think on them gals when we're far, far away.

'Cast loose yer tops'ls next !' he cried,
To'gall'nts'ls and royals,
Yer jibs and stays'ls see all clear, haul aft each sheet, me boys,
As we run before the gale, we will crowd our lofty sail,
And we'll think on them gals when we're far, far away.

Chorus: Oh, we'll think on them gals when we're far, far away.

Twas in the pleasant month of March, with a strong sou'easter blowin'
There wuz Kate and Jane and lovely Sue, tears from their eyes were flowin'
As they saw our lofty ship, runnin' head before the wind.
And we'll think on them gals when we're far, far away.

Chorus: Oh, we'll think on them gals when we're far, far away.

The Bosun's Locker Stan Hugill

Vol. 3 No. 1

Sailors in their songs and shanties normally, unlike farmers, shepherds and other folk singers, called a spade a spade – hence the difficulty of printing their songs in their entirety. However, as well as using unprintable words, sailor songs also contain a nautical terminology or *double entendre* which certainly equals, if not outdoes the sexual imagery used in shore folk songs as commented on by J. Reeves in his *'Idiom of the People'*.

The very fact that a ship is feminine in gender obviously was a good start for any mariner with imagination! As sailor songs developed already existing nautical terms soon came to be used to explain the chasing, courting, capturing and conquering of the feminine quarry.

My grandfather wrote in his songbook, which unfortunately was destroyed during the blitz on Liverpool, a sailor version of how to dance the Lancers (or it may have been the Quadrilles). The nautical imagery here was wonderfully apt, such as 'Short board':

> Gentleman makes a short board,
> Lady bears away on a starboard tack,
> comes head to wind,
> Rounding-to abreast the gentleman.

and so on. In one of Clark Russell's works a sailor giving evidence bewilders a judge with his salty spiel:

> "Aye, aye, yer 'onor. I was running free up such-and-such a street when four points on me starboard bow this craft hove in sight bearing down straight for me I brought up sharply with a round turn, heaving to until the strange craft came line abreast o' me........"

Or something like it – it is years since I read it.

An old sea-song (naval rather than merchant service) which shows respectable use of nautical phraseology is the *Seaboy's Farewell*, often sung by the men of the wooden walls of a Saturday night.

> Hush, hush ye winds till I repeat a parting signal to the fleet whose station is at Home
> And waft the seaboy's simple prayer an' oft may it be whispered there, while foreign climes I roam
>
> Here's to Father, reverend hulk, in spite of metal, spite of bulk, must soon his cable slip,
> Before he's broken up I'll try the flag of gratitude to fly, in duty to the ship.
>
> Here's to Mother, first-rate she, who launched me on life's stormy sea and rigged me fore and aft,
> May Providence her timbers spare and keep her hull in good repair, to tow the smaller craft.
>
> Here's to George the jolly-boat an' all the little craft afloat
> When they arrive at sailing age may wisdom be their weather-gauge to guide them on their way.
>
> Here's to all on Life's rude, stormy main, perhaps we ne'er may meet again,
> When summoned by the Board above, we'll anchor in the port of Love, an' all be moored together.

But it was in his amorous years netted in shanty and forebitter that Sailor John gave vent to his finest (or worst!) imagery. In verses such as:

> We closed alongside boys, I hauled in me slack,
> I busted me bobstay an' then changed me tack,
> Me shot locker's empty, me powder's all spent,
> Me gun needs repairing it's choked at the vent.
> (*Ratcliffe Highway*)

> He shifted her main tack an' he caught her flat aback,
> They rolled from the lee to the weather,
> And he laid her close 'longside, oh, close hauled as she would lie,
> Twas tack 'n' tack through hell an' stormy weather.
> (*The Flash Gals o' the Town*)

It is not possible here for me to give a full treatise on this most intriguing subject but with as much research as possible I present the following limited vocabulary of words and phrases used by Sailor John in his shanties and forebitters – all of them having two meanings, a shipboard one and a sexual one.

The phrase 'cut o' her jib' is obviously the type of face Jack's girlfriend possesses, and 'fire-ship', 'flash packet' and 'chowlah' are John's usual words for his kind of love. Female breasts are called 'catheads', the original use of the word being that given to two heavy baulks of oak projecting one from each bow to which the anchor was 'catted', i.e. hauled up clear of the 'drink'. 'Spars' are female limbs – a 'Giblet Pie' was a girl with long legs – and 'stern' or 'stern-sheets' described her 'derriere'. 'Bluff in the bow' meant her vital statistics were worth taking notice of, while 'round in the counter' suggests she is well-cushioned.

There were many other nautical words, terms and phrases used by Jack to soften the details of his amorous adventures in Shantytown, but in the main Jack was forthright in his obscenity so that most sailor songs are impossible to put, unexpurgated, into print.

Some of these words and terms have been used in folk songs over the air, on TV etc., without, I feel, the singer realising their meaning – although I fancy that Robin Hall and Jimmy MacGregor, judging from their faces, understood the true meaning of 'bobstay' when they sang it in *Doodle let me go girls* on the BBC 'Tonight' programme some time ago!

The Bosun's Locker Stan Hugill

Ratcliffe Highway

Now as I wuz a-walkin' down Ratcliffe Highway, A flash lookin' packet I chanct for to say, Of the port that she hailed from I cannot say much, But by her appearance I took her for Dutch. Singin' too-relye-ad-die, too-relye-ad-die, Singin' too-relye-ad-die, aye, too-relye-ay!

Her flag wuz three colours, her masthead **wuz low,**
She wuz round in the counter an' bluff in the bow
From larboard to starboard an' so sailed she,
She wuz sailin' at large, she wuz runnin' free.
Chorus: Singin' etc.

She wuz bowlin' along wid the wind blowin' free.
She clewed up her courses an' waited for me;
I fired me bow-chaser the signal she knew,
She backed her main towps'l an* for me hove-to.

I hailed her in English she answered me clear,
'I'm from the Black Arrow bound to the Shakespeare'
So I wore ship wid a what-d'yer-know,
'An' passed her me hawser an' took her in tow.

I tipped her me flipper an' took her in tow,
An' yard-arm to yard-arm away we did go;
She then took me up to her lily-white room,
An' there all the evening we drank an' we spooned.

(Several double entendre verses here omitted!)

Now all ye young seamen, take a warn in' I say,
Take it aisy me boys when yer down that Highway;
Steer clear of them flash gals on the Highway do dwell,
'Or they'll take up yer flipper an' yer soon be bound to hell.

The Bosun's Locker Stan Hugill

Vol. 3 No. 2

During the last three years, off and on, I have contacted many folk song clubs, both singers and members, and have been pleasantly surprised at the interest shown in sailor songs and shanties. Most groups, at some time or other, attempt a shanty, sailor or whaler song, and many I must admit, put them over quite well.

I have often been asked how a shanty should be sung. Well to begin with, the day of the shanty as a work song obviously has gone, therefore the query seems to be in two parts: should it be sung aping in the manner in which it was handled in its heyday by half-frozen tars hauling at halyard or sheet, or by drink-merry matlows trundling round a pawling capstan heaving up a weed-hung anchor, or should it be sung in the manner adopted by broad-chested baritones when singing *Drake's Drum* or *Hearts of Oak* at some boiled-shirted charity concert.

To answer this I think that the advice I gave in the first of these articles fills the bill: "'Tis impossible to sing a shanty without the feel of a rope or capstan bar in one's mit" was the cry of old shellbacks, but although it is impossible to recapture the full atmosphere of shantying without the background of canvas and hemp, the effort being made nowadays is, in my opinion, the finest ever achieved, and many landlubbers and landlubber groups are now producing shanties almost as good and as true as they were in their native salt....
a) Remember – a strident voice is preferable to a gentle one,
b) Free time in the solos is a true part of shantying,
c) Strict time in the refrains is essential,
d) Let's hear the WORDS.

And to this I add – leave out, for heavens sake, the toy capstan!

Shanties were essentially chorus songs, and a shanty without a chorus is like an egg without salt, so it is absolutely necessary to dig up a chorus. As I usually go to the clubs solo, the first thing I try to do is to rope the audience in by making them practise the chorus before I start the song. But if you intend to shanty regularly try to have a group with you so the chorus rings out in the proper deep-sea fashion.

Another shanty singing trick is the overlapping of the last word of the solo line with the first word of the refrain – a ruse common with other types of folk singing.

Harmony was <u>never</u> used at sea, unless some natural harmoniser did a little, and in this latter case it was normally either a Negro or a Taff who sang in such fashion. And in the hauling songs one other trick was the singing of each alternate stanza an octave higher or lower – something also found in Negro singing.

The days of sail have departed so no-one now can haul or heave on a ship's deck, hence the slowness advised by some 'authorities' in the singing of a hauling song no longer applies. But, on the other hand, don't sing as though each sailor work song was a hornpipe.

As an interest in the working of a capstan has been evinced in certain quarters I will attempt to explain the mechanics of this symbol of the sailing ship.

The very earliest device for heaving the anchor was a horizontal barrel between two stout upright baulks of timber. The rope cable was wound around this barrel four or five times and the barrel was hove around by

57

The Bosun's Locker Stan Hugill

means of spokes fitted into holes in the barrel. This device was known as a windlass, and although used on Drake's ship is even to be found today aboard Chinese junks, where it is used for working cargo. From this early form of windlass the brake-windlass evolved – a type of mechanism found aboard many deepwater sailing ships down through the centuries, finishing up around the latter half of the nineteenth century, and on English coasting schooners existing up to the Second World War. It was worked by two long levers or brakes – their up and down motion giving such a windlass its sailor name of the jiggitty-jig windlass. The anchor chain was wound round the barrel as the rope cable was in its prototype.

With the invention of the capstan, the horizontal barrel was positioned upright and in the earliest ones the nine-stranded cable-laid rope was attached to the heavy wooden stock anchor and was wound several times around the barrel, being kept in position by the buttresses on the barrel called whelps.

In the Navy the cable-laid rope was of such great proportions that it was impossible to wind it around the upright barrel. The result was two capstans were used – one huge, in the waist of the ship, around which the men trundled, and a smaller one some distance away from it. Linking the two capstans and wound round each was an endless rope called a messenger. From the messenger to the great cable-laid anchor rope – which came in through the bow hawse pipe, ran along the deck beside the two capstans and entered the huge cable tier below deck through another pipe – short ropes called nippers were tied. Young lads had to follow these nippers as they moved slowly between the two capstans, as they reached the big one before they began to go round its barrel they would 'fleet' them i.e. shift them back to position on the big cable near the small capstan. This job was repeated until all the large cable was hove in. It was

from such a task that the word 'nipper' entered the English language as a name for a small boy.

When anchor **chains** took the place of cable-laid ropes the chain **did not go round the capstan barrel but beneath** the fo'c'sle-head to where stood a great windlass such as one finds on the fo'c'sle-head of a modern steamer, although in this case there was no steam to make it go! The chain came in over this windlass in metal grips called cable-holders or gipsies and went down straight into the cable locker below the deck. From this windlass a metal shaft went up through the deck of the fo'c'sle-head and was the axis around which the fo'c'sle-head capstan revolved. The men pushed the capstan around with bars working the windlass underneath, bringing in the anchor 'clank-clank', one link at a time. Most of these capstans were double-headed, that is they had two sets of pigeonholes (see drawings). In the upper holes the bars were placed when the anchor was to be hove; when the job was merely heaving some rope like a tack or sheet taut this would be wound round the barrel and the lower pigeonholes alone were manned.

In many ships of later days and in Yankee packets smaller capstans, around the barrels of which ropes for working the ship were wound, were to be found on the main deck, sometimes as many as six, and in some Yankee ships one was also to be found on the poop. When a sailing ship was being moored, hauled through locks or from one side of the

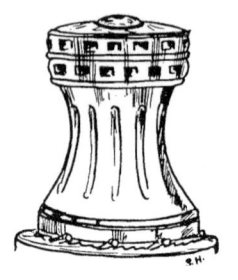

The Bosun's Locker Stan Hugill

Can't Ye Dance The Polka?

As I walked down the Broadway, one evenin' in Ju-ly, I met a maid who axed me trade, an' a Sailor John sez I .. Then away, you Santee, my dear Annie, Oooh!, ye Noo York gals, Can't ye dance the polka?

To Tiffany's I took her,
I did not mind expense;
I bought her two gold earrings,
An' they cost me fifteen cents.

Chorus: Then away you Santee,
My dear Annie,
Oooh! ye Noo York gals,
Can't ye dance the polka?

Sez she you Limejuice sailor,
Now see me home you may,
But when we reached her cottage door,
She this to me did say.

My flash man he's a Yankee,
Wid his hair cut short behind,
He wears a pair of long seaboots
An' he's Bosun in the Blackball Line.

He's homeward bound this evenin'
An' wid me he will stay,
So git a move on sailor boy,
Git crackin', on yer way!

So I kissed her hard and proper
Afore her flash man came,
An' fare ye well, me Bowery gal,
I know yer little game.

I wrapped me glad rags round me,
An' to the docks did steer,
I'll never court another maid,
I'll stick to rum an' beer.

I joined a Yankee blood-boat
An' sailed away next morn,
Don't ever fool around wid gals,
Yer safer off Cape Horn!

dock to another, the mooring ropes would be wound around the barrel of all capstans needed, just like they are around the drum-ends of the winches of modern steamers.

This long rigmarole, I hope, will clear up the query as to where the rope went round the capstan. In the case of anchor chains – they didn't!

As well as men pushing away at the bars there was also an individual sitting on his behind hauling in the incoming rope, over which the men had to step at each revolution.

Some capstans – mainly in the Navy, but also some old East Indiamen – had to take in a wire or rope from one bar's end to the next. This helped to keep the bars in place and also extra hands could seize a piece of it and help to put more 'beef' into the job. Such a wire or rope was called a 'swifter'.

Old hands always liked to be near the barrel of a capstan when trundling since they hadn't so far to walk, the outboard ends of the bars being left to the new and young hands who would have to tramp a much bigger circle. But in the case of the pawls of the capstan being stripped – that is the metal flaps which prevent the capstan 'walking back' being suddenly torn off by a great groundswell lifting the vessel up on its summit in some open roadstead – it was always the old hands who got killed, the younger ones being thrown clear as the capstan rushed round in reverse. Such a catastrophe usually occurred in the open roadsteads of the west coast of South America.

Vol. 3 No. 3

Quite recently I have been asked to review a new American book entitled *'Songs the Whalemen Sang'* edited by Gale Huntingdon. This is a collection drawn mostly from songs scribbled down by the whalemen themselves in their private journals which have been preserved in the many maritime museums and whaling museums of America's eastern seaboard. Judging from this authentic collection it would appear that the 'blubber-hunters' sang many other kinds of songs besides the typical whaling ones of the chase and capture of the mighty Cachalot. This fine-looking volume has arrived at an opportune time when whaling songs appear to be in great demand among the folk groups. And from this and other collections we realise that a great many whaling songs have been preserved – Gracias a Dios! – for posterity.

However, in the case of ditties of another tough body of old-time sailors, the Sealers, this is not so. To my knowledge no book has ever appeared purporting to be Songs the Sealers Sang, and I know of no sealer song included in the numerous books of sea-songs, forebitters, shanties and so on, nor in the ordinary folk collections. However, when I was gathering together material for my shanty book, Mr D. MacDonald loaned me a most interesting pamphlet, published in St. John's, Newfoundland in 1925, of songs sung by the old-time Sealers. Although text only is given, the tune of each song is named, usually some well-known air. One of the most interesting to me was that called *Wadham's Song*, an early 'pilot verse' of Newf'nland's rugged and treacherous coastline, of the same class as those I mentioned in an earlier *'SPIN'* once used on the British coast by fishermen, coasters and others. The tune to which this song was sung is similar to that of 'I'll tell Ma when I get home, the boys won't leave the girls alone'. The song apparently is named after its author who wrote it in 1756. It was placed on record in the Admiralty Court in London soon after it was composed, since it was considered the best contemporary coasting guide for that wild coast.

Wadham's Song

From Bonavista to the Cabot Isles, the course is north full forty miles,
When you must steer away Nor' east, till Cape Freels, Gull Isle, bears West-nor-west.

Then North-nor-west thirty three miles, three leagues off shore lies Wadham's Isles,
Where of a rock you must beware, two miles Sou-sou-east from off Isle bears.

Then Nor-west-by-west twelve miles or more, there lies Round Head on Fogo Shore,
But Nor-nor-west, seven or eight miles, lies a sunken rock near the Barrack Isles.

Therefore, my friend, I would you advise, since all these rocks in danger lies,
That you may never amongst them fall, but keep your luff and weather them all.

As you draw near to Fogo Land, you'll have fifteen fathoms in the sounding sand;
From fifteen to eighteen, never more, and that you'll have close to the shore.

When you abreast of Round Head be, then Joe Batt's point you'll plainly see;
To starboard then three or four miles, you'll

The Bosun's Locker Stan Hugill

see a parcel of damned rugged isles.

When Joe Batt's Arm you are abreast, then
Fog Harbour bears due West;
But untold Fortune, unlucky laid, a sunken
rock right in the trade.

So West-nor-west you are to steer, till
Brimstone Head doth plain appear,
Which over Pelley's Point you'll see, then of
that danger you are free.

As you draw within a mile, you'll see a house
on Syme's Isle;
The mouth of the channel is not very wide,
but the deepest water is on the larboard
side.

When within Syme's Point you have shot,
then three fathoms of water you have got,
Port hard your helm and take care, in the mid
channel for to steer.

When Pelley's Point you are abreast,
starboard haul and steer Sou-sou-west,
Till Pilley's Point covers Sym's stage, then you
are clear I will engage.

Apropos contemporary books covering folk song in general I would declare the most enlightening to be one I recently received from its publishers, University Books Inc., New York. Its author, G. Legman, whom I claim as a rather good friend, has been acclaimed 'the most learned and most controversial figure in the field of American folklore and 'the principal living specialist in erotic folklore'.

This book *'The Horn Book'* is a *must* for everyone interested in folk song, unexpurgated, as sung by the sailor, peasant, labourer, fisherman and crofter, not to mention the bloods and bucks of olden times. He gives the real facts about erotic literature and folklore instead of 'the fakes and fantasies' that he declares now pass for authentic material. His chapter on Burns' *'Merry Muses'* is most enlightening and will shock many Scotsmen, and those on 'The Bawdy Song' and 'Folk songs and Folklore', will certainly cause some eyebrow lifting among those folk singers who think they know the lot.

In relation to Sailor Songs he makes mention of – apart from an unpublished MS of the present writer – the only unexpurgated English book of Sailor Shanties, called *'A Collection of Sea-songs and Ditties'*, 'from the stores of Davy Jones', the only known copy of which is in the collection of the Kinsey Institute in America. It has been attributed to either Frank Shay who wrote *'American Sea-songs and Shanties'*, or to David W. Bone, author of *'Capstan Bars'*.

'The Horn Book' is rather expensive costing 12 dollars, 50 cents, but if you really want to know the true background of folk song, this is the only book in English up to date that gives it.

Vol. 3 No. 4

Tony and Beryl – that indefatigable and unsinkable pair of editors – writing in the last *'SPIN'* apropos folk song in schools, suggest that 'folk music can be a basis to build on, and not necessarily only musically' but 'as a wider project embracing history, geography, etc.'. This statement has put me in a romantic mood – not in the one of Love, but in its original sense of racing clippers, and pigtailed mariners, of buccaneers and treasure. Here we go then, to give a rough outline of the ships and their trades and the men who sailed them, in an endeavour to recreate the atmosphere in which the shanty was born.

As I have pointed out previously the shanty was probably a product of the beginning of the nineteenth century. With the cessation of the Napoleonic Wars and the American War of 1812, merchant ships developed and merchant seamen found new freedom. No longer was the sailor liable to be torn from his ship or home by a roving press-gang, or piratical press tender 'lying off the Bar o' Shields' or elsewhere and pressed into fighting service in the 'King's Navee' – a service where shantying was taboo. Now, unhampered by such fears, the creating and singing of shanties replaced the erstwhile hauling and heaving to numbers and the bosun's pipe (and cat-o-nine-tails).

Following hard on the heels of the Post Office 'Coffin Brigs' – the first regular, though rather unseaworthy 'mail packets' to cross the Atlantic or Western Ocean from Britain to the U.S.A., came the Packet Ships, the first emigrant ships carrying mail worth so calling. In ships of the Blackball, Swallowtail, Red Cross, Black Cross and other lines many a thousand of rather forlorn Irish, Scandinavian and German emigrants crossed the Atlantic and had their first view of the New World from the rough shed in Castle Garden:

Twas at the Castle Garden, oh they landed me ashore,
Heave away, me Johnnies, heave away!

Liverpool was the great jumping-off port for the 'Amerikay', and here, around the Prince's Dock and elsewhere, the confused scenes of Packet Ship departures were daily occurrences. Be-kirtled, sea-booted and kerchiefed females from Mid-European countries, with babies slung at their hips and their bearded, fur-hatted husbands at the sides, clay-pipe smoking Paddies in knee-breeks and big buckled leather belts, carters with their baggage-drays, bustling ship's chandlers and beaver-hatted agents, and tarpaulin-wearing mariners smelling of tar, all thronged the quays. A forest of masts and yards greeted the eye at all points of the compass, with nimble topmen aloft loosing sails and leading down gear prior to sailing. As well as the fast Packet Ships there were many slowcoaches, also bound for the States. The emigrants had to supply their own food for the passage, 'meal' being the main diet, either bought from the marine chandlers on the dockside, or sold aboard the ships. It was the Irish pronunciation of the word 'meal, i.e. 'male' which made the emigrants in the shanty *We're All Bound to Go!* think they were travelling on a 'mail' ship.

Oh, yes I've got a packet ship, and today she does set sail,
With five and fifty emigrants and a thousand bags of male (meal).

The Bosun's Locker Stan Hugill

The seamen aboard such ships – known as the Packet Rats – were mostly Liverpool or New York Irish, the toughest seamen, probably, the world has ever seen. Good seamen at sea who deteriorated ashore. The afterguard, that is the captain and mates, of such ships were even tougher, and 'handspike hash and belayin'-pin soup' were the order of the day. One gang of Packet Rats known as the Bloody Forty, signed on the famous Packet Ship the *'Dreadnought'* – the Blood-boat of the Atlantic – with the expressed intention of trimming the whiskers of its master Captain Samuels. However, Samuels turned the tables and tamed the Bloody Forty.

Aboard such ships shantying was highly developed, and many well-known ones such as *Blow the Man Down* and *Leave Her Johnny*, had their beginnings there, as also did many forebitters. The Irish produced many from the minor shore tunes of their Celtic homeland; other have been culled and adapted from the singing of the emigrants – when they weren't seasick! – Scandinavian songs, German hymns and Slav folk songs. A further development of the shanties occurred when these Packet Rats deserted their ships in New York and Boston (preferably when the bitter North Atlantic winter was approaching) and headed south to the warmer climate of the Gulf Ports of New Orleans and Mobile, here to work shoulder to shoulder with Negro hoosiers screwing the bales of cotton into the holds of the Cotton Droghers. From the Negroes they learnt new work songs, songs used in heaving around the big jackscrews, and the Negroes learnt new work songs from the Jolly Tars. Many of the songs sung on the waterfronts of New Orleans and Mobile had come down from the Mississippi and Ohio rivers by way of the boatmen and were 'River-Songs'. *Shenandoah* once sung by the 'Long Knives' and the 'Blue Bellies', cavalrymen, frontiersmen and mountainmen, probably took this route to the wharves of the Gulf Ports and was incorporated in the sailorman's repertoire by the present white hoosiers or cotton-stowers, erstwhile Western Ocean Packet Rats. These latter when they returned to sea, probably signed on a wooden Cotton Drogher bound for Liverpool or Le Havre, often called 'coffin ships', as their sides veritably burst open thanks to the cotton bales being screwed too tightly. They carried such work songs with them, introducing them into the crews of the ships in which they next signed.

In fact the Gulf Ports could be called Shanty Marts for it was in them that the exchange and barter of River-songs, Negro work songs and Irish shanties occurred. A shanty like *Lowlands* came from Britain, was taken by the Negroes of Mobile and transformed into *Dollar and a Half a Day* and in such guise came back to the land of its origin. Good examples of shanties with the hallmark of the Gulf Port Shanty Mart on them are *Johnny Come Down to Hilo* and *Clear the Track*, both having Irish airs with Negro words and phrases in their refrains. The West Indies, too, produced shanties; work songs used by the islanders and introduced aboard sailing ships by coloured crews shipping out of Barbados and Jamaica in the Rum and Sugar Droghers. *Sally Brown* probably comes into this category.

In the West Coast of South America trade, in the Cape Horners, which around the seventies and eighties loaded saltpetre in Chile, several new shanties were born; shanties with pseudo-Spanish wording in the refrains and a Latin touch in their tunes. These are in the main not so well known in the folk song world.

The seamen of the Western Ocean Packets produced many forebitters too, and some of these were born aboard the old East Indiamen, but strangely enough, the Flying Fish Sailors, i.e. the men in the Tea Clippers out to China and Japan, produced few if any shanties peculiarly their own, although one or two were born in the Australian Wool Clippers.

The Bosun's Locker Stan Hugill

The Coolie Ships were vessels running a triangular course from Liverpool out to India with general cargo, thence across to Trinidad with indentured coolie labourers, and back to Liverpool with rum and sugar. These ships had Lascar seamen and the afterguards and crews spoke a mixture of Hindustani Bat and English. Such a lingua franca must have produced shanties, but apart from a solitary hauling song I have collected called *Eki Dumah*, I doubt if any exist today.

Aboard the Whalers, specialised songs of the trade came into being as early as the latter part of the eighteenth century but no shanties were born. The great shanty making period was from the 1820s until the sixties and seventies, after this few new shanties came into being, although marches from the Crimean, Zulu, and Boer Wars were taken by seamen, adapted and used at the capstan head.

The Fourteenth of February

On the fourteenth of Febru'ry, we sailed from the land, In the bold Princess Royal, bound for Newfoun'land, We had forty-five seamen for a ship's compan-y, The wind from the east'ard, To the west'ard steered we.

We'd hardly been sailin' but a day two or three,
When the man from our masthead strange sail he did see.
She came bearin' down on us with her tops'l so high,
And under her mizen peak black colours did fly.

An' when this bold pirate had hove alongside,
With a loud speakin' voice, 'We are comin'!' he cried.
'We come from fair London bound to Callao,
So hinder us not in our passage to go.

'Back yer maintop'l an' heave yer ship to,
For I have a letter to be carried home by you.
'I'll back my maintop'l an' heave my ship to,
But only in some harbour an' alongside o' you.

The Bosun's Locker Stan Hugill

or **The Princess Royal**

On the fourteenth of February we-e sailed from the land, In the bold Princess Ro-oy-al— bound for Noo-oo-foun' land, We had for-ty five sea-e-me-en- for a ship's compa-nee-ee, An' the wind from the ee-east'ard, To the we-est-ard steered we.

He chased us to the wind'ard and through the long day,
An' he chased us to the loo'ard but he could not gain way
An' he fired long-shot after us but he could not prevail,
An' the Bold Princess Royal showed a clean tail.

Go down to yer grog, m'lads, go down every one,
Go down to yer grog, m'lads, go down one an' all,
Go down to yer grog, m'lads, an' be of good cheer,
For as long as we've sea-room, we've nothing to fear!

Vol. 3 No. 5
'Songs of American Sailormen'

Published recently by Oak Publications INC. New York, at $2.95, it is a nicely turned-out, unabridged, paperback edition of the original work by Joanna Colcord, published in 1938, itself an enlarged edition of *'Roll and Go'* by the same lady, published in 1924 by Bobs Merrill Co., Indianapolis.

Miss Colcord was born aboard her father's ship – this statement seems to come from Jack is every inch a sailor! – while among the romantic islands of the South Seas, and, up to the age of eighteen, lived in deepwater surroundings, her companions being American seamen of the Old School. In such an atmosphere she, obviously, imbibed much nautical knowledge. And of course she learnt her shanties.

When Miss Colcord first published her *'Roll and Go'* in 1924 – with the exception, perhaps, of Captain John Robinson, whose collection *'Songs of the Sailorman'* first appeared in the magazine *'The Bellman'*, in 1917, she was one of the few collectors in America who had first-hand knowledge of the subject. She added to the shanties, and in particular to the forebitters and whaling songs in her later work, the result being an almost complete treatise on shantying from the American angle. In this paperback edition the addition of guitar chords makes it an indispensable volume for modern folk singers interested in shanty singing – and what folk group nowadays is not? However, if anyone expects to find the bawdy or near bawdy versions of shanties in this work he will be unfortunate. I doubt somehow whether such versions would ever have been heard by Miss Colcord (unless by accident), for sailors were, in the main, respectable enough not to sing their spiciest lines when women were aboard. However, I would have thought that some of the tunes Miss Colcord failed to find for certain songs in her earlier book – I am thinking mainly of *Rolling Down to Old Maui* – she could have found from other printed collections, thereby making this paperback edition more valuable still. *'Songs the Whalers Sang'*, for instance, gives the tune of the whalers' song cited.

Missing lines, too, such as the first line of verse 6 of *The Coast of Peru* could have been inserted, and her wish that *Come Down you Bunch of Roses, Come Down* could be resuscitated, has of course, been granted in several modern collections. *The Lass of Mohea* (usually Mohee) given here is more sentimental and less outspoken than some of the versions I have heard, and her version of *Abel Brown the Sailor* (*Abram Brown*) is not the form of tune of the sailor-over-hand song, but one taken from the gramophone records of the early thirties.

On page 98 Miss Colcord gives Captain Robinson's *John Cherokee*, and states that 'Eckstrom and Smyth give a fragment of this song, with the refrain *Jan Kanaganaga, too-li-aye*.' This is of extreme interest to the reviewer, firstly because I have a rather different version, in tune, of *John Cherokee*, and, secondly because this is the only reference I have ever seen in print to my collected *John Kanaka-maka tulai-e*. As to one being the refrain of the other, this, of course, is just plain rubbish; the two shanties are entirely unrelated, and I learnt both, many years ago, from a wonderful coloured shantyman called Harding the Barbadian, a man steeped in shanty tradition, and a real seaman who would never have been guilty of

The Bosun's Locker Stan Hugill

making two shanties out of one.

However, apart from these few criticisms, this is a fine book, with all the well-known shanties and some unusual ones, as well as many forebitters or fo'c'sle songs, and those, too, of the whalemen. Her chapter on the Singing Sailor explains the types of shanties, and covers the troublesome query of the origin of the same 'shanty'. In the main body of the book between the songs Miss Colcord gives racy and smooth-running commentary, with reference to her singers, although in the main, the songs are as she heard them herself at sea, or from her father, a master mariner of the seventies.

Finally this book is probably the only collection wherein the songs sung by American freshwater sailors – the men of the Great Lakes – are to be found. There must have been many hundreds of these songs in the heyday of the Lakes schooners, but where are they now?

Vol. 3 No. 6
Liverpool Sailor Songs
(in reference to Liverpool place-names.)

Liverpool being a port of fair antiquity, is naturally referred to in many of the shanties, and I propose to give couplets and stanzas from various shanties – many of true Liverpool birth, others claimed, often erroneously by Liverpool – in which Liverpool place-names, docks, pubs and characters are mentioned.

The first Liverpool street that comes to mind is naturally, Paradise Street. This district, the street itself and the alleys, jowlers and 'weints' which at one time tentacled from it, is often mentioned in shanties and forebitters. In the Liverpool halyard shanty *Blow the Man Down*, in the version in which Jack chases the flashpacket, and in that in which he is accosted by a 'fat Irish bobby', Paradise Street is the scene of both the 'chase' and the 'meet'. In the now popular Liverpool forebitter *Maggie May*, in the older version, Paradise Street is given as the usual hang-out of this famous, or infamous, sailor-whore, with Canning Place as another area of her soliciting – probably, although the song doesn't say so, at the feet of the statue of Mr Huskisson, a famous whores' parade a hundred years ago.

When I ran into her, I hadn't got a care,
I wuz cruisin' up and down ol' Canning Place;
She wuz dressed in a gown so fine, like a frigate of the line,
An' I being a sailorman gave chase.
Oh, Maggie, Maggie May, they have taken you away,
To slave upon Van Diemen's cruel shore;
You robbed many a whaler an' many a drunken sailor,
But ye'll never cruise down Paradise Street no more.

Later versions give Lime Street, a street mentioned in the following capstan song:

Our advance note's in our pocket, boys, it sure will take us far,
Heave away me Johnnies, heave away, away!
An' now a cruise down Lime Street, boys, an' to the American Bar,
Heave away me bully boys, we're all bound to go!

The American Bar, of course, has been known to generations of sailors from all over the Seven Seas, as also was its one-time famous Ma Egerton. W. Tapscott, mentioned in the Packet Ship version of this shanty, was a well-known Liverpool emigrant agent of Oldhall Street. Versions giving the Salthouse Dock, the Albert Dock and Clarence Dock, as the berths from which the emigrants sailed, have also been handed down to us:

As I wuz walkin' out one day, down by the Salthouse Dock,
I met an emigrant Irish gal conversin' wid Tapscott.

The Salthouse Dock is also mentioned in the *Liverpool Packet*, although the Waterloo Dock was sung by some shantymen:

An' now we are leaving the sweet Salthouse Dock,
All the boys an' the gals on the Pierhead do flock,

In this song, too, there is reference to the Rock Light:

An' we'll round the Rock Light where the salt

The Bosun's Locker Stan Hugill

tides do flow,
She's a Liverpool Packet, O Lord let her go!

In the capstan shanty *Jamboree*, the Rock Light also appears, as does, in some versions, Fort Perch Rock over at New Brighton. The Bar, too is referred to, while Dan Lowrie's, a sailor 'dive' (some say playhouse) appears in the same song.

Park Lane (or Parkee Lane) is to be found in many shanties, in particular in *Roller Bowler*, which also, in Sharp's version, has Playhouse Square:

Oh, the first time that I saw her,
Hooraw, you roller bowler!
Oh, the first time that I saw her,
'Twas down in Parkee Lane (or Playhouse Square).
Timme me high rig-a-jig, an ' a ha-ha!
Good mornin', ladies all!

Most of all the streets already given are to be found in what was known as the South End Sailortown; the North End Sailortown was centred around Union Street, mentioned in *Roving Jack*, the Liverpool song unearthed by Jackie Macdonald and Bridie O'Donnell. Close to Union Street once stood Rosemary Lane, but I don't think this is the one mentioned in earlier forms of *Bellbottomed Trousers*. I rather do believe that this is the Rosemary Lane in London (now Royal Mint Street) near the London Docks:

I lived in good service in Rosemary Lane,
I keep the goodwill of my master and dame;
Till a sailor came there one night for to lay,
And that was the beginning of my misery.

Marybone or Marylebone, however, sung of by Sailor John, *is* the Liverpool and not the London one. Sailors often called it 'Marrowbone':

I dreamt a dream the other night, I t'ought I wuz at home,
Oh, there wuz me an' my Judy, back home in Marybone;
A-sitting' in a pub, me boys, a jug o'ale in hand,
But when I woke, I found no joke, on the Banks o' Newf'n'land.

Not far from this district lies Great Howard Street, once the habitat of Paddy West, the famous Liverpool boarding-house master:

As I wuz a-rollin' down Great Howard Street,
I strolled into Paddy West's house;
He gave me a plate of American Hash,
An' swore it wuz Liverpool scouse.

Great Howard Street, too is sometimes substituted for Paradise Street in *Blow the Man Down*. Other Liverpool crimps and boarding-house masters mentioned in song are Paddy Doyle, with a shanty to himself:-

Timme way hay high ya,
We'll pay Paddy Doyle for his boots!

Rapper Brown, given in one version of *Go to sea no more*:

Now as I wuz rollin'down the street I met ol' Rapper Brown
I axed him then to take me in, he looked at me wid a frown,
Sez he, Last time ye wuz paid off, wid me ye chalked no score,
But I'll take yer advance, an I'll give ye a chance, an' I'll send yiz to sea once more.
and John da Costa:

Oh, watch yer step me bully, for John da Costa's around,
If yer not careful, he'll ship yer out, bound for ol' Puget Sound.

Other streets are given in the now famous *Leaving of Liverpool*:

The Bosun's Locker Stan Hugill

Farewell to Lower Frederick Street, Anson Terrace and Parkee Lane
I'm bound for Californ-i-a, an' may not see you again.

In the forebitter *The Liverpool Judies* the Bramley Moor Dock is referred to:

An' now we've arrived in the Bramley Moor Dock
An' all of them flash judies on the pier head do flock;
The barrel's run dry an' our five quid advance,
An' I guess it's high time for to git up an' dance.

And the Princes Dock is given in a verse sung by some singers of *Maggie May*:

Oh, the rain came down in torrents, as in my pants an' boots and socks
I made my way down to the Princes Dock.

In this version the poor, robbed sailor makes a few pennies for his carfare home by singing under the famous 'clock'. In the old Liverpool forebitter *The Ebenezer*, Liverpool Bay is mentioned:

'Twas pump her bullies, night an' day,
To help her git to Liverpool Bay.

The halyard song, *Roll, Alabama, Roll*, is the only shanty to my knowledge in which any place 'over the water' is mentioned, i.e. Laird's shipyard, although 'Wallasey Gates' were sometimes sung about in the homeward-bound song *Goodbye fare-ye-Well*.

Other Liverpool-connected shanties, although they may not mention any particular Liverpool place-name or character, are: *The Blackball Line*, certain versions of *Stormalong, Across the Western Ocean, Haul the Bowline* (*Kitty comes from Liverpool*), *The Sailor's Way* (forebitter);
as well as the rarer shanties of the Liverpool–West Coast of South America Nitrate and Guano trades:
Serafina, Paddy Lay Back, Blood Red Roses, The Gals o' Chile, The Companayro, Homeward Bound, Randy Dandy O! and the *Saltpetre Shanty*. And of course some versions of *Rio Grande*:

So fare-ye-well me Liverpool gel,
We're bound for the Rio Grande!

The Bosun's Locker Stan Hugill

Bound for South Australia

[Musical notation with lyrics:]

Them Liverpool gals ain't got no combs, Heave a-way! heave away! They comb their hair wid codfish bones, An' we're bound for South Australia! Heave away my bully, bully boys, Heave away! Heave away! Heave away, why don't ye make a noise? An' we're bound for South Australia.

Toxteth gals don't sleep on beds,
They all doss down on finny addie heads.

Everton gals make damn fine cooks,
They're good at catching kippers on hooks.

[Musical notation with lyrics:]

Park Lane gals ain't got no combs, Heave away! heave away! They comb their hair wi'd salt-fish bone, An' we're bound to South Australia! Heave away, me bully, bully boys, Heave away! haul away! Heave away, why don't yiz make some noise? An' we're bound for South Australia!

South End gals don't wear any frills,
They're skinny and tight as a finny addie's gills.

Our Old Man don't set no sail,
He's a Liverpool man wid a sait-fish's tail.

O, South Australia's a bloody fine place,
To git blind drunk is no disgrace.

This shanty was often sung at the capstan head as well as at the pumps – hence the use of the word `haul` as well as `heave` in some refrains. There were many versions of both words and tune and in my book I give several more. The words here are those given me by an old Liverpool Sailor Paddy Delaney, but the song was equally popular in Yankee as well as English ships. The former often sang `an` we're bound for California.

This shanty was often sung at the capstan head as well as at the pumps – hence the use of the word 'haul' as well as 'heave' in some refrains. There were many versions of both words and tune and in my book I give several more. The words here are those given me by an old Liverpool sailor Paddy Delaney, but the song was equally popular in Yankee as well as English ships. The former often sang 'an we're bound for California'.

It is now more or less agreed that sailors in the China tea trade did not produce any new shanties, nor did they sing shanties to any extent – except perhaps at anchor heaving. The theory I gave in an earlier article was that since the ships were small and the crews large – some crews were even doubled when racing – the need for shanties didn't exist. But if so much 'beef' aboard the tea clippers silenced the shantyman, the singing sailor was in no wise mute. The sailor naturally picked up and adapted songs in 'furrin lingoes in the port he wuz in' to quote a phrase from a shanty. On the China coast Pidgin English songs often rang in his ears – and for John to hear was for John to learn, and sing at fo'c'sle 'banyans'. This being the case several Pidgin English songs have been handed down to us as part of Saltwater Jack's repertoire. Before I give some examples let me yarn a little about this lingua franca known as Pidgin English.

The clipper ship men and the early steamboatmen were all familiar with the broken English of the China coast, spoken from Macao to North China. Expressions like 'can do' meaning 'it's possible', 'maskie' for 'O.K.' and 'chow-la' for 'grub' in general were so tenacious that they were even to be heard aboard Blue Funnel ships of the 1930s.

Some of the earlier words, at one time extremely common, words such as 'boberi' meaning 'foolish talk', and 'fai-ti!' meaning 'hurry up!' died out in more recent years. Some of the so-called Pidgin English was not in fact English at all, but stemmed from odd Spanish and Portuguese words, corrupted in the mouths of Chinese coolies and with the passing of years. 'Joss' for an idol comes from the Spanish 'Dios' meaning 'God'; 'junk', a native boat is from the Portuguese, 'junco'. 'Mandarin' is a Spanish word as is 'compradore' or 'agent'. 'Boberi' of course is the Spanish word 'bobería' meaning 'silly talk'. Other Pidgin English words were Chinese mainly from the Cantonese dialect: 'shangyen': cigarette, 'samshu': wine, 'laoyeh': mister, and 'lao-dah': a boatman. English words were, naturally, sprinkled through the vocabulary, sometimes recognisable with just an ending of 'ee' or 'lee', sometimes completely 'China-sized'. 'Pidgin' itself is the English word 'business' but in the main it was an understandable lingua franca used all along the China coast. On the Japan coast it was used a little since some of the ship-working coolies were Chinese, but there was another 'bat' called the 'Yokohama dialect' that was heard along the waterfront in the sixties and seventies of the nineteenth century. It consisted largely of genuine Japanese words linked together in un-Japanese fashion. For instance a lighthouse was called a 'fune-haiken-sarampam-nai-rosoku', which reads 'ship-see-no-boat candle'. And a sailor who left his ship and got a job ashore as a teacher of English in a Japanese school, a common happening in the nineteenth century, would called be a 'damn-raise-shito' or a 'damn-your-eyes-man' on account of his frequent oaths even when in front of the class.

South Sea Island Pidgin was, of course based entirely on English, and a lingo of great early traders, sailors, whalers and Blackbirders in the so-called Black Islands of the Pacific. Examples are: 'One-legged Whitefella Mary' meaning a white woman, and, 'Whitey man him fightem hands b'long him, box hime sing out flenty' being a description of a chap playing a piano.

And now follow three examples of Pidgin English sailor songs:

Me Have Got A Flowerboat

Me have got a flowerboat, come sailing Chu-ki-ang Sampan girlie play to you all the same sing-song'

Lao-yeh, you likee me?
Tzia-tzia velly good.
Foreign man to Canton come,
Me got planty chow.

Home side have got pidgen
Me savvy, me can tell,
 Bring me master chicken,
Chi-da velly well.

Suppose he likee samshu,
It all the same, can-do,
Chop-chop me fetch him,
Big-big Da-Bing-Yu.

You no likee Yang-yen,
Me lightee little pipe,
He go smokie Shang-yen,
B'long velly velly tiled.

Chu-kiang	The Pearl River at Canton.
Lao-yeh	Master, Mister.
Tzia-tzia	Flower-boat or sing-song girl.
Pidgen	Work or profession.
Chi-da	A chicken
Samshu	Rice-wine, or perhaps more strictly bean-wine
Da-Bing-Yu	Big bottle of wine.
Yang-yen	Opium.
Shang-yen	A cigarette.
Tiled	Tired.

The Bosun's Locker Stan Hugill

Chinee Bumboat Man

I'll sing ye a story o' trouble an' woe, That'll cause ye to shudder an' shiver, Concernin' a Chi-i-nee bumboat man, that sailed the Yang-tze River. He wuz a heathen o' 'igh degree, As the josshouse records show – His family name wuz Wing Chang Loo, But the sailors all called him Tim Crow-ee-eye-oh-ee-eye, Hitchy Kum, Kitchy Kum, yah! yah! yah! sailorman no likee me, No savvy the story of Wing Chang Loo, too much of the bober-i-ee, Kye-eye!

'She had two eyes like pumpkin seeds, an' slippers two inches long;
But Ah Chu Fong loved a pirate bold, with all her heart an' liver
He wuz capitan of a double-decked junk, an' he sailed the Yangtze River-
eye-iver-eye

Chorus: Hitchee-kum, kitchee-kum, yah, yah,yah!
Sailorman no likee me,
No savvy the story of Wing Chang Loo
Too much of the bober-eye-ee, Kye-eye!

When Wing Chang Loo heard o' this, he swore an 'orrible oath,
'If An Ch marries that pirate bold, I'll make sausage meat of 'em both.'
So he hoisted his blood-red battle flag, put into the Yangtze River,
He steered her east an' south an' west, till that pirate he did did diskiver-eye-iver-eye

The drums they beat to quarters, an' the cannons did roar,
The red-'ot dumplin's flew like lead an' the scuppers they ran with gore;
The pirate paced the quarter-deck with never a shake nor a shiver,
He waz shot in the ass wid an 'ard-boiled hegg, an' it pinitrated his liver-eye-iver-eye

The dyin' pirate feebly cried, 'We'll give the foe more shot,
If I can't marry Ah Ch Fong, then Wing Chang Loo shall not.'
When a pease-pudding 'ot 'it the bumboat's side, it caused an 'orrible scene
It upset a poto''ot bow-wow soup, an' exploded the magazye-eenee-eye-eenee!

75

The Bosun's Locker Stan Hugill

Sampan Girl

From Canton to Macao, Hong Kong to Lu-li-a-o, The sojers and the sailors, they singee all ab luv. For dingee, dingee, ding, dong, for dingee, dingee, ding, dong. You are a sampan girlie and come from Hong-Ki-Kong.

Oh, you-hoo likee me-hee,
A manadarins daughter?
You sojers an' sailors,
When you come to Hong-Kong.

Chorus: For dingee, dingee, ding-dong, etc.

I no-ho likee you-hoo,
You no-ho likee me-hee !
You all belong to sojers,
You no belong to me.

Chorus: For dingee, dingee, ding-dong, etc.

The Bosun's Locker Stan Hugill

Vol. 3 No. 6
Reflections on Refrains

The recent showing on T.V. of the Cambrian *'Hob-y-deri-dando'* folk song series and its Anglicised version *Deri-dando* caused me, like Barney's Bull, to do some ruminating on the refrains of folk songs in general and shanties in particular.

Was there any real meaning to any of these apparently meaningless concatenations of phonetic syllables?

The name of the T.V. series just mentioned is the refrain of a well-known Welsh song, the North Wales version of which was often used as a shanty aboard Welsh ships out of Liverpool:

Ar y fford wrth fynd I Lundain
Hob-y-deri-dando!
etc.

On expressing my English opinion that this refrain is obviously meaningless a competent Welsh teacher informed me that I was wrong. 'Hob', he said, in Mediaeval Welsh means 'pig', 'deri' is the Mediaeval Welsh plural of 'derw', an oak, and 'dan-do' means 'under the roof'. The whole refrain therefore, he declared, was an allusion to sides of bacon hanging on oak beams under the roof.

But isn't this a little too pedantic? Isn't it merely a merry jingle of lively syllables? 'Derry dando' and 'derry down' were common refrains in English folk songs, dating back to Elizabethan times. 'Hay down, ho down, derry derry down!' was often heard across the English countryside as was 'Down, down, down derry down!' in many a sailing ship's fo'c'sle as all hands roared the chorus of a forebitter. And, I rather think, until James Reeves got crackin', generally accepted as a nonsensical refrain. Reeves, however, after research suggests that this 'derry down' bit may have some connection with an old-time rather obscene dance called the *dirrydan*. I wonder?

In a once popular French capstan shanty called *La Margot* the refrain is 'Biribi!' Feeling it incumbent upon me – a collector must not shirk his duty! – I went into the possible meaning of this word coming up with:

Biribi: Slang for disciplinary companies in the French Army stationed in North Africa.
Biribi: A prohibited game of chance.

However, after my wanderings through French dictionaries and so on, I finished up believing it to be nothing more than a meaningless phrase, possibly allied to the Italian 'Chiribirribin' or 'Ciribiribi' in the song of that name. An allied Scandinavian meaningless refrain is 'Karre varre vip, bom, bom!' or 'Cherry verry vip bom, bom!', a phrase, part of which appeared in a Yankee pop song of a few years back. It was often heard in Swedish halyard and capstan shanties.

The most popular refrain in English folk song probably is 'fal-de-lal-la' and its associates. The meaning of the word 'fal-de-ral' or 'fal-lal' given in the dictionaries as a trifle, gewgaw or gaudy ornament, in all probability comes from the use of such 'ornamenting' a song and not the other way about. Even at sea the 'fal-lal' refrain is not absent. It is to be found in the *Drummer and The Cook*, a capstan shanty with strong shore connections, and also in *Portland Street* – Timme fal-de-lal-day, fal-de-lal-day, fal-de-lal-dal, de-dal-day! – another capstan song of shore origin. Scandinavian seamen had many songs with 'fal-de-lal' choruses, and the

77

The Bosun's Locker Stan Hugill

Germans, both ashore and afloat, used similar links of syllables:
'Song volle-ralle-ralle-rala!'
and
'Holla hi, holla he, holla ho!'

A variant of 'holler' is found in 'Holla baloo balay!' the shanty once popular with baritone singers. 'Holla' is also a variant of the 'hooraw!' 'hooray' or 'Hurrah!' of our own seamen's wild 'Hooraw Choruses'.

But if many of these Welsh, French, German and English 'fal-de-lals' and so on are more or less meaningless what about Irish examples – the 'whack fol the rols', 'too-rel-lye-addies' etc.? It has been suggested that many of these are broken-down forms of Irish Gaelic, but may they not be meaningless syllables too, stemming from the old mouth-music, popular at a 'jig' when the fiddler was absent or overdosed with potheen? Yes, I know 'too-relye-addie' is to be found in *Botany Bay* and *Villikins and his Dinah*, which some will declare to be Cockney in origin, although I expect the airs and refrains, at least, came over with Irish emigrants. *Ratcliffe Highway*, a song with 'too-relye-addie' in the refrain, is definitely an Irish one. A good 75% of sailor forebitters had their origins in the Old Sod.

Perhaps collectors in the past have tried to find sensible meanings to many of these refrains, which, in the minds of their peasant and sailor composers never existed. *Gently Johnny, My Jingalo*, one classic shore example, is thought to have some connection with the 'Jongleurs' of mediaeval France – 'gentil joli jongleur'. At sea the word 'Hilo' or 'hilo' is another. Some declare it is the port of Hilo, in the Hawaiian Islands, although this harbour did not become well-known to seamen until the latter days of sail when the sugar traders called there. Others say the guano port of Ilo, in Peru, or Iloilo in the Philippines are the places indicated. And there are a few who think it should read 'high-low'. Take your pick!

Johnny come down to Hilo, poor ol' man
Hilo Johnny Brown, Stand to yer ground
Timme hilo, me Ranzo ray!
Away, you hilo-o-o!

All these are shanty examples and its use in the last refrain is nothing more, I feel, than the so-called 'hitch' or yodelling sound good shantymen would put into their singing. Some collectors, trying to give sense to senseless shanty refrains, have spelt 'way' – a common word in many choruses – 'weigh' suggesting the weighing of the anchor, but this in *hauling* songs such as the following is ridiculous:

To me way, hay, hoo ro ya! (*Blackball Line*)
Timme way, hay, blow the man down (*Blow the Man Down*)
Timme way, hay, high ho! (*A Long Time Ago*)

Negro songs – and shanties – have many meaningless refrains:

Ah ho' way ho, are yuh mos' done?
Doodle let me go gals, doodle let me go!
Hooraw me looloo boys, doodle let me lone!

And I doubt if anyone, no matter how hard he tried, could make them meaningful. And I wonder if it is possible to bring light to the chorus of a one time popular forebitter:-

Doo me amma, ding me amma,
Doo me amma day!

Maybe, in time, some student will work it out to have connections with 'l'amour'!
In ancient sea-songs, harking back to the days of the first Elizabeth, the word 'rumbelow' often appears in refrains, and

78

much time has been spent trying to give it a sensible meaning. Perhaps it has none. Maybe it was used because it rolls off the tongue nicely!

The earliest seamen in all probability sang out at rope and windlass in a manner imitative of the cry of the seagull, of the sighing of the wind in the rigging, of the flapping of the sail, or the susurrus of the water around the bow. These cries became the refrains of latter-day more complex and musical shanties, as well as being kept alive in the wild 'sing-outs' used when hauling on a light hand-over-hand.

If this is the route by which most of the refrains found in shanties came, is it not possible a similar development could be found for many of the refrains of shore folk songs?

Perhaps the peasant, the rural worker, the miner and the lumberman, imitated the cries of the birds, the lowing cattle, the noise of the shuttle and cage or the crashing of tall timber and so on in their refrains.

It is a thought and though perhaps not as pedantic as some would like it, still I feel a lot nearer the truth.

The Bosun's Locker Stan Hugill

Paddy Lay Back (or Valpariso Round the Horn)

'Twas a cold an' dreary mornin' in December (December), An' all of me money it wuz spent; (it wuz spent); Where it went to Lord I can't remember (remember); So down to the shippin' office went (went, went). Paddy, lay back, Paddy lay back! Take in yer slack, take in yer slack! Take a turn around yer capstan, heave a pawl, heave a pawl... ! 'Bout ship, stations, boys, be handy, be handy! For we're bound for Valparaiser round the Horn!

That day there was a great demand for sailors (for sailors)
For the Colonies and for 'Frisco and for France, (an' for France)
So I shipped aboard a Limey barque the Hotspur (the Hotspur)
An' got paralytic drunk on my advance ('vance, 'vance)

Chorus: Paddy lay back (Paddy lay back)!
Take in yer slack (Take in yer slack)!
Take a turn about yer capstan – heave a pal – heave a pawl!
For we're bound for Valparaiser round the Horn!
Now I joined her on a cold December mornin'.
A-frappin'o' me flippers to keep me warm.
With the south cone a-hoisted
To stand by the comin' o' a storm

Now some of or fellers had been drinking '.
An' I meself wz heavy on the booze:
An' I wuz on me ol' sea-chest a thinkin'
I'd turn into me bunk an' have a snooze.

I woke up in the mornin' sick an' sore,
An' I knew I wuz outward bound again:
When I heard a voice a-bawlin' at the door,
'Lay aft, men' answer to yer names!'

'Twas on the qarterdeck where first saw 'em,
Such an ugly bunch I'd niver seen before;
For there wuz a bum an'stiff from every quarter'
An' it made me poor ol' heart feel sick an' sore

There wuz Spaniards an' Dutchmen an' Rooshians
An' Johnny Crapoos just across from France;
An' most of 'em couldn't speak a word of English,
But answered to the name of 'Month's Advance'.

I wish I wuz in the 'Jolly Sailor',
Along wid Irish Kate a-drinkin' beer;
An' them I thought what jolly chaps were sailors,
An' with me flipper I wiped away tear.

I knew that in me box I had a bottle,
By the boardin'-master 'twas put there;
An' I wanted somethin' for to wet me throttle,
Somethin for to drive away dull care.

So down upon me kness I went like thunder,
Gropin' like a pig at any trough,
An' what wuz my great surprise an' wonder,
Found only a bottle o' medicine for a cough.

P.S. There has been a slight alteration in the last couplet as to the medicin found by John!

80

"A shanty without a chorus is like an egg without salt"
(Old sailor saying)

Many ex-seafarer writers have declared, I myself among them, that never again would it be possible for a couple of hundred voices to respond to the lone solo of the shantyman as in the days gone by, when a homeward-bounder was heaving up her anchor in some bone-dry West Coast port such as, Antofagasta or Caleta Colosa. In such a time and place the crews from dozens of ships laying in her tiers would board the homeward-bounder to help man the capstan. At such a time the shantying would be something to marvel over – something old shellbacks revive only in memory. And I along with all others have often sighed for such a sight and sound, declaring with nostalgia that such could never be even faintly resuscitated.

Other retired seafarers, members of nautical clubs and factions throughout the country, have often declared that it is not possible nowadays to hear even a single shanty by a solo singer sung as it would have been sung in the great days of sail. A certain Commander Woolard, a real old-timer and official of the Cape Horn Society, bemoaned this fact when he wrote to the BBC to play some shanties for an old octogenarian shipmate in hospital and was offered, I believe, *Tom Bowling* and *Hearts of Oak* or something in this strain.

However, all of us were wrong! 'Tis a pity these old-timers were absent from the Keele Folk Festival. My outstanding, although perhaps a little hazy, memory of this great and enjoyable get-together is the incident around 2 or 3am Sunday morning, June 18th. At this time, filling the landing leading to the balcony of the Walter Moberley Hall, and squatting on two curved staircases leading up to the landing were two hundred or so of the finest shanty singers the world, I reckon, has ever seen. Talk about the Packet Rats, and the Flying Fish Sailors, and the West Coast Johns and other South Spainers – why this crew was the saltiest, roustiest, full-bloodiest, seagull-scattering crowd that ever raised a 'Hooraw chorus'. These young men and women were magnificent and their shantying the equal of that of any gathering of salts anywhere or any time! And the great pity is I doubt if a tape-recorder was in hearing distance.

Roll on the next KFF!

* * * * *

A style of shantying in which the sailor met the lumberman was that used where both were stowing timber through the bow ports, or on to the deck of timber droghers. Unfortunately very few such shanties have come down to us.

'Wuz ye ever in Quebec, launching timber on the deck?'

was a common line to such songs, and Quebec was one of the earliest of the timber ports where such shanties were heard. From the middle of the nineteenth century bluff-bowed wooden droghers ploughed the Atlantic in what was known as the Western Ocean Timber Trade. Certain ships were virtually built from the cargo and taken apart on reaching Europe. Quebec in its early days was not a sailor-resident port, and crews for such ships were often wanting. Hence the reason shanghaiing boarding-house masters and crimps of all kinds flourished here earlier than elsewhere in the New World. Of such a

The Bosun's Locker Stan Hugill

type were the notorious Jim Ward and Mike Huck. In summer the timber droghers loaded around the Miramichi River and Chaleur Bay ports.

>Wuz ye ever in Quebec,
>Hieland laddie, bonnie laddie!
>Launching timber on the deck,
>Me bonnie hieland laddie O!

>Wuz ye ever in Mirramashee,
>Where ye tie up to a tree?
>(See *SPIN* Volume 2 No: 3)

Donkey Riding, a variant of *Hieland Laddie* was also used by timber stowers both in Canadian and New Brunswick ports and in British ports such as Liverpool and Glasson Dock.

>Wuz ye ever in Quebec,
>Launching timber on the deck,
>Where ye'd break yer bleedin' neck,
>Riding on a donkey!
>Way-hay, an' away we go!
>Donkey riding, donkey riding!
>Way-hay, an' away we go
>Riding on a donkey!

There exist many versions of this type of timber-drogher's shanty, most using similar texts but with different tunes. One I had from Seamus Ennis, who collected it in Ireland, runs:

>Were ye ever in Quebec?
>Bonnie lassie, hieland lassie!
>Were ye ever in Quebec?
>My bonnie hieland lassie-O!
>I was often in Quebec,
>Throwing timber up on deck,
>
>*Chorus:* Although I am a young maid,
>That lately left my mammy-O!

Whall has a similar version, his chorus being:

>Because she was a young thing
>Lately left her mammy-O!

At a later day these Canadian and Nova Scotian timber ships – brigs, barquentines and brigantines, and even schooners – ran down to Demerara and Buenos Aires. This trade lasted up till and after the First World War. From Georgia, too, Doboy Sound in the main, hard-pine ships went all over the world, and, when with indiscriminate cutting ('letting daylight in the woods' it was called) this source ran dry, the yellow fever ports of Florida, Pensacola, Apalachicola, Pascagoula became the haunts of the pitch-pine ships. The 'Quebec Fleet' would come to these harbours annually, and ashore the tough tobacco-chewing, rum-swigging French-Canadian and Irish stevedores, men who settled their grievances by knifing and kicking and eye-gouging, ran riot in between stowing the ships. Groggeries and brothels sprang up everywhere and in Pensacola, around Lower Palafox Street, there grew up one of the toughest Sailortowns in the world. It was against such a background that the timber gangs when working aboard the pitch-pine droghers lustily roared out the song I give – *Roll The Woodpile Down*.

In the Mississippi ports of Gulfport and Biloxi, many British ships loaded timber for Europe. Around the turn of the century many British ships loaded sawn planks and pit props in Baltic ports such as Frederickstadt, Sundsvaal, Riga etc. and for Melbourne and Port Adelaide in the 'Colonies'. Most of the songs used by the timber-stowers have, unfortunately, been lost, but around the Baltic ports many such Swedish, Norwegian and Finnish songs have been saved from oblivion. I give several in my *'Shanties from the Seven Seas'*. Around the turn of the century timber was also loaded in Portland, Oregon, but apart from a single line in a shanty referring to this, no special song used in this trade has ever been discovered.

The Pacific Islands, too, had their Sandalwood trade (a heaven-sent gift to the Joss-houses of China) but no songs seem to have stemmed from this romantic occupation. On the other hand, if we look to a similar class of traders, the Logwood Cutters of Campeachy Bay, the Mahogany stowers of Realign, Cajole, Puerto Arenas and other Southern Mexican and Central American ports, we find one or two working songs have survived. In my book I give:

> Haul away for Campeachy Bay,
> Dance gal, gimme de banjo!
> Oh, haul away, an' stretch out fer yer pay-ay,
> Dance gal, gimme de banjo!

This was once well known in the Honduras Logwood trade, and the Danish sailorauthor Rasmussen gives, in his book *'Sea Fever'*, two lumber-stowing songs used by the stevedores of Laguna de Terminos:

> A de hala hombre poquito más,
> Down below for rolling go!
> Rushow manitana, manitana, tana si,
> Rushow manitana, tana.
> Hala hombre hala aria poco,
> Sing Sally O, Oh bound for Rio! etc.

and

> Chyrra me Yankee, Chyrra me rao,
> What's de matta de loggin' no go?

This was used for freeing the logs in a 'jam'. Peter Kennedy was fortunate enough to tape Rasmussen singing these songs when the Dane visited England a few years ago.

Roll the Woodpile Down

'Way down south where the cocks do crow, ch. 'Way down in Florida! The gals they all dance to the ol' banjo, An' we'll roll the wood-pile down!
Full chorus
Rollin'! rollin'! Oh, rollin' th' whole worl' round! That brown gal o' mine's down the Georgia Line, An' we'll roll the wood-pile down!

When I was a young man in me prime
Chorus: Way down in Florida!
I chased them yaller girls two at a time,
Chorus: An' we'll roll the woodpile down!
Rollin', Roll in', Rollin', the whole worl' round!
Thet brown gal o' mine's down the Georgia Line,
An' we'll roll the woodpile down!

We'll roll him high an' we'll roll him low,
We'll heave him up, and away we'll go.

O, rouse on bust 'er is the cry,
A black man's wage is never high.

O, Curly goes on the ol' ran-tan,
O, Curly's just a Down-East Man.

O, one more heave an' that'll do,
We're the bullies for to kick 'er through,

* A Negro version of this song gives for the refrain:

> Haul the woodpile down!

And Taylor Harris gives 'Trav'ling ' instead of 'Rollin' in the chorus.

The Bosun's Locker Stan Hugill
Vol. 3 No. 10

In this issue Tony has asked me to write a short comment on the record *'Farewell Nancy'* (Topic 12TII0). So here goes . . . When I played the LP of sea-songs and shanties entitled, in Dibdinian fashion, *'Farewell Nancy'*, my first impression was that here we have a record fulfilling what it purports to be. However, on replaying, I began to feel that the choice of songs perhaps could have been bettered. Two, if not three, are songs of the sea rather than sea-songs, if you get my meaning. In the windbag days sea-songs were sung at leisure aboard ship, some genuine forebitters of sailor origin, others of doubtful lineage. Songs of, or about, the sea were, and still are, often found far inland sung by rural types rather than by seamen. In this latter category I would place *Lovely Nancy*, *The Nightingale* and *One Morning In Spring*. The *'Bold Princess Royal'*, with its many tune variants, seems to have been equally popular with deepwater seamen and rustic singers alike. Lacking, too, is the true capstan shanty, the type that has four-line verses followed by a full chorus. One or two of these would have helped to justify the secondary title, *'Sea-songs and Shanties'*. These are the only moans I have – all the rest is praise.

The singers are an excellent choice; all singing as though they really enjoy the job. As a shantyman Lou Killen could not be bettered. His strong, strident and salty solos would have made him an excellent forehand on halyard or sheet in the old days. The version he sings of *The Wild Goose* shanty, whilst not as musical as the better-known version with different refrains –

    I'm shantyman of the working party,
    Timme way, timme hay, timme hee, ho, hay!

So sing lads, pull lads, so strong an' hearty,
An' sing hilo me Ranzo way!
– has a real kick to it, and I should say its Ranzo refrain would really have got any shipboard chore soon accomplished. His *Hilo, Johnny Brown* is also well done and differs but little from the regular shipboard version. *Heave Away, My Johnny*, although new to me, both tune and words having been 'devised' by A. Lloyd for the film, *'Moby Dick'*, I enjoyed immensely. By the way, Bert would have undoubtedly made a good shantyman, having the knack of improvisation. The main Negro dance or game song given in *'Folk songs of Jamaica'* by Tom Murray, and turned into a boat-rowing song in the same film, went down fine – with me anyhow. This was *Hill 'n' Gully Rider*. Lou's singing of the *Ship in Distress* is also well executed, but, for myself, I rather prefer Lloyd's version on the *'Singing Sailor'* LP. Instead of singing the usual (folk-club) words about the 'smart Yankee packet' in 'Frisco Bay to *Row, Bullies, Row*, Ian Campbell in fine voice gives the Western Ocean shanghaiing version, usually, but not always, sung to a different tune. His singing of the West Indian version of *Lowlands Low* is very effective, the chorus coming in smartly in proper shanty fashion. *Hog-eye Man* I felt was a little weak in the refrains – not enough emphasis on the 'Row the boat ashore!' Lloyd writes that Vance Randolph found some bawdy versions of this up the 'wide Mizzourah', these being at present in the Indiana Sex Institute. I too, have the bawdy version of the sailor's song (no letters of enquiry, thank you!) which I have given to the author of the *'Horn Book'*, Gershon Legman, which will eventually see the light o' day when he publishes – soon I

The Bosun's Locker Stan Hugill

hope – his Ballad Book. Of course, no-one better could have been found than Bob Davenport for the singing of *Billy Boy,* but I do not think he was too happy with *Tom's Gone to Hilo,* to my mind one of the hardest shanties to put over on dry land. The refrain in *Poor Old Horse* is perhaps a little weak; on the other hand, that of *Goodbye Fare Ye Well* is one full of gusto.

Cyril Tawny's presentation of the old naval ballad *The Bold Benjamin* is excellent although I do feel a chorus by the gang may have been an improvement. His strict traditional way of singing – such as 'pidlow' for pillow – in *The Nightingale* is a joy to hear, but it is his *Fire-ship** that really intrigues me. Perhaps this is because I always doubted whether anyone would have the nerve to present a song about V.D. in plainer language than that used in *The Young Sailor Cut Down in His Prime*. Mind you, the story of the sailor's voyage to, and wreck on, the Island of Cytherea is given in nautical terminology, but still the theme is plain even to the most moronic listener. Here, too, I do feel the crowd in the chorus should have joined him. Pity, too, Red Sullivan didn't get a chance in solo work. And what can one say about Dave Swarbrick's fiddle and Lou's concertina? Just that they are the right instruments and the right players for the job. All this plus A.L. Lloyd's clear and knowledgeable sleeve notes make this a fine record. And seeing that we are an island race, with our heritage the sea, let's have more and more like it!

* At some later date I intend to write an article on these Fire-ships and Ratcliffe Highway songs, all of which hark back to nigh Elizabethan times.

Lowlands Low

Our packet is the Island Lass, Lowlands, Lowlands, Lowlands low! There's a nigger howlin' at the main topmast, Lowlands Lowlands, Lowlands low!

The Ol' Man hails from Barbados,
Chorus: Lowlands, Lowlands, Lowlands low '.
He's got the name O Hammertocs,
Chorus: Lowlands, Lowlands, Lowlands low !

He gives us bread as hard as brass,
Our junk's as soft as Balaam's ass.

The monkey's rigged in the sojer's clo'es,
Where he gottem from God 'lone knows.

We'll haul 'em high an' let 'em dry,
We'll trice 'em up into de sky.

Lowlands, me boys, an' up she goes,
Git changed, me boys, to yer shore-goin clo'es.

This was a halyard shanty very popular in ships that carried chequerboard crews, i.e. one watch White and one watch Black. I learned it from an old West Indian shipmate called Tobago Smith.

The Bosun's Locker Stan Hugill

Vol. 4 No. 1
Another folk process

Were shanties, or any sort of work song used around the coast of Britain – in the 'narrow sea' sailing vessels?
A friend of mine has pointed out that in *'Shipping Wonders of the World'* there is a paragraph which reads:
> 'The sailing coasters were often slipshod in their shanties because they did not carry enough men. Although they had a number of shanties, these were seldom heard in deep-sea ships, and the usual habit was to adopt the music hall ditties of the day.'

Where this information came from I am at a loss to know, but, after research, I am afraid I have to disagree. My findings, gathered from talks with English coasting schooner and ketch men, are that no sort of work song was ever used aboard British fore 'n' afters – they were usually run far too short-handed to raise a song of any kind, although sing-outs were used, occasionally, when hoisting sail. However, in earlier times to which the above paragraph may refer, in the days of such coastal square-riggers as the Geordie Colliers and brigs and pit-prop carriers, work songs were probably sung, and, as the above declares, they may have been music hall ditties, or else adaptations from music hall ditties. This, of course, is Runciman Terry's feelings in regard to the song which his great uncle said was raised at the windlass of many a Geordie brig – *The Drummer and the Cook*. Also the so-called capstan song he calls *My Johnny*:
> In the middle of the sea, my boy is floating free,
> So far away from me, my love
may come into this category.

The North East coast version of *Billy Boy*, too, Terry declares was most used aboard the Northumbrian Colliers, and this is, of course, most certainly a shore rather than a sea-song. Various forms of *Lowlands* I feel were first used as coasting shanties as well in collier brigs, and so on, but before they ventured into deep water.

East Anglian and Scottish fishermen had some net-hauling songs; Bob Roberts points this out in regard to *Windy Weather* and *Still I Love Him* but these were never heard outside of fishing and barge circles.

There was of course some slight movement of coastwise songs to deep water. *The Fishes* is one instantly brought to mind, but a far greater movement, I feel, was that in reverse – from deep water to the coast. The barge, fisher and rural waterway folk singers, such as Bob Roberts, Sam Larner and Harry Cox, all sing songs traditional in these trades but which, at some time or another, must have come from the deepwater fo'c'sles of square-riggers before they were trimmed and salted to suit the fore 'n' aft trades. The so-called *Cruising Round Yarmouth*, which in the chorus in some strange manner transplants the hero to London, is obviously the deepwater forebitter, *Ratcliffe Highway*. *Maggie May*, in which 'North of Blythe' and 'the pool' (of London) are strange geographical locations, is another deep-sea-song transplanted.

In the forebitter often called *The Flash Gals of the Town*, the couplet about 'he shifted her main tack and he caught her flat aback' becomes 'he shifted her main tack like a coaster or a smack', showing the fore 'n' aft influence of the coastwise seamen.

This 'folk process' is one which as yet has

remained sealed to the folk song world, and is one which would probably produce a lot of interesting data for the research worker who has both the time and the means to follow it up.

I have mentioned in previous articles that I have found some excellent contacts through my book with members of the Dutch Cape Horn Society. One in particular, a Mr K. Suyk, Jnr, has been searching extensively in all directions for genuine Dutch shanties. There is a collection in existence – mainly from the island of Terschelling – by a chap called Jaap Kunst, but most Dutch salts say that these were rarely sung on shipboard, the texts being mainly about 'flowers, cows and such sweet things'. A consensus of opinion of all the members of the Dutch Cape Horn Society seems to be that all Dutch shanties were obscene, and unlike English and American shanties, had no clean versions.

Mr Suyk wrote me an interesting letter in regard to this matter, which I quote here:

'A great-uncle of one of my friends, who was an old sailor and had rounded Cape Horn in sailing ships, did note, many times, a lot of Dutch sea shanties together with their music. He wrote them all in exercise books and put them in his sea chest in the corner of the loft. Many years passed and the old sailor died. My friend once nosed in that chest, looked into the exercise books and was taken aback with the obscene language. He loves old folklore and did not want to throw them away, so he left them in the sea chest in the corner of the loft. Some time later, his sister, married to a clergyman, cleaned the loft, and the clergyman opened the sea chest with the exercise books inside. The good man had such a fright when he read the sea shanties that he took the stuff with a pair of tongs and burned them in the stove. Anyway it is a pity that again another bit of folklore has vanished'.

This, of course, is a repetition of what has occurred, and is still occurring unfortunately, in many parts of the world, and thanks to such narrow and Puritan attitudes a tremendous amount of valuable material has been irrevocably lost to the serious folk song student.

* * * * *

After some thought I have decided to give the first verses and tune of one of these Dutch shanties – a genuine one – that has recently been recovered. It has a good melody and could be transformed into an acceptable sea-song, perhaps!

In the old days before the cutting of the canal, ships would lie in the roads at Hellevoetsluis instead of coming up to Rotterdam, and the crimps would bring the crews out in small boats to the roads from the boarding houses in Rotterdam's Schedamschedyk. The 'Baggerman House' was a famous sailor pub standing on the shore opposite to the Hellevoetsluis Roads. An old sailor, Captain Spaandarman, eighty-odd years of age, gave this shanty to Mr Suyk.

The Bosun's Locker Stan Hugill

The Iron Man
(De Ijzere Man)

At Hel-le-voet-sluis there is a house, Hur-rah the Iron-Man! There the dam-sels Beggarman they are at home, Hurrah the Iron Man! Now, we'll sing merrily fal-de-ral-de-ra, Who's coming now with us? We are sail-ing for Am-er-ic-a, the ship lies in the roads, We are sailing for Am-er-i-ca, the ship lies in the roads.

In Hellevoetsluis daar staat een huis,
Chorus: Hoera die Ijzere Man !
 Daar zijn do dames van Baggerman thuis
Chorus: Hoera die Ijzere Man !

Full Chorus: Dan zingen wij vrolijk
            Falderal - dera,

Wie gaat er met ons mee,
Wij varen naar Amerika, het schip ligt op de ree,

En in dat huis daar staat een stok,
Hoera etc...
Daar krijgen de dames mee op hun kop
Hoera etc....

ENGLISH TRANSLATION

At Hellevoetsluis there is a house,
Hurrah the Iron Man!
There the damsels Baggerman they are at home,
Hurrah the Iron Man!

Full Chorus: Now we'll sing merrily,
            Falde ralde ra

Who's coming now with us ?
We are sailing for America, the ship is in the roads,

And in that house there is a stick
Hurrah etc. . . .
And with it these girls on the head are hit,
Hurrah etc....

The Bosun's Locker Stan Hugill

Vol. 4 No. 2

FOLK MUSIC FESTIVAL IN HAWAII
By John M. Kelly, Jr.
Published by Boston Music Co; & Chappell,
London.   Price 12/6d.

Readers who have enjoyed Michener's magnificent novel *'Hawaii'* will have learned how mixed is the blood of the present inhabitants of this glamorous group of volcanic islands in the North Pacific.

Recently *'SPIN'* received for reviewing a well-set-up paperback volume entitled *'Folk Music Festival in Hawaii'* compiled, edited and annotated by John M. Kelly Jnr. Tony looked at it, Beryl waded through it, and both exclaimed: "STAN!"

And why did they saddle me with the reviewing of this unusual folk song book?

Well, the book is divided into the folk songs of Hawaii, Samoa and Tahiti, of Japan, Korea, China and the Philippines, winding up with folk songs from America. And what, sez you, has all this to do with Stan the Shantyman? Only that, Tony suddenly remembered that I'd been around the South Seas, and Beryl believed I once was familiar with written and spoken Japanese. And this was sufficient for them to declare me to be the reviewer – whether I liked to review or not.

The truth is I do speak and read Japanese and once made an academic study of Japanese drama, puppet-play, song, poetry and general literature, in the hallowed halls of the School of Oriental and African Studies, London University. As a hobby, in my youth, I once dabbled in comparative Polynesian dialects, including Maori, Hawaiian, Samoan and Tahitian, although I'm a bit rusty nowadays. Chinese – Cantonese mainly – like Chop Suey I've dipped into. I once tried to learn Korean but gave up in despair, and as far as the lingoes of the Philippines, I was best at picking the Spanish bits out of Tagalog such as the following shop sign 'Relojería og Platería' – in which I had to guess that the 'og' was the Spanish 'y'. So having tossed into your lap, dear reader, my doubtful qualifications, I will endeavour to have a bash at reviewing (perhaps in my case, this is hardly the right word) this charming little book.

The first section of the book concerns Hawaiian folk songs. These can be divided mainly into *oli* or chants harking back to pagan days, *himenes* or songs based on the then new melodic system introduced to the Islanders by the Calvinistic missionaries, *hulas*, chants accompanying the native dances, and *meles*, under which the greatest number of native songs can be classed.

One of the *oli* given is based on a prayer to Pele, the goddess of fire, known throughout Polynesia as Pere or Fe'e, her habitat usually being some fiery volcano. Several *himenes* are given, and, naturally, since the word is the Polynesian rendering of our word 'hymn', their melodies are reminiscent of Welsh chapel chorals. This form is found throughout the South Seas, even among the Maoris of New Zealand. In Samoa, *himenes* are usually accompanied by an intriguing form of hand clapping, which the writer, in his youth, once had the pleasure of witnessing.

Hulas, of course, nowadays are recognised instantly having entered the Western world in the nineteen-twenties along with the *ukulele* and the Hawaiian guitar. I don't know whether readers realise that

89

The Bosun's Locker Stan Hugill

'ukulele' is Hawaiian for 'jumping flea'. This was the description the natives gave of an early Portuguese sailor's fingers as they jumped along the strings of this, to them, peculiar instrument. Until the arrival of the white man all the Hawaiians had in the way of musical instruments were drums, flutes, nose flutes and Pandean pipes. Stringed instruments didn't exist. It will be noticed from the examples given that Hawaiian royalty were great songwriters. *Wailana* (p.14) was composed by King Kalakaua, and *Ainahau* (p.24) by Princess Like-like, and Prince Leileiohoku wrote *I Love Your Eyes* (Aloha no wau i ko maka) (p.15) The famous *Aloha Oe,* now known all over the world, is said to have been written by Queen Liliuokalani when imprisoned by the Americans for having rebelled against their occupation of the islands.

A couple of Samoan songs are also included – one an *himene*, and the uncaptioned photograph on page 25 shows natives dancing the famous *sivasiva*, or war-club dance. Of course the Polynesian tongue is very melodious, consonants are few and all words finish with a vowel. Sentences can be formed entirely of vowels, which makes for a race of natural singers.

The Japanese section comes next and this is very representative of Nipponese folk song. The photograph prefacing this section shows native dancers performing with taiko or drum accompaniment. The characters read *Minion Matura* or Folk Festival. It will be noticed that a lot of these Japanese songs are called 'bushi' (really 'fushi'): *Tosa-bushi, Kuroda-bushi, Chakkiri-bushi* and so on, while others are known as *Uta*. To the uninitiated I feel the best way to describe the difference although not academically – is to say that the latter are general songs, whereas the former are those of the countryman, fisherman, miner and so on, in other words, *true* folk songs. An *uta* really means a poem of thirty-one syllables.

The first song in the series is about a common native song subject; the cherry blossom or *Sakura*, while others are those sung during the Bon ceremony, a sort of return of the ancestral ghosts kept around the 14th, 15th, and 16th. July. It is a ritual of probable Chinese origin, in which dancing in a rotary fashion by long lines of people, under the cherry trees, and the singing of songs accompanied by pipes and drums are the main features.

A fisherman's shanty for hauling in the herring nets from Hokkaido, Northern Japan, is an interesting item. In the refrain is the word *dokkoisho*, which the collector gives as having no specific meaning, but I know for certain that this equals our sailors' 'heave-ho!' and is common in Japanese fisherman and sailor songs.

The next six Korean songs I'm afraid I am insufficiently competent to write about, but I know a little about the Chinese songs which follow. The *Flower Drum Song* is very ancient and has many variants. It is probably the most widely known of all Chinese folk songs.

On page 54 a very famous war-song is given. This is the *Chang Cheung Yiao* or *Great Wall Song*. The Great Wall of course is that of China, which the natives call the Wan Li Chang Cheung or '10,000 li wall', and this song was to be heard everywhere wherever groups of soldiers or patriotic citizens gathered during the years of the Sino-Japanese War of 1931-1945. I myself have heard it many times in the thirties. Songs sung during the planting or transplanting of rice in the paddy fields are also included in this section.

The Philippine songs are in three languages – Tagalog, Viscayan, and Iggorote, the speakers of the first lingo being Catholic in belief, the second Moslem and the third Pagan, and, naturally, thanks to Spanish influence over a great number of years these folk songs have a Latin lilt.

The final section of the book is given over to American folk songs commonly heard in

Hawaii, sub-divided into White and Negro. Many well-known ones are included such as *Buttermilk Hill, Hole in My Bucket, Deep Blue Sea* and *Oh, Mary, don't you Weep*, as well as some of the lesser-known variety. There are some nautical songs included such as *Haul Away, Joe* and *High Barbary*. *Buttermilk Hill* has this comment:

'One of the popular songs of the Revolutionary War, *Buttermilk Hill* is a direct paraphrase of an Irish love song *Shule Aroon*, which became popular about 1699.' The most popular concert version of the Irish song was in English, but with a chorus in Gaelic, and many American versions contain traces of this Gaelic language, treated as nonsense syllables. One comic version sung by Negro Minstrel troupes, travelled to England and became a British sea shanty.

The shanty, of course, referred to is that fine, stirring capstan song, *Clear the Track Let the Bulgine Run*, which I should say is hardly British, being the Irish air of *Shule Agra* (or *Aroon*) given American Negro words in the refrains. 'Transatlantic' would describe it better I feel.

Clear the Track (Let the Bulgine Run)

Oh, the ol' Wild Cat of the Swallow Tail Line,
Chorus: Ah-ho ! way-ho ! are you mos' done?
She's never a day behind her time,
Chorus: Soo, clear the track an' let the bulgine run!

Full chorus:
To me high rig-a-jig in a jauntin'-car,
Ah-ho ! way-ho ! are you mos' done ?
Wid Eliza Lee all on me knee,
Soo, clear the track an' let the bulgine run

Oh, we're outward bound for New York town,
'Them Bowery gals we'll waltz around.
Oh, them Bowery gals will give us fun,
Them New York dives is home from home !

Oh, them gals is walkin' on the pier,
Let's all git ashore an' 'ave'some beer.

When we've stowed our freight at the West Street pier,
We'll be homeward bound to our Liverpool beer.

When we all gits back to Liverpool town,
I'll stand yiz whiskies all around.

Oh, in Liverpool town them gals hang around,
An' it's there me Liza will be found.

The Bosun's Locker Stan Hugill

Vol. 4 No. 3
Shanghaied!

Shanghaied!

Since shanghaiing is a constantly re-occurring theme in sailor shanties and forebitters – one that crops up in many of the sailor songs sung in the folk clubs, with many singers and a good percentage of the audiences not having a clue as to what the operation was or how it was carried out – I have decided in this issue of *'SPIN'* to elucidate the matter to the best of my ability.

In the King's Navee, in time of war (and sometimes in times of peace), the impressment of men was the method employed by My Lords of the Admiralty to ensure their fleets were fully manned. This meant that certain small groups of tough seamen under a young officer, usually a lieutenant and known as a 'Yellow Admiral', were used to scour the ports and countryside roping in, willy-nilly, brawny yokels or city counter-jumpers with equal determination, often at the point of the cutlass, pressing them to do service in one of Old England's Wooden Walls. Obviously, what with the poor grub, bad living conditions, lack of normal shore recreations, flogging and hazing (such as seen recently in the film of Melville's book *'Billy Budd'*), men rarely volunteered to join the Navy in the eighteenth and early nineteenth centuries.

So the 'Lobsters' or press-gangs were called in to enforce enlistment. Often the gangs would, in their tenders, meet the homeward-bound merchant ships, off the Nore and farther down the Channel, board them, and impress nearly all the crew. This, in the old records, was often called 'trepanning', or 'crimping'. Trepanning is a medical word for cutting open a skull; how it got to be used for this abducting of men into the Navy no one knows. Crimping – a word probably of German origin – was also used for the kidnapping of crews for merchant ships. Whenever there was a shortage of manpower for merchantmen, predatory sailor-boarding-house masters and crafty publicans of waterfront taverns, both usually referred to as 'crimps' would, by means of knock-out drops in the seamen's ale, render suitable lodgers and customers unconscious and have them trundled down in a cart to the waiting ship. Such crimps would take the kidnapped man's Advance Note in payment for delivering the 'body'.

The Advance Note was a system whereby the sailor was able to trick himself out at the tailor, chandler, or in most cases, the tavern, catering for his pre-voyage needs. This system had been in operation for years prior to the mid-nineteenth century when a slightly different system of ship crewing came into existence.

Whereas before this, the ships definitely needed crews thanks to a genuine shortage of men, after 1849 an artificial supply and demand was created by the crimps. This happened around 1850 on the 'Barbary Coast', the Sailortown of San Francisco.

The crimps would board an inbound ship and with the aid of their tough, ex-boxer runners, rot-gut whiskey, obscene postcards, soap-in-the-galley soup, aphrodisiacs and rosy tales of glamorous girls, potent booze and nothing-to-do jobs paying fabulous wages ashore, entice the crew to their boarding houses almost before the vessel was made safely fast alongside.

Then, when a ship was ready to sail, very often the ship from which the men had been lured – the crimp would guarantee her master a new crowd for a substantial fee. If the men refused to leave the delights of the 'Barbary Coast' they would be doped with laudanum, opium, or some other concoction such as Shanghai Cigars, or straightforwardly bludgeoned, and taken to the outward-bounder, dead to the world, in the bottom of a Whitehall rowboat. This system had its crimps, runners, carters, and lawyers (in case of legal trouble) and shipping masters, the police and local government officials were all tied up in it at times, everyone making a fat living out of the sailor body. Crimps were so powerful they even sent letters (some still in existence) to British shipping companies informing them of the ease with which they could obtain crews in 'Frisco if they agreed to pay the price – a high one! – the crimp demanded. In other words, blackmail!

This system, and this system only, was the true shanghaiing of the shanty and forebitter. The word 'shanghai' was first employed by a certain reverend gentleman, who vilified the crimps from a rostrum in the vice district of San Francisco in 1850. At first a 'Shanghai Voyage' meant one for which it was difficult to obtain men. Sailors didn't mind being shipped aboard vessels going to Europe or the Eastern States or South America, because it would always be easy for them to obtain another berth from such places to return to the home port, but they didn't fancy being dumped in Shanghai, China, as this was a port most difficult to ship out from except perhaps aboard a Chinese junk. Of course, in later years, when the tea clippers were around, Shanghai became a more popular port. As the words 'shanghai' and 'shanghaiing' became popular the older term 'crimping' more or less died out, although the word 'crimp' was still retained.

By the end of the nineteenth century this system of dragging men off a ship and re-selling them to another vessel became general throughout the major ports of the world and in the Sailortowns of New York, Buenos Aires, Valparaiso, Antwerp, Cape Town and so on. This system produced some amazing characters, crimps like Shanghai Brown and Chicken Devine of 'Frisco, Tommy Moore of Buenos Aires's Boca, Johnny da Costa of

The Bosun's Locker Stan Hugill

Liverpool, and the Portuguese Consul of Rhode Island. Women like Ma Smyrden of Liverpool, Mother Fairvelt of New York, Bremer Mary of Iquique, Chloroform Kate of 'Frisco and Meg Gallup of New York. Not to mention the infamous taverns that sprang up in the wake of the Shanghai Game: the 'Black Horse' in Marseilles, the 'Norwegian Flags' in London, the 'Hole in the Wall' in New York, the 'House of Blazes' in Cardiff, the 'Bucket of Blood' in 'Frisco and the 'Liverpool Bar' in Buenos Aires. This list of course is a mere drop in the ocean, there were thousands of such pubs and saloons, and hundreds of such crimps and their women counterparts throughout the ports of the Seven Seas, and until they were eradicated, the life of a sailing ship tar was that of a dog.

Recently my friend Gershon Legman sent me a pre-publication copy of a type facsimile edition of Burns' *'Merry Muses of Caledonia'* edited by him. This is a wonderful book and of great interest to folk singers and collectors, in particular Scottish ones! Apparently there have been over thirty publications bearing this title *'The Merry Muses'* but many of them have been incomplete, many phoney, some privately printed and others very difficult of access for the ordinary citizen. But this edition of Legman's (University Books, New Hyde Park, New York) claims, and rightly so, to be the only unexpurgated and completed text of the one and only copy of the first edition of Burns – a work never before reprinted. Legman, in the Spring of 1959, came over from France on a flying visit of barely more than a week, and visited London (the British Museum mainly), Stratford-on-Avon and Edinburgh, and in this hasty journey discovered, accidentally, the long-forgotten *'Cunningham Manuscript'* making possible, as he writes, 'a serious assessment of the part played by Burns in the creation of this collection (i.e. *'The Merry Muses'*), long known only in spurious and incomplete editions'. This type facsimile of the original edition of Burns is, to quote the dust cover, 'a pioneer collection of unexpurgated folk songs'. A fine historical introduction, a chapter on 'Notes', a bibliography and a very interesting glossary of Scottish dialect words and terms found in the songs make this an excellent buy for all interested in FOLK.

Vol. 4 No. 4
The Press Gang

The Pressgang (from an old print.)

In my last locker while on the subject of shanghaiing and crimping, I referred briefly to naval impressment – the traditional manner in which the Navy crewed her ships from time immemorial. The 'press' was a word to scare the pants off both landlubbers and merchant seamen. Any man – and not always able-bodied – between the ages of fifteen and fifty-five and over was liable to impressment.

Not only did the press work the taverns and waterfront areas of the ports, but also, actually more so, did it comb the inland areas and rural villages. The press-gang, or 'lobsters' as its members were contemptuously called, consisted of six to eight men with, usually, a lieutenant or 'Yellow Admiral' in charge. Rural crossroads and bridges were favourite spots for them to lie concealed awaiting their prey. According to the local library, they even turned up in the little Welsh village where I now reside, Aberdovey,

whipping off two shepherds from their flocks without so much as a 'by yer leave'.

The Yellow Admirals were a crafty lot and well-known for their habit of swindling. And by this I mean swindling H.M.N. (His Majesty's Navy). They were allowed 'footage' money for the distance they travelled in seeking their prey. This they would 'cook'. Also they would declare they had pressed more men than was actually true, thus getting extra 'perks' on non-existent bodies. They would enter taverns, schools, and even churches after men and boys.

In Liverpool they entered the old Custom House, and, in London, India House, seeking their prey. East Indiamen were granted 'permissions' by the Navy (exemption, in theory) for their crews from impressment. But, in actual fact, this did not work, and many a merchant Indiaman, nearly home after a twelve-month voyage, would have her crew whipped off by the press tender, lying at the

The Bosun's Locker Stan Hugill

Nore or in the Channel, and transferred aboard a three-decker. Once a great sea fight took place between a heavily armed East Indiaman and a naval frigate resulting from the man-of-war endeavouring to impress the Indiaman's crew. The merchant ship, I'm glad to say, won the engagement.

A common place for the press to wait, according to the numerous songs of the period, was outside a church, grabbing the bridegroom before the poor chap had time to consummate his marriage. Sometimes, if the old broadsides are to be believed, a bridegroom would be dragged from his connubial bed.

At one period in the eighteenth century a gang of women worked the streets of London rigged out as regular press-gang, and tailors, (who have always been lampooned in folk songs and ballads as licentious, less than human tradesmen) were their special prey. They are said to have pressed fourteen of these poor devils from their cross-legged positions while still grasping needle and thread. This occurred at a certain period when the press-gang was considered a respectable method of crewing naval ships, and everyone (except the victim) highly patriotic towards it. But most times the press was dreaded. It was this pressing of men that was one of the causes in bringing about the mutiny at the Nore.

But the Navy didn't always win. During the Napoleonic Wars when naval manpower was in short supply and even the press was not bringing in the goods in sufficient quantities, the Navy offered a bounty to all seamen (mainly merchant and fishermen) willing to join for a voyage. Many smart seamen took advantage of the offer which was paid on joining a man-o'-war. As soon as the next port was reached these 'bounty seamen' would jump ship, and the Admiralty lost both man and bounty, and few were ever netted again.

One may see in junk shops nowadays a few old glass-bottomed drinking mugs. The custom of putting glass in the bottoms of beer mugs came about in these days, thanks to the press-gang. Before this type of mug was evolved, the press-gang would enter a tavern and offer a likely-looking man a drink, at the same time the officer would surreptitiously slip a shilling into the beer. When the intended victim had swallowed his pint the lieutenant would point out the shilling and inform the poor beggar that since he had accepted the King's Shilling he was now well and truly in the Navy. The glass-bottomed mug was introduced so that the press could not carry out this trick.

The poor in those far off days were nearly all louse-bound, hence when men were roped in by the press the first thing to happen to them when they boarded the man-of-war was the act of cutting off their hair and a form of de-lousing. One could always tell at a glance the pressed men from the volunteers, the former wearing their hair short, the latter sporting a pigtail or queue. Many broadsides relating to the press-gang were churned out and sold on the streets of London. Ballads such as:

(a) Of late near the Strand, we well understand,
Six lasses that took a brisk frolic in hand;
'Twas thus, I profess, they in seamen's dress,
Not far from the Maypole, resolved to press fourteen tailors.

(b) This jolly young sailor, as true is reported,
Had been but a very few weeks on the shore;
But as he and his love together was walking,
By a large press he from her was tore.

(c) Oh, cruel was thy parents that envied our love,
And cruel was the press-gang that gave me such a shove;
That took me head and heels and put me

in a sack,
And to the waterfront one took me on his back.

(d) Oh, cruel were the winds that took my love from me,
Oh, cruel was the press-gang that took him off to sea,
And cruel was the little boat that rowed him from the strand,
And cruel was the great ship that sailed out from the land.

(e) Farewell our wives and dearest children,
Our friends and relations we must bid adieu,
For the press-gang they have pressed us,
For to fight the daring foe.

The North East Coast is an area from which many press-gang songs have come down to us.

(a) Oh, the lousy cutter,
They've taen my laddie from me,
They've pressed him far away foreign,
Wi' Nelson ay 'ont' the salt sea.

(b) William Taylor was a brisk young sailor,
He who courted a lady fair;
Bells were ringin', sailors singin'
As to church they did repair.

Thirty couples at the wedding,
All were dressed in rich array,
Instead of William being married
He was pressed and sent away.

(c) Where hes tit been maw canny hinny?
Where hes ti' been maw winsome man?
Aw've been ti' the norrard, cruisin' back and forrard,
Aw've been tit the norrard, cruisin' sair an' lang,
Aw've been ti I the norrard, cruisin' back and forrard,
But daurna come ashore for Bover and his gang.

I've known for a long time that many people interested in the shanties sailors once sang would give the eyes out of their heads to hear the real words that came out of the mouths of lusty shantymen. Well, very soon their wish will be granted. Recently I had a letter from my friend and fellow-counsellor in folk song, Gershon Legman. This great authority is not so well known in print in the folk song world owing to his belief that no folk song should be expurgated, and this naturally has prevented him from putting his finds to paper. At last, thanks to the greater freedom given publishers of erotica and bawdy song during the last few years, he has come into his own. In the coming months and years, I prophesy, he will be well to the fore – in fact he is already being quoted in this month's *'Playboy'* in an article about sex in films! But to the letter. In it he tells me that he has been given the editorship of a new folklore and song journal; *'The Journal of Erotic Folklore'* * to start publication in the autumn. In the first issue he is printing thirty-three real versions of the shanties which he obtained from me in 1954 (I think). So lovers of 'real' shanties stand by for a treat!

* Had a letter today with the journal's latest title: '*THE NEW KRYPTADIA*'

The Bosun's Locker Stan Hugill

Married to a Mermai-ed

There was a gay young farmer, Who liv'd on Sal'sb'ry Plain, He lov'd a rich Knight's daughter dear, and she lov'd him again. The knight was so distress-ed, That they should sweethearts be, That he had the farmer soon press-ed, And he whipped him off to sea. — Singin' Rule Britannia! Two tanners make a bob, Five make two and six, and one for his Knob!

'Twas on the deep Atlantic midst the equinoctial gales,
The young farmer fell overboard among the sharks an' whales;
He disappeared so quickly, headlong down went he,
And he went out Ol' sight, like a streak O' light, to the bottom of the deep blue sea.

Chorus: Singin' Rule Britannia!
Two tanners make a bob, five make two an' six,
And one for his knob.

We lowered a boat to find him, we thought to see his corpse,
When up to the top, he came with a shock, and said in a voice so hoarse,
'My shipmates and my messmates, oh, do not weep for me,
For I'm married to a mermaid at the bottom of the deep blue sea.

He said that as he went down, great fishes he did see,

And they seemed to think as he did wink that he was rather free;
But down he went so quickly, thinkin' 'tis all up with me,
When he met a lovely merma-id at the bottom of the sea.

She came at once unto him, she gave him her white hand,
Saying, 'I have waited long me dear, to welcome ye to land,
Go to your ship an' tell 'em, ye'll leave 'em all for me,
For your'e married to a merma-id at the bottom of the deep blue sea.

The wind was fair the sails were set, the ship was runnin' free,
When we all went to the capen bold, and told what we did see;
He went unto the ship's side and loudly bellowed he,
'Be happy as you can my man, at the bottom of the deep blue sea!

Vol. 4 No. 5
Shanty and Seasong discs

In the last issue of *'SPIN'* a 'Scottish exile' in the U.S.A. wrote a letter inquiring about shanty records. Our imaginative editor thought the answer to this inquiry would make a fair article and dropped me a line to tell me so. Down gets I to research and here's the result.

The earliest efforts at putting shanties on wax were those of HMV and Columbia, during the twenties. They were all 78s and HMV had B as the serial letter. Obviously they are more or less collectors' pieces now, and very difficult, if not impossible to acquire. I possess HMV B 2940 *'Walk Him Along Johnny'* (which apparently has only just been discovered by the clubs!), *Johnny Come Down To Hilo, Shallow Brown, Miss Lucy Long* – and HMV B 3782 – *Stormalong, Roll The Woodpile Down, Sciacamunnista Lampa* (a hauling song from Sicily) and so on. The solo singer is the baritone John Goss and the chorus The Cathedral Quartet. Of course, these records were produced long before the so-called folk revival and the fashion of singing them – plus piano accompaniment – follows that of all Victorian and Edwardian concert sea-song singers. The versions are those of Terry (*'The Shanty Book'*) and Taylor Harris (*'Six Sea Shanties'*). Of the early Columbia records I only possess, unfortunately, one – Columbia 4689 *'We're All Bound To Go, Hogseye Man,'* etc. This has as shantyman Raymond Newell, with male chorus and piano. It is rather strange after forty years of being on wax *The Hogseye Man* has only recently made the folk song scene!

The next shanty record to appear was much nearer to the real thing. This is the Stanley Slade, ex-Bristol shantyman, disc which was the first postwar release in this country, HMV B 10605. It was recorded in collaboration with the BBC and the EFDSS, and the accompaniment is the accordion of Sandy Moir. Here we have *Mister Stormalong, Sally Brown, Haul Away Joe, Mobile Bay* and *Can't You Dance The Polka?* The diligent seeker may be able to acquire a secondhand copy.

Towards the end of the thirties and the early part of the forties Alan Lomax, Sam Eskin, and others recorded several old shantymen, mainly at Sailors' Snug Harbour, Staten Island, New York, for the University of Wisconsin and the Library of Congress, Washington, D.C. They are excellent examples of real shantying, although in most cases the singers were past their prime. Unfortunately these records are for non-commercial use only. They're edited by Duncan Emrich and their serial numbers are American Sea-songs and Shanties (1) AAFSL26 and (2) AAFSL27.

Shanties and forebitters included are: *Haul The Bowline, Blow, Boys, Blow, Drunken Sailor, Reuben Ranzo, A-Rovin', Heave Away, Sailors' Alphabet, Paddy Doyle, Paddy Get Back, Dead Horse, Do, My Johnny Boker, When Jones's Ale Was New, Whisky Johnny, Rolling Home*

and so on, which Sam Eskin, a powerful

The Bosun's Locker Stan Hugill

American singer, plus guitar, sings on one side The singers, all septuagenarians and octogenarians, are Dick Maitland, Sailor 'Dad' Hunt, Captain Leighton Robinson (over eighty), and Noble B. Brown, as well as other aged seamen. Booklets are supplied with each disc giving a fund of information on shanty singing: and details about the singers.

To emphasise the difficulty landsmen have in understanding shanties I must cite an incident in the singing of *Paddy Get Back* – the famous American folk expert and collector, Alan Lomax is the recorder and questioner. Dick Maitland, the shantyman, who has gone to some trouble explaining how this capstan shanty was used, is then asked by Lomax: "And show us where the pull comes..." Maitland carries on talking about the chorus but with persistence Lomax queries: "And that's where they pull?" Maitland now rather sharply comes back with, "There's no pull in a capstan shanty! They're walking round the capstan with the bars!"

By the fifties many more shanty records appeared. Folkways released their FP19 in loggers' songs and on the other shanties such as: *Rio, Clear The Track, Heave Away My Johnny, Boney, The Sailor Loves, A Hundred Years Ago*, etc.

Some are from Whall, Terry, Sharp and the P.S.N.C. Magazine. Another LP by Folkways, FA 2312, is that in which the great Canadian folk singer Alan Mills gives the solo to thirty-two shanties and forebitters, with his Shantymen singing the refrains. Included are:-

Rio, Cheerily Man, Dead Horse, Ten Thousand Miles Away, Blow, Boys, Blow, New Bedford Whalers, Can't You Dance The Polka?, Fire Down Below, Boney, Hilo Somebody, Galloping Randy Dandy-O!, The 'Shannon' and the 'Chesapeake' and many more.

Alan Mills, at one time, sang with John Goss (The London Singers), and some of the latter has obviously rubbed off on him, but I prefer his presentation (with guitar accompaniment) to that of Goss. A book of words is included with the disc. Both these Folkways records are, I believe, still available. In England The Workers' Music Association Ltd. (Topic) brought out the first, in my opinion, commercial record in which the shantying was realistic. This was *'The Singing Sailor'* (TRL3) now, unfortunately, deleted. The singers were Ewan MacColl, A.L. Lloyd and Harry Corbett (Yes, of Steptoe and Son!), with Alf Edwards on the concertina and Brian Daly on the guitar. Some of the songs are:-

The Ship in Distress, Johnny Todd, Haul The Bowline, The 'Dreadnought', Santy Anna, Row, Bullies, Row, The 'Flying Cloud', Lord Franklin and *Blow The Man Down*.

This is the first record in which forebitters are given realistic treatment and, although unobtainable now, much of its material was redone by Topic on their more recent LPs 8" T7 and T8. These were followed in turn by three EPs, *'Blow The Man Down'* (A8), *'A Hundred Years Ago'* (A9) and *'The Coast of Peru'* (A10), but the most recent issues of these three discs are numbered TOP 98, TOP 99 and TOP 100 respectively. A continental friend of mine however, has informed me that a French release of the original Singing Sailor called *'Chants de Marins Anglais'* is still obtainable in France.

In similar vein to these is TOP 27 on which Stan Kelly of Liverpool sings sea-songs and shanties in the Scouse idiom. This record is called *'The Liverpool Packet'* and includes the now-famous *Maggie May, Lowlands Away, Hullabaloo Balay*. Of other salty records of the fifties Decca presents Burl Ives in his *'Down To The Sea In Ships'* (DL 8245) offering, among others, *The Sailor's Grave, The Eddystone Light, High Barbaree, Red Red Roses, Highland Laddie* and *The Golden Vanitee*.

Peter Kennedy (EFDSS) has recorded and edited *'A Pinch of Salt'*, in which the well-known folk singers Cyril Tawny, Bob Roberts,

Seamus Ennis, Isabel Sunderland, Steve Benbow, etc., sing *British Submarine, Maggie May, The Handsome Cabin Boy, Santy Anno, Fine Girl You Are, Henry Martin, Paddy and the Whale, Tom's Gone to Hilo* and *Time For Us To Leave Her.*

This record (HMV CLP 1362) includes modern naval songs, canal songs and songs of the Lifeboat Service. A Columbia LP (1103) called *'High Barbaree'*, with Johnny Webb and other soloists singing *Shenandoah, According to the Act, Chinese Bumboatman, Blow the Man Down,* and so on has rather too much orchestral backing for my liking, but otherwise has some good material. In 1961 my own record *'Shanties from the Seven Seas'* (Stan Hugill with the York and Albany chorus), CLP 1524, was released. It has fourteen shanties including *Stormalong, The Ebenezer, Valparaiso Round the Horn, Paddy West, John Kanaka, The Liverpool Packet* and *The 'Campanayro'.*

The most recent-to-date disc on sailor songs is Topic's *'Farewell Nancy'* (12T110). Lou Killen, Cyril Tawny and others sing quite authentically *The Wild Goose, The Fire-ship, Lowlands Low, Hilo, Johnny Brown, Goodbye, Fare-ye-well* and *The Bold 'Princess Royal'.*

Bob Roberts, the master of the sailing barge *'Cambria',* around 1960, recorded for the Talking Book series a record (2/1501/26) called *'Windy Old Weather'.* On this disc, Bob accompanies himself with his squeezebox and sings *The Bargeman's ABC, Poor Old Horse, Captain Kidd, Johnny Todd* – and so on. And on the Collector disc JEB6 (*'Stormy Weather, Boys'*) he gives us *The Collier Brig, The Single Sailor, New York Girls, The Gray Hawk,* etc.

Other records that contain sea-songs are Folkways: *'Folk songs of Newfoundland'* (FP-831): *The Squid-Jiggin' Ground, Jack Was Every Inch a Sailor* and *I's the B'y That Builds the Boat* sung by Alan Mills.

Another example is Folkways: *'Bay State Ballads'* (FP47/2) on which Paul Clayton sings *Cape Cod Girls, Huzza for Commodore Rogers, The Ocean Rover, Seaman's Grave,* and other sea-songs of Massachusetts.

Of course, many records by the Spinners, Lou Killen, Ewan MacColl and Bert Lloyd contain sea-songs and shanties among other material. Of foreign discs, France and Germany have the best productions. In France the following are well known: *'Chansons de la Mer'* (RCA F 130003 and F 130028), on which Les Compagnons du Large sing: *Sur la Route de San Francisco (Rio), Les Filles de la Rochelle, Passant par Paris, Valparaiso, Jean Français de Nantes, Pique la Baleine, Sur le Pont de Morlaix, L'Archevêque de Bordeaux, De la Mer du Nord à la Bretagne.*

(Pathe AT 1057) which are orchestral offerings of the shanties only, and the most authentic of the four discs, the LP *'Chansons de Bord Françaises'* (Pathe ATX 109). These latter were collected by Capt. Armand Hayet and are sung by Marcel Nobla and his 'Bordée' or 'Watch'. They include: *La Danae, Valparaiso, La Margot, Quand la Boiteuse va au Marché, Pique la Baleine, Passant par Paris, Jean François.*

Germany has *'Rolling Home'* by the Kiel Holtenauer Lotsenchor 'Knurrhahn' (Polydor 20263 EPH). Here we have: *A Long Time Ago, De Hamborger Veermaster, Roll the Cotton,* etc.

This is a truly traditional record. Other German sea-song records are *'Wind und Wellen'* (661600 Fontana); Bernard Jakschart und die Seelords on Elektrola 040 412, singing: *Rolling Home, De Hamborger Veermaster, The Samoa Song;* and the record Telefunken No: 4771 with *Rolling Home, O, Jonny, In Amsterdam.*

Also Polydor 20263 EPH and Polydor 109 EPH (Burl Ives and the Ralf Hunk Singers), and Philips 429345 BE (Norman Lindoff and choir) with *Rolling Home, Blow the Man Down,* etc.

And with this I feel I have exhausted the topic of sea-song and shanty discs ...

The Bosun's Locker Stan Hugill

Vol. 4 No. 6
The Bosun's Locker

Many sailor songs and ballads are based on the exploits of the Barbary pirates and their, at times, European captains.

Who were these Barbary pirates, these Corsairs, Riffs or Sallee Rovers?

They were the maritime-minded inhabitants of the North African states of Algeria, Morocco, Tunisia and Tripoli. They held the whole Christian World in fear for over two hundred years and even longer. Their haunts were referred to as the 'Barbary Coast' or 'High Barbaree'. Some say that the name 'Barbary' originated with that of the Berber tribes inhabiting these parts, but the writer feels he has a more tenable theory.

One of the earliest of these North African pirates was Kheyr-ed-Din, nicknamed Barbarossa or 'Red Beard'. He was born in Mytilene, an island off the coast of Turkey, and, during the sixteenth century, his flamboyant beard was feared by every seaman in the Mediterranean Sea. He sacked the galley of the King of Naples, and with the aid of 20,000 Berbers, attacked the North African town of Jigelli, then Algiers. From then onwards he became the most notorious 'pirate' chief of the Coast. He sacked the ports of Italy, Spain and Sardinia with impunity. He was king of the Corsairs before the white pirates took over the coast, and I think the name 'Barbary' was given to the Coast by these European pirates in honor of Barbarossa. Two other early Moslem pirates were Dragut and Occhiali. These Corsairs were all Mohammedans, and most European pirates who joined them abjured Christianity and became Moslems if only nominal ones.

The name 'Corsair' is of French origin, and the name 'Riff' comes from the Riff tribesmen of Algeria and Morocco, now found in our language in the term 'riff-raff'. And 'Sallee' comes from the port of 'Sallee', or 'Safee' as it is given in some of the old ballads.

Theoretically, these Moslem pirates were ruled by the Sultan of the Ottoman Empire, but actually they swore allegiance to no one but themselves. They amassed great treasure and lived in opulence. Their main reason for piracy, however, was not just the collecting of treasure, but the collecting of slaves. Although these sea rovers had molested shipping well before the seventeenth century, it wasn't until the end of the Spanish wars and the resultant peace, during which English and other seamen found themselves out of work and out of adventure, that the Barbary pirates really became powerful. This was thanks to the adventure-seeking English and Dutch seamen turning pirate and joining the ranks of the Sallee Rovers. They were known as *renegades* or as it runs in many old ballads 'runnagades' and they brought to Barbary the arts of navigation and of maritime warfare. About this time in Spain, the Moriscoes or Moors, who hated the Christians, were being kicked out of the country en masse. They crossed over to North Africa and brought their shipbuilding skills to the pirates' lairs. At first these pirates used long sleek and swift galleys carrying oars and lateen sails, but the European seamen who joined their ranks taught them the art of square-rigged sailing thereby enabling them to venture farther afield. They even managed to sail as far as the Thames even in the sixteenth century.

The Bosun's Locker Stan Hugill

Sir Henry Mainwaring, a wonderful English scholar, who was a B.A. at 15, being of a roving disposition, sailed a small galley to Marmora on the Barbary Coast. Here he joined the sea rovers, becoming a *renegad* and Moslem. However, he was a humane man, and, as his power grew, he ordered his Corsair compatriots to leave his countrymen's ships alone. The Spaniards, whom he attacked incessantly, hated him. The Spanish king, as a last resort, offered him an award of several thousand ducats if he would join forces with him, but Mainwaring refused. At a later date he accepted a free pardon from King James of England. In fact, he was one of the very few *renegades* ever to return to his native land in good health. After receiving his pardon, his first job was that of pirate hunting. (A sequence later paralleled by Harry Morgan, who after being pardoned undertook to clear the Caribbean of pirates.) While Mainwaring was scouring the Channel for the Breton pirates of St. Malo – pirates such as Hankyn Lyons and Pety (Petit?) Pyllson – as well as Flemish and Italian sea-robbers, he came across three Barbary Coast galleys, fought them, and released many hundreds of European slaves from bondage at the oars.

Pirates such as the Dutchman Danseker (or Simon Denzer) and Ward, the 'Pyrate of the World', were a different kettle of fish. They were true *renegados* and Barbary fiends, remaining so until their timely demise. Captain Smith, writing of these days, declares that the 'Moors scarce knew how to sail a ship', and it was the nautical know-how of such European pirates as these two, that brought the port of Sallee into such prominence by the early seventeenth century,.

Ballads from the reign of James I concerning the exploits of Danseker and Ward are still with us. Ward started life as a fisherman in Faversham, and as a pirate attacked English, Turkish, Maltese, Venetian and French ships with impunity. He was accused in the ballads of 'drunkeness and letchery' and of 'the filthy sin of sodomy'. He built a castle in Tunis and was the captain of twenty-four ships. In the Roxburghe Ballads is to be found one of his songs:

English Ward and Danseker begin greatly now to jar,
About the true dividing of their goods,
Both ships and soldiers gathered,
Danseker from Ward is fled,
So full of pride and malice are their bloods.

This verse is about Danseker who helped Ward to capture the ships, *'London'*, *'Charity'*, *'Bonavanture'*, *'Pearl'* and *'Trojan'*. He fell out with Ward, and the two parted company.

Another well-known ballad about Ward is that entitled *A Famous Sea Fight between Captain Ward and the 'Rainbow'*.

In 1620, James I sent a fleet, under Sir Robert Mansell, against these Barbary pirates with the intention of releasing some of the 1500 enslaved Christian seamen, slaves who were mainly chained to the oars of the galleys of Argier, Tunis, Sallee and Tituane. The MS of a ballad in the Bodleian Library entitled *The Lamentable Cries of 1,500 Christians now Prisoners in Argiers under the Turkes*, tells us something of the plight of such slaves. Part of it runs:

Being boorded so, and rob'd, then they are tide
On chaines, and drag'd to Argiers, to feede the pride
Of a Mahumetan dog (eight in a row)
(Each eighth man to the Argier King must goe)
And the eighth part of what's tane is still his prize,
What men he leaves are anyones who buyes
And bids most for them, for they then are led

103

To market, and like beasts sold by the head,
Their masters having liberty by law
To strike, kick, starve them, yet make them draw,
In yoakes, like oxen, and if dead, they beate them,
Or they are throwne for beasts and ravens to eat them.
He that's condemned to the oar first his face,
Eyebrows, and head close shaven (for more disgrace
Cannot betide a Christian) then, being stript
To th' girdle (as when roagues are to be whipt),
Chain'd are they to the seats where they sit rowing,
Five in a row together; a Turke going
On a large plancke between them, and though their eyes,
Are ready to start out with pulling, he cryes
'Worke, worke, you Christian curres', and though none needs
One blow for loytering, yet his bare back bleeds,
And rises up in bunches, which the Turke
With a bulls-pizzle gives him, crying still, 'Worke,
Worke, dog', whilest some so faint, at the oare they dye,
Being cast (like dogs) over-boord presently.

At different periods, annual tributes to keep the sea rovers from molesting their ships and seamen, and high ransoms for men in slavery, were paid out by the Christian nations. In 1624 a collection of money was made in England in order to ransom some of these poor seamen slaves, and in 1637 the ship *'Rainbow'*, (already referred to) sailed into Sallee and rescued nearly 400 English seamen from slavery. In the mid 1690s the famous Captain William Kidd sailed from Plymouth in the privateer *'Adventure'*. He held a commission under the Great Seal to seize Barbary pirates. As everyone knows he turned pirate himself, was captured in Boston and in 1701 he was hung at Execution Dock. The old ballad about his adventures called *Captain Kid's Farewell to the Seas*, or *Famous Pirate's Lament* has survived to the present day, but has suffered a little in its wanderings. Its original tune was that called *Coming Down* and here are a couple of verses for to compare with the ones heard in folk clubs:

My name is Captain Kid, who has sail'd, who has sail'd,
My name is Captain Kid who has sail'd;
My name is Captain Kid, what the laws did still forbid,
Unluckily I did, while I sail'd.

We steered from sound to sound, while we sail'd, while we sail'd,
We steered from sound to sound, while we sail'd;
We steered from sound to sound, a Moorish ship we found,
Her men were stript and bound, while we sail'd.

This ballad has, in its entirety, 22 verses!

In 1758 a ship called the *'Lichfield'* ran ashore on the coast of Morocco, all hands being taken into slavery. A ballad was composed about the incident. It is a ship song and called *Captain Barton's Distress on Board the 'Lichfield', being under Slavery for Seventeen Months and Fourteen Days*. It is given on p. 214 of C.H. Firth's *'Naval Songs and Ballads'*. According to the old records the slaves were eventually freed on payment of a ransom of 170,000 dollars. The last verse of the ballad runs:

Now my brave boys, to Old England we're bound,

We will have stores of liquor our sorrow to drown,
We will drink a good health, success never fail,
Bad cess to the bawds, and whores of Kinsale.

Kinsale was the port they arrived at after being delivered from Corsair slavery – and, like true seamen, it would appear they suffered as much at the hands of the harlots of Kinsale as they did at the hands of the Barbary pirates!

Other ballads from these days dealing with the Barbary Coast are *The Argier Slaves Releasement*, or *The Unchangeable Boatswain* which are to be found in the Roxburghe Ballads, and *Captain Mansfield's Fight with the Turkes at Sea*.

However, the one ballad that started out at an even earlier date than any of these and survived, orally, the centuries, becoming a nineteenth-century sailor forebitter and, at times, shanty, is that known in folk clubs as *High Barbaree*. Originally it was named *The Sailor's Onely Delight*, and it is to be found in both Child and the Roxburghe Ballads. It is sometimes called *The Salcombe Seaman*. The tune, or one of its many tunes, was registered in March 1611. The ballad tells the tale of a certain Diggory Piper, who in 1596, was granted letters of marque, and sailed from London in a ship called the *'Sweepstakes'*. His companion ship in the song is the *'George Aloe'*. They met a French Corsair out of Barbary and sank her after a tough fight.

By the time this ballad had reached the nineteenth century sailing shipman the names of the ships concerned had become the *'Prince of Luther'* and the *'Prince of Wales'*. And many new tunes had developed, although the text rarely altered.

By the nineteenth century, England and America, being rather fed up with these North African pirates and the tributes and ransoms they had to pay them, decided to bombard the Barbary forts. In 1803, the United States Navy blockaded Tripoli, and in 1804 the Tripoli fort surrendered. It was about this time that the U.S. Frigate *'Constitution'* or *'Old Ironsides'* engaged these Barbary pirates. My boys are at present engaged in making a plastic model of this famous ship, which is still afloat in Boston harbour. In 1816 the British bombarded Algiers, and James Catnach printed a broadsheet about the incident. By 1831 the French had marched into Algiers and taken many of the Barbary States, bringing to a close two centuries or more of piracy, slavery of Christian seamen, and the exacting of ransom and tribute from Christian nations. Many famous men were slaves of these pirates including Cervantes of *'Don Quixote'* fame and St. Vincent de Paul.

It is interesting to note however, that spasmodic piratical attacks occurred even in the twentieth century, the last, I believe, being in 1906, when a Moorish pirate attacked an English ship right under the lee of the Rock of Gibraltar and the nose of the British Navy!

The Bosun's Locker Stan Hugill
High Barbaree

There were two lofty ships, from ol' England they set sail – Blow high! Blow low! An' so sail'd we. One was the Prince of Luther and the other Prince of Wales, Sailing down along the coast o' High Barbaree!

Aloft there, aloft, o our gallant cap'n cried,
Chorus: Blow high, blow low, an' so sail'd we!
Look ahead, look astern, look a-weather an' a-lee,
Chorus: Cruisin' (Sailin') down along the coast of High Barbaree!

I see naught upon the starn, an' there's naught upon the lee,
But there's a lofty ship to wind'ard an' she's sailin' fast 'n' free.

O, hail her, O, hail her, our gallant cap'n cried,
Oh, are you a man-o-war or privateer cried he.

Oh, no I'm not a man-o-war or privateer cried he,
But I'm a salt sea pirate an' I'm lookin' for me fee.

For broadside, for broadside we fought on all the main,
Until the Prince of Luther shot the pirate's mast in twain.

For quarter, for quarter, them rascal pirates cried,
But the quarter that we gave 'em was to sink 'em in the tide

Vol. 5 No. 1
Yo Ho 'n' a Bottle of Rum

Strangely enough, apart from those singing of the Barbary Coast, few songs based on the lives of pirates are to be found in print and fewer still appear to have been handed down orally. As I showed in the last issue of *'SPIN'*, the infamous sea-robbers of North Africa were the only ones well represented in song and ballad. Pirates *must* have had songs – probably in great numbers – but, somehow or other they were never recorded nor handed on traditionally. Robert L. Stevenson's famous *'Treasure Island'* stave, 'Fifteen men on a dead man's chest' is thought to be some fragment of a real pirate's song and not just a composition of the 'Tusitala', but unfortunately, no real proof has ever been offered.

The terrible fiends of the Spanish Main, Morgan the 'Sacker of Panama', Rackham, Montbars, the 'Exterminator', L'Olonnois, Homigold, Mansveld and so on, have never a word in song. Neither have the female pirates, Anne Bonney and Mary Read. The sea rogues of the West African coast – England, Roberts and Howel Davies the Wild Welshman – although their nefarious exploits are well recorded in print, strangely enough, never appear to have become famed in song. Of the pirates of Madagascar – Avery, Surcouf, Misson and Tew – only Avery has special mention.

Avery, (Every as he is named in some ballads) or Bridgman, as he is sometimes called, in May 1694 seized a merchantman, the *'Charles the Second'*, laying at anchor off Corunna. Avery set the captain and sixteen seamen ashore, renamed the ship and sailed for Guinea. Avery's 'Jolly Roger' when he embarked on the piracy game, was a black flag sporting a white skeleton; a dart striking a red heart in one of its hands and an hourglass in the other. Under this flag quarter would be given, but when the rogues hoisted a red flag then every enemy's throat was slit:

> …yet call out for quarter before you do see,
> A bloody red flag out which is our decree,
> No quarters, no quarters to take
> To save nothing living, alas, 'tis too late,
> For we are now sworn by the bread and the wine,
> More serious we are than any divine.

Avery's most famous feat was when he captured and sacked the Great Mogul's treasure ship the *'Gang-i-Sawai'* but his end was a death ashore in the back streets of Bristol, an impoverished wreck. His men were not so fortunate perhaps since there exists a ballad (in the Pepys Collection) telling of the pirate Joseph Dawson and five of Avery's crew being executed at Wapping in 1696.

> We robbed a ship upon the seas,
> The *'Gunsway'* called by name
> Which we met near the East Indies
> And Rifled the same;
> In it was Gold and silver store,
> Of which we had a share,
> Each man six hundred pounds or more,
> Let pyrates then take care
> (*The Pirates' last farewell to the World*)

The Bosun's Locker Stan Hugill

One of the very few buccaneers to have a ballad built around him was Teach, or 'Blackbeard' as he was usually called. Edward Teach was born in Bristol in the latter part of the seventeenth century, and probably commenced his piratical career under Hornigold. Lieutenant Maynard brought his wild career to an end. After a savage battle the pirates believed that they had wiped out the man-o'-war's crew, and boarded her silent decks. Maynard, however, had hidden his men at salient points around the ship, and as the pirates came aboard, they found themselves in a trap. Blackbeard, with his usual halo of slow matches flaming from his black hair and whiskers, and smelling of rum and gunpowder (his favorite tipple) was suddenly surrounded. Maynard almost cut him to pieces with his sword and another seaman crashed a pike on his head. Then, as he died, the man-o'-war's men slashed his head off and stuck it on the jackstaff on the bowsprit. This happened on the twenty-first of November 1717. Maynard showed the head at Bathtown and then sailed to Jamestown with it still glaring from the prow. The only man of Blackbeard's crew that escaped Execution Dock was Israel Hands (whose name was used by Stevenson in *'Treasure Island'*) since he happened to be ashore at the time of the fight. He had been crippled by a 'playful' shot in the leg from Blackbeard's pistol, and in later years became a beggar displaying his crippled leg around the lanes of Wapping.

Here are some relevant verses from the ballad *The Downfall of Piracy.*

> Maynard boarded him and to it
> They fell with sword and pistol, too
> They had courage and did show it
> Killing of the pirate's crew.

> Teach and Maynard on the quarter
> Fought it out most manfully,
> Maynard's sword did cut him shorter,
> Losing his head he there did die.

> When the bloody fight was over,
> We're informed by letter writ,
> Teach's head was made a cover
> To the jackstaff of the ship.

> Thus they sail'd to Virginia,
> And when they the story told
> How they'd killed the pirates many
> They'd applause from young and old.

A well-aired pirate song around the clubs is *Henry Martin*:

> There were three brothers in merry Scotland,
> In merry Scotland there were three,
> And they did cast lots which of them
> would go, would go, would go,
> And sail as pirates all on the salt sea.

Henry Martin never existed but his prototype Sir Andrew Barton did. The Scot, Jon Barton, had three sons. They obtained letters of reprisal against the Portuguese for the seizure of their father's treasure ship. They enjoyed to

108

the full their attacks against the Portuguese under the privilege of the letters, but eventually they made a habit of it. One son, Andrew, for example, used to raid English ships, seize their goods and say that they were Portugal's. In 1511 Henry VIII sent Lord Edmund Howard and Lord Thomas Howard to capture these pirates. According to the ballad, Andrew didn't fire any guns in the ensuing battle, but relied upon 'beams', which he lowered on the decks of the enemy. Full explanation of their use, however, is not given in the ballad:

> With beams from her Top-castle,
> As also being huge and high;
> That neither English nor Portingall,
> Can Sir Andrew Barton pass by.

and

> Let no man to his Top-castle goe,
> Nor strive to let his beames down fall.
> Then did he one Gordian call,
> Unto the Top-castle for to goe,
> And did his beames he should let fall,
> For I greatly fear an overthrow.

(Andrew Barton, *'Douce's Ballads'* 1,19; III, 84, Child, 167)

The Scots have always been averse to having Barton called a 'pirate'. He was killed in 1512. The old forebitter *The 'Flying Cloud'* is a song of slavery and piracy but, although correct in its background, neither the ship nor its captain, have ever been identified.

> And now our money is all gone,
> We must go to sea for more,
> But each man listened to the words,
> The words of Capt'n Moore,
> There's gold and silver to be had,
> If with me you'll remain,
> Let's hoist the pirate flag aloft
> And sweep the Spanish Main.

In sailing ship fo'c'sles of the nineteenth century a pirate song, which probably had its origin on the music hall stage, called *The Pirate of the Isles* was very popular with the men.

> I command a sturdy band of pirates bold and free,
> Our Isle's our home, my ship's my throne
> My kingdom is the sea;
> The flag is red at our royal-masthead,
> At all my foes I smile,
> No quarter I show, where'er I go
> But soon a prize we'll take in tow.

It was not based on the exploits of any particular pirate and could be called an 'art song' rather than folk or ballad.

Foreign seamen, from my own observations, appear to have rarely sung about pirates. Among French sailormen *Le Grand Coureur* was very popular, and was, at times, sung at the capstan. I give it in my *'Shanties from the Seven Seas'*. The song is a humorous one, with much play on words, and has no bearing on any known pirate. In fact it appears to be based on a mythical Breton pirate such as sailed forth into the Channel from Dunkirk and St. Malo in the sixteenth and seventeenth centuries.

The most famous German pirate was Stortebeker, who with three other infamous sea-robbers, Manteufel, Moltke and Godeke (Godekins) formed a brotherhood called 'The Friends of God and the Enemies of the World'. They were eventually defeated by a fleet of cogs belonging to the Hanseatic League. Stortebeker and seventy of the 'Friends' were executed at Hamburg in 1402. German seamen still sing a song about his savagery, the first verse of which runs:

> De Stortebeker und God eke Michele,
> De rovenden beide to lieken Deel,
> To Wader und to Lanne
> Bet dat et Gott van hemmel,
> Verdroot dor mussen se lieden grote Schanne.

The Bosun's Locker Stan Hugill

Songs about privateers – a more respectable form of piracy – are also very few, although ballads inviting men to enter on board privateers in times of war are more numerous. The reason for this was probably because during times of war privateers men became more honoured, particularly so during the wars with France and America. One with which I am familiar is *The 'Polly' Privateer* – a Liverpool ship carrying letters of marque – which begins:

> Come all ye gallant seamen, come listen unto me,
> Whilst I relate a bloody fight, just lately fought at sea;
> As we set sail from Liverpool to the salt seas we did steer,
> To try our hard fortunes in the '*Polly*' privateer.

Another, a slipsong from the Madden Collection of ballads in Cambridge University Library goes:

> Why should we here our time delay in London void of pleasure,
> Let's haste away for Biscay Hay and ransack there for treasure,
> Here we must creep and play bo-peep, to shun the damn'd press-masters,
> We live in strife, we die in strife, confined by catchpole bastards.

(*The 'Blandford' Privateer*)

The Lowlands Low, our song for this issue, has no true locale. The Barbary Coast may have been the scene of the song, but, since some versions give a Spanish pirate and others 'a Turkish gahally', and some just a 'false galley' the incident may have occurred (if it did!) anywhere. Some say Sir Walter Raleigh was the cruel 'cozening lord' who was master of the ship. Our version was supposed to have stemmed from a ballad called *Sir Walter Raleigh Sailing in the Lowlands,* although Child reckons that traditionally, the *'Golden Vanitee'* (our version) may be as old as this supposedly early ballad. 1682-85 is usually given as the date of the Sir Walter Raleigh version but Ashton places it around 1635. The theme is the same in the old and 'new' versions, but the 'modern' tune will not fit the old one. Child has four versions. In one the ship is called the *'Sweet Trinity'*.

One unusual version runs:

> There was a gallant ship and a gallant ship was she,
> Eck iddle dee, and the Lowlands low,
> And she was called the *'Golden Vanitee',*
> As she sailed in the Lowlands low.

The Bosun's Locker Stan Hugill

The Golden Vanitee

There once was a skipper who was boastin' on the quay, Oh, I have a ship and a gallant ship is she, Of all the ships I know she is far the best to me, an' she's sailin' in the Lowlands low, In the Lowlands, Lowlands, She's sailin' in the Lowlands low!

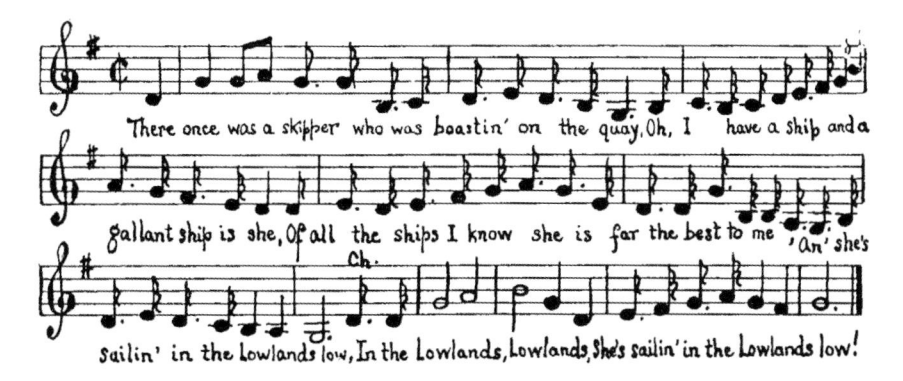

Oh, I had her built in the North Countree,
An I had her christened the Golden Vanitee
I armed her an' I manned her an' I sent her off to sea,
An' she's sailin' in the Lowlands low.
Chorus: In the Lowlands, Lowlands,
She's sailin' in the Lowlands low.

Then up spoke a sailor who'd just returned from sea,
Oh, I was aboard of the Golden Vanitee,
When she was held in chase by a Turkish pirateer,
An' we sank her in the Lowlands low.

For we had aboard of us a little cabin boy,
Who said what will you give me if the galley I destroy,
The Turkish piratee no more she shall annoy,
I will sink her in the Lowlands low.

Of treasure and of gold I will give to thee a store,
An' my pretty little daughter who wait'eth on the shore,
Of treasure an' of fee as well I'll give to thee galore,
If ye sink her in the Lowlands low.

So the boy bared his breast and he plunged into the tide,
He swam until he came to the rascal pirates side,
He climbed on deck an' went below, by none he was espied,
An' he sank her in the Lowlands low.

He bored with his auger, he bored once and twice,
An' some were playin cards an' some were playin' dice,
An' the water flowed in an' dazzled their eyes,
An' he sank 'em in the Lowlands low.

Now the cabin boy did swim all to the Starboard side
Sayin' Capen take me up I am drownin' in the tide,
I will shoot you, I will kill you if ye claim my child as bride,
I will sink you in the Lowlands low. . . .

So the cabin boy did swim all to the larboard side,
Sayin' shipmates take me up I am drownin' in the tide,
An' they hauled him up so quickly but when on deck he died,
He was drowned in the Lowlands low.

They laid him on the deck and they sewed him up in hide,
They lashed him in his hammock which was so strong and wide,
They said a short prayer o'er him and they sank him in the tide,
He was buried in the Lowlands low.

The Bosun's Locker Stan Hugill

Songs of the 'Wooden Walls'

The great naval sailing ships-of-the-line known as 'Wooden Walls' came into being in the seventeenth century. They were the battleships of the period and were crowded with men. The last to be built, in all probability were the twelve 100-gun ships decided upon by My Lords of the Admiralty in 1758. Of these the *'Victory'* of course, is still with us. She was launched in 1765.

Wars with the Dutch and French were mainly those in which these ships were 'gainfully employed', although at the time the *'Victory'* was launched there existed a peace between us and the Johnny Crapauds. However, by the seventies the French and ourselves were at it again, with the press-gangs busy manning those huge floating forts. The lighter and faster frigates rarely needed pressed men. Seamen proper did not mind 'entering' the frigates as prize money was plentiful, but in the 'Wooden Walls' the latter was almost negligible, hence pressed men formed a goodly part of their crews.

These men were referred to as 'Landsmen'. When they felt in the mood for a 'tween-decks sing-song – which probably wasn't often – they would sing those ditties currently popular ashore. Such songs, however, are beyond the limits of this article, and we must confine ourselves to the type of song sung by the regular seamen of such ships. These, like those of the Merchant Service, were referred to as 'forebitters'. In this case, however, the fore-hilts from which the generic term arose were not the fo'c'slehead as in merchantmen, but came from what merchant seamen call the 'fife-rail'. This was found at the foot of the foremast (and at the main and mizzen masts too). In the ships-of-the-line it consisted of a stout construction of timber through which all the gear of the foresail and foreyard led and was belayed. Its top rail, on which the lead-singer would perch, would be about four feet above the deck, and therefore formed a fine rostrum around which the sailors would squat on coils of rope or on the trucks and brackets of the gun carriages. However, in many naval ships this singing at the forebitts was not allowed. In ships-of-the-line such as the *'Victory',* immediately next below the upper or main deck was a gundeck – a deck bearing different names at different periods. Part of it was exposed to the sky owing to there being a large aperture in the upper deck above it between the fore and main masts. This aperture was spanned with several beams, these in turn being skids on which were nested two or more ships' boats and the longboat. In many ships the seamen carried out their sing-songs on this deck, between the guns, and when in port, their carousing.

As I have stated in previous articles, the six to eight dogwatch during which in merchant ships, merchant seamen held their sing-songs, in naval vessels was the period when was given the order "All hands to dance and song" or "All hands to dance and skylark (or frolic)". It was an order by My Lords of the Admiralty, which had to be obeyed. The reason for it was the belief that the vicious disease of the sailing ship sailor, scurvy, could be kept at bay by violent movement, a reasoning proved to be a fallacy in the light of later research. This belief brought about the vigorous dancing of the hornpipe and so on, and the nautical rough and tumble known as 'frolic'.

Admiral Cyprian A.G. Bridge believes that

we should have to go back to the sixteenth century before finding a period when 'nothing but nautical folk song was heard on the forecastle'. Also, on what proof I do not know, he believes that the old seadogs of King Billy's reign were averse to singing 'obscenities', and that it was not until the middle years of Queen Victoria's reign that music-hall song with its *double entendre* was permitted by an audience of naval matlows. Well, if this is true, (and I doubt it) the seamen of the British Navy made up for it in later years! Nevertheless it is true that if what we call 'dirty songs' were sung in those far-off days, apparently none have come down to us. Songs of 'pure' love, of tokens, of female sailors, of battles, and of the press-gang and so on, still exist in plenty, but *double entendre* or straightforwardly obscene ones are markedly absent.

As to the style of singing, Admiral Bridge, writing in 1906, declares that the old-fashioned naval manner of singing forebitters still existed at that time on Norfolk Island in the Pacific. The islanders, overflow descendants of the *'Bounty'* mutineers, apparently cast the hymns they sang in their island church in the traditional forebitter style. This must have been the last place in the world where the forebitter manner of singing was still enacted.

The sailor songs from the days of the 'Wooden Walls' best known today are, I should say, those stemming from the days of our hectic wars with the French and with the American colonists, songs such as *Admiral Benbow*, *The Saucy 'Arethusa'* and *The 'Shannon' and the 'Chesapeake'*.

> Oh, we sailed to Virginia and thence to Fayal,
> Where we watered in our shipping and then weighed all;
> Then in view of the seas, boys, seven sail we did espy,
> And we manned our good capstan and weighed speedily.
>
> Now the first we came up withall was a brig and a sloop,
> And we asked if the other five were as big as they looked
> Then turning to wind'ward, as near as we could lie,
> We met French men-o'-war, boys, oh, a-cruising hard by.

This song was a great favourite, its theme being based on the bravery of Benbow and the cowardice of Captains Wade and Kirby who left Benbow to engage the French on his own. *The Saucy 'Arethusa'*, although a shore-manufactured song, was entirely accepted by the men of the 'Wooden Walls'. The seafight of which it sings happens to be the first engagement of the thirty-seven years war between the French and us. Admiral Keppel's fleet of twenty-seven ships, of which the *'Arethusa'* was one of three frigates, came across two Frenchmen in the Channel. War hadn't actually been declared but Keppel decided to attack them so as to prevent them carrying information about his fleet back to France. The *'Arethusa'* took on one of the ships, *'La Belle Poule'*, and although she lost less fewer men than the Frenchman, nevertheless she sustained more damage. This happened in 1778.

> Come all ye jolly sailors bold, whose heart's are cast in honour's mould
> Whilst British glory I unfold, hurrah for the *'Arethusa'*!
> She is a frigate tight and brave, as ever stemmed the dashing wave,
> And her men are staunch to their favourite,
> And when the foe does meet our fire, sooner than die we'll all expire,
> On board the *'Arethusa'*!

The American War of 1812 and Boston

The Bosun's Locker Stan Hugill

harbour form the background of that very popular number *The 'Shannon' and the 'Chesapeake'*. The fight between these two naval ships, the *'Shannon'*, a British frigate, and the *'Chesapeake'* an American, took place on a lovely sunny day in 1812, with half of Boston's populace sitting on the shore enjoying the spectacle and the bands playing noisily in competition with the cacophony of shot and shell. The defeat and capture of the *'Chesapeake'* was the one signal victory of the British in the War of 1812.

> Oh, the *'Chesapeake'* so bold, sail'd from Boston we've been told,
> For to take the British frigate neat and handy O!
> All the people in the port, all came down to see the sport,
> And the bands were playing Yankee doodle dandy O!
>
> *Chorus:* Yankee doodle, Yankee doodle, dandy O!
> All the people in the port came down to see the sport.
> And the bands were playing Yankee doodle dandy O!

Of course, over and above these rather well-known songs many nautical ballads, once popular in the 'tween-decks of the navy have disappeared from ken and voice. Obviously it is impossible in such a short article to cover all of these, but I will give a stanza or two of those I consider representative of the type of song sung by the tarry pigtailed mariner at the forebitts or whilst sitting on the breech of a gun. First let us take songs dealing with the old-time sailor's tendency to drink. There were many ditties about beer, 'swipes', 'flip', punch and later, rum. A rather rollicking forebitter from the early 1700s runs:

> All hands up aloft, swab the coach fore'n'aft,
> For the punch-clubbers straight will be sitting,
> For fear the ship roll, sling off a full bowl,
> For our honour let all things be fitting.
> In an ocean full of ale, we tonight will all sail,
> In the bowl we're in sea-room, enough we ne'er fail.
> Here's to thee, messmate,
> Thanks Honest Tom,
> 'Tis a health to the King,
> Whilst the larboard man drinks,
> Let the starboard man sing:
>
> *Chorus:* With full double cups we'll liquor our chaps,
> And then we'll turn out with a who-up-who, who,
> But let's drink e'er we go,
> But let's drink e'er we go.

The full song is to be found in *'Durfey's Pills to Purge Melancholy'*, (1719).

A later song, *The Mariner's Compass*, gives the impression that the British Navy ran on grog – and it probably did!

> Sam Spritsail's a lad you'd delight in.
> For friendship he's ever agog,
> Loves his King, loves his wench, loves fighting,
> And he loves, to be sure, he loves grog.
> Says Sam, says he, life's a notion.
> And he wants from the spirits a jog,
> The world is a wide troubled ocean,
> And our rudder and compass is grog.
>
> *Chorus:* For grog is our larboard and starboard
> Our mainmast, our mizzen, our log,
> At sea, or ashore, or when harbour'd,
> The mariner's compass is grog.

Of course, in those days some form of alcohol was served daily aboard naval ships. (Coffee

The Bosun's Locker Stan Hugill

and tea were yet to come as nautical beverages.) In earlier days it is recorded that many of the British commanders cruised only 'as long as the beer lasted'. In the reign of the first Elizabeth and during that of the Stuarts each sailor was allowed four quarts of beer per day. Under later monarchs this was watered down to 'swipes' or 'small beer' or 'flip', an acidy concoction that gave seamen dysentery. In the eighteenth century rum was imported from the West Indies and this took the place of beer at sea. At first pure rum was handed out, but on the recommendation of Admiral Vernon or 'Old Grog', it was watered down and for ever after was called 'grog' after the Admiral. The songs of Charles Dibdin, although they found little favour at sea, helped to disseminate the belief that all naval seamen were drunk more or less all the time.

Songs of Nancy and Polly and Susan found equal favour among the Jack Tars, and many 'token' songs, too, songs mentioning broken rings or torn hankies were popular on the lower deck. We have, just to mention a few: *The Welcome Sailor*, *The Distressed Sailor's Garland*, *Fair Phoebe and the Dark-eyed Sailor* and *Pleasant and Delightful*, now making its round of the folk clubs. This latter and *Fair Phoebe* were well known even in my dad's time, and I have both in his handwritten songbook.

A term of contempt used at sea in the old days was "You Port Mahon Baboon!" This probably came in use after 1755 when a chap called Blakeney was holding a fort at Port Mahon against the French. Admiral Byng was supposed to have backed him with his fleet but instead the Admiral sheered off with the result that we lost to the French. Many songs came into the forecastles of naval ships singing of Admiral Byng, one with the chorus:

> To the block with Newcastle and the yardarm with Byng!

Another ran:

> Here's a health to brave Blakeney, so stout and so bold,
> Who the fort of St. Philip so bravely did hold.
> Had he been reinforced by Admiral Byng
> He'd not yielded St. Philip unto the French King.

At sea nowadays, on British passenger liners, the ship's bugler plays the tune known as *The Mighty Roast Beef of Old England* to announce dinner. It is an air of great age and was used for many songs in the eighteenth and nineteenth centuries. *The Bold Blades of Old England* was an early one.

> Come rouse up me lads, let us haste to the Main,
> And load home our chests with the dollars of Spain,
> For as we have beat them we'll do so again,

'Twixt-deck Sing-song

115

The Bosun's Locker Stan Hugill

And it's oh, the bold blades of Old England.
And, oh, for the bold British blades!

A later one was:

Now fill up a glass while a bumper we have,
To Howe, Jervis, Duncan and Nelson the brave,
All bold British tars that now rule the waves,
Huzza for the bulwarks of England,
And huzza for the bold British tar!

Sea battles, such as those of the Nile, of Copenhagen, of Trafalgar, all produced a welter of songs but these, perhaps, did not find such favour among the salts as did ones dealing with actual sea-life. For one thing they were, in the main, shore-composed by famous printers of broadsides such as Catnach, Such and so on, and were all 'true-blue' and rather too patriotic for the half-starved, badly paid, impressed and well-flogged naval matlows of the 'Wooden Walls'.

I have chosen an actual naval seamen's tune for our music this time but, before we reach it, let me give you some stanzas from two more similar in construction and sentiment. The first one, *The Saucy 'Scylla'*, is about a tough frigate on the Bahama station engaged in a search for slave-ships.

After quarters was over, there was one thing more,
All hands to reef tops'ls, which grieved us full sore,
'Men, man the rigging,' our lieutenant would cry
'Rise up and lay out your reef-points to the tie.'

In less than two minutes our tops'ls must be reefed,
All sail set above them so snug and complete,
For black-listing and drilling grieved us to the heart,
For our six-watered grog it just measured one quart.

The second is about the frigate *'Vanguard'*:-

Then down from the mast to the gangway you must repair,
And there is the gratings rigged ready to punish you there.

Chorus: Then let us sing the *'Vanguard's* praise,
Proclaim her valiant name,
Cruel usage I have met with,
Since I sailed in the same.

Here we have one of the songs dealing with

La Pique or The Fancy Frigate

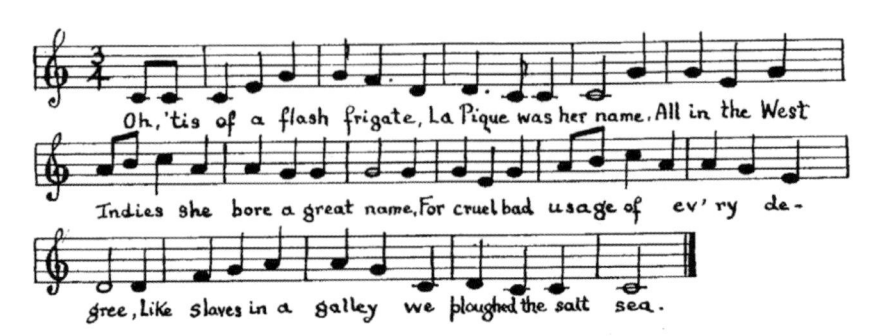

Oh, 'tis of a flash frigate, La Pique was her name. All in the West Indies she bore a great name. For cruel bad usage of ev'ry degree, Like slaves in a galley we ploughed the salt sea.

The Bosun's Locker Stan Hugill

'fancy frigates' oft cursed by the men of the 'Wooden Walls'. I have this from my father's songbook and I give rather more verses here than I did in my *'Shanties from the Seven Seas'*. Its tune was later used by merchant seaman for the capstan shanty and forebitter, *The Liverpool Packet*.

At four in the mornin' our work is begun
To the cockpit the waisters for buckets must run;
Our fore and main topmen so loudly do bawl,
For sand and for holystones, both large an' small.

Oh, master Make-clever you know very well,
He comes up on deck and he cuts a great swell;.
It's 'Bear a hand, here, boys', and 'Bear a hand there',
And in the lee-gangway he takes a broad sheer.

Half a dozen cuts here, ye'll be sure he goes on,
You're sure of a hiding, boys, yes, every darn one,
For marine or for sailor he cares not a damn,
But he'll lash you as long as you're able to stand.

Our decks being washed down and mopped up quite dry,
'Tis lash up your hammocks, our bosun do cry;
Our hammocks are lashed, black clews an' black shows,
And all of one size, boys, through the hoops they must go.

Our hammocks being stowed and our breakfast all done,
We're ranked in divisions with our white caps all on;
With our speeguls and lashings, so black they must shine,
With our white frocks and trousers we must all be in line.

Our divisions officer now makes his round,
Not a hole, nor a mark in your clothes must be found
For an hour or more in this way we must be,
Our ropes flemished down, both in port and at sea.

Divisions being over the next thing comes on
Jack-o-clubs now is a-calling for swabs in his song;
Three or four dry swabs then each cook he must find,
An' the bright copper hoops on our mess-kits must shine.

'Tis pulling and hauling all the four hours round,
On deck or below, there no peace to be found;
Either paint room or store room you're sure for to clear,
To find out what blacking or paint is to spare.

Pass the word for the painters, fore- 'n-aft is the cry,
By booms, nor by gangway I would have you draw nigh;
Nor yet in the ports would I have you be found
For six strokes or more to your name 'twill go round.

Our pikes and our cutlasses are as bright as the sun,
Our shot-racks are copper, boys, yes, everyone;
Our pommelins and handspikes, belayin'-pins also,
With our bright iron stanchions we cut a brave show.

Neither combings, nor hatchways I'd have you go near,
From the bell or cook's funnel I'd have you

The Bosun's Locker Stan Hugill

steer clear;
Nor yet in the galley I'd have you to go,
For a black thunder squall, boys, will take you in tow.

And now look aloft, oh, me boys, every one,
All hands to make sail, going large is the song;
From under two reefs in our tops'ls we lie,
Like a cloud all our canvas in a moment must fly.

There's tops'ls, topgallants'ls, staysails also
There's stuns'ls on both sides, aloft and alow;
There's royals, an skys'ls, stargers so high
By the sound of one pipe everthing it must fly.

An' now, me brave boys, comes the best o' the fun,
It's hands about ship and reef tops'ls in one;
Our hands go aloft when the helm it goes down,
Lower away tops'ls as the mainyard goes round.

Trice up an' layout an' take two reefs in one,
In a moment of time all this work must be done;
So 'tis man your head braces, your halyards an' all,
An' 'Hoist away tops'ls! ' an' 'Let go an' haul! '

Now your quids of tobaccy I'd have you to mind,
If ye spits on the deck, sure your death-warrant's signed;
If you spits over bow, over gangway or starn,
You're sure of three dozen just by way of no harm.

But worse than all this, I have known them to stop,
A week's wine or grog if you spill but one drop;
Either forward or aft I would have ye keep clear,
Or the bell, or cook's funnel, will fall to your share.

Come, all brother seamen, where'er ye may be,
From all fancy frigates I'd have ye steer free;
For they'll haze ye, an' work ye, 'till ye ain't worth a damn,
Then they'll ship ye half-dead to your dear native land.

Vol. 5 No. 3

Owing to the fact that I have failed to get a certain song transcribed in time for press I have had to shelve this month's intended article. I scratched my topknot for some time wondering with what to replace it, then suddenly, while doing a job-o-work and humming an old sea ditty to myself, the thought struck me: why not an article on certain words and terms that crop up regularly in nautical ballads both ancient and modern? Sez I to meself, sez I, "That's it!" and here it is. . . . .

Firstly (what an awful word!) let us take a four-point bearing at those crowd-embracing and encouraging cries that appear both time and time again in shouts used at the capstan and cordage, and in sailor song either in the refrains or in the stanzas –usually, in the latter case, to make them scan. In more modern songs 'me boys' or 'brave boys' would be the sort of thing:

Heave, me boys, an' bust 'er!

Come, me boys, now don't be silly,
Pack yer bags an' join the Lily.

The man up in the barrel there, wid a spyglass in his hand,
"There's a whale, there's a whale,
 there's a whalefish!" he cries,
An' she blows at every span, brave boys,
An' she blows at every span.

Expressions including the word 'boy' appear to me, on research, to have been favoured both by ancient and modern sailor composers, although the 'brave boys' one begins to fade after the first few years of the nineteenth century. Another expression that has spanned the years of nautical ballad and song is 'my lively lads'. An early example, probably from the sixteenth century is the following:

The Boatson (Bosun) he's under the deck,
A man of courage bold,
To th' top, to th' top, my lively lads,
Hold fast, my hearts of gold!

The rather romantic 'my hearts of gold' bit, however, never survived the years. Although a popular expression with sea-ballad makers for many years, it would seem to have died a natural death by the end of the eighteenth century. In the last issue of *'SPIN'*, I gave a song (the tune of which was that of *The Roast Beef of Old England*) that used the expression 'bold blades' – *The Bold Blades of Old England*. A similar phrase occasionally found in old naval broadsides was 'my noble blood'. Here it is in a press-gang song of the eighteenth century:

What ship, honest brother sailor?
You must stop and let us know,
If you're entered* or protected**,
You must tell us before you go,
Here's warrants to impress you;
Ne'er repine, my noble blood,
We don't want for to press you,
It's for your King and Country's good!

* 'Entered' means to have already joined the Service.

** 'Protected' signifies having had a 'protection' granted by High Authority excusing one from being 'pressed'.

The Bosun's Locker Stan Hugill

'Blood', of course, was a shore phrase – as was 'blade'. The bloods, blades, bucks, beaus, hearts and sparks of shoreside in the eighteenth century, although they were in the main, good swordsmen and brawled often, hardly fulfilled what these terms implied at sea – tough but illiterate, hail-fellow-well-met he-men. In fact they signified the opposite, that the bearers of such names were mainly dandified, effeminate, foppish layabouts. In their drinking, of course, both were equal! By the beginning of the nineteenth century a change becomes noticeable in the use of many of these terms. For example, 'My Hearts' becomes 'Me hearties' and by the forties 'me buckos' and 'me bullies' dominate the scene. 'Bully' is probably a word that has come through from the past. In the form 'bully-boy' it is to be found in the ancient ditty *We Be Three Poor Mariners,* the chorus of which runs:

> To them we dance this round, around,
> To them we dance this round,
> And he that is a bully-boy,
> Come pledge me on this ground!

But then again Ireland may be its home. In the forties of the nineteenth century the Irish Potato Famine sent thousands of poor Irish peasants across to Liverpool. This was the period in which ships began to be manned by Irish seamen and Irish seamen began to compose their shanties and forebitters. And with them came the 'buckos' and 'bullies'. Anglophiles, however, may contend that 'bucko' is nothing more than the good old English word 'buck'!

It would appear that, even on cursory examination of sea-songs and nautical ballads prior to 1800 that the encouraging words used were 'my hearts', 'my hearts of gold', 'my braves', 'my bully boys' and 'my bold blades' and the like, whereas by the nineteenth century the words that took their places were 'me hearties', 'me bullies' and 'me buckos'. An awareness of this kind of thing helps greatly, I feel, in the establishing of an approximate age of a sea-song or ballad. A knowledge of the expressions used in working ships must also aid the tyro in judging the age of a song. This angle of research has been, as yet, barely touched upon. For instance if a song like the following uses the word 'cap-stal' for 'capstan' (cf. German 'Kapstal') its birth must certainly be before the eighteenth century.

> Then to take our lading in,
> We moil like Argier slaves,
> And if we to complain begin,
> The cap-stal lash we have. *

* This means to be tied to the capstan and flogged.

Of course many of the names of the ropes and parts of the rigging have always been the same from earliest times to the end of sail, but in the earliest songs the spellings. were different.

'Boilings' for 'bowlines' (ropes to haul tight the edge of a sail)
'Cun' for 'con' (handling a ship, steering)
'Passarado' for 'passaree boom' (used to stretch the foot of a stuns'1)
'Tallee' 'to haul' (tally on the fall)

But in the actual handling and the steering of a ship there is the greatest diversity of terms; those used before 1800 and those used after are, very often, entirely different. From earliest times until eighteen hundred we have one set of terms, and from eighteen hundred, in many cases until the present day, we have another. For instance even nowadays we have the nineteenth century sailing terms with us as used by modern yachtsmen.

With the wind ahead we have: 'by the wind', 'on a tack';
and with the wind astern: 'running free', 'jibing', 'wearing', and so on.

But in the very old ballads we find many

weird expressions for similar manoeuvres. For instance:

> Steady, steady, now 'tis lof,
> And don't falloff and thus no near.

This is what we now call 'sailing by the wind'. And similarly:

> You nimble fellows at the helm,
> Pray keep her under your command,
> A good rack full and away with her,
> No near, my boys, no near you can.
> ('Distress'd Sailor's Garland' – circa 1725)

This probably means what we now call 'full and by', i.e. close to the wind but don't let the sails shake.

After the latter end of the eighteenth century the great lower yards of sailing ships, both naval and merchant, were fixed permanently to the masts by means of metal trusses and slings (i.e. they could not be lowered down to the deck and they had *no halyards*). Prior to this they were moveable. They could be lowered down to the deck, or rather on to the gunwales, if necessary, and the halyards with which they were hoisted or lowered were called 'jeers'. In the earliest vessels the rope that formed the tackles of these jeers was rove through a top block or pulley called a 'ram's head' and a bottom set of sheaves set in a post called a 'knight'. Flogging at the fife rail was often carried out, being known as a 'drubbing at the jeers' (geers). The grating apparently wasn't rigged as in later days – or in *Reuben Ranzo*! So any song singing of a flogging (drubbing) at the jeers (geers), and there are many, must go back well before the mid-eighteenth century.

> The Quartier must Cun,
> Whilst the foremast-man steers;
> Here's a health to each port where'er bound,
> Who delays 'tis a bumper,
> Shall be drubbed at the geers,
> The depth of each cup therefore sound.

Of course this research into the age of sea-songs from the angle of nautical terms is an inexhaustible subject, so we will bring our *'good ship'* to an anchor by pointing out that in sea-songs of the nineteenth century 'goodly ship' is the term used, but in more ancient ditties it is 'goodlike' (or 'godlike') ship!

A "Drubbing at the Jeers"

The Bosun's Locker Stan Hugill

Blow, Boys, Blow

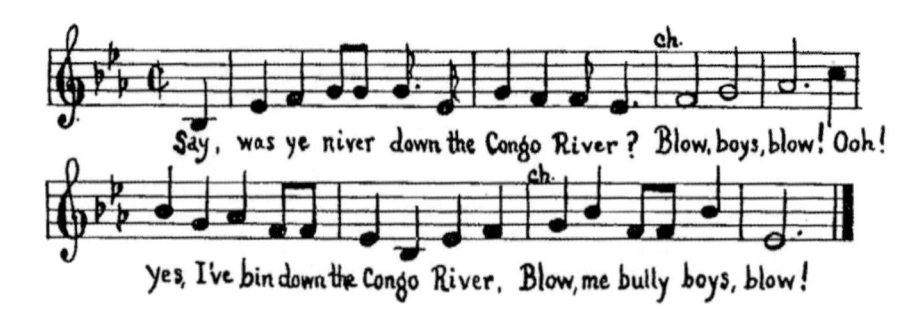

Say, was ye niver down the Congo River? Blow, boys, blow! Ooh! yes, I've bin down the Congo River, Blow, me bully boys, blow!

Congo she's a mighty river,
Chorus: Blow, boys, blow!

Where the fever makes the White Man shiver,
Chorus: Blow, boys, blow!

 A Yankee ship came down the river,
As she rolls down her tops'ls shiver.

How d'yer know she's a Yankee clipper?
By the blood and guts that flow from her scuppers.

Her masts and yards they shine like silver
Her masts and yards they shine like silver

\\'ho d'yer think's the skipper of her?
A boss-eyed, bandy bastard from the Bowery.

Who d'yer think's the Chief Mate of her?
Saccarappa Joe from Hell's Half Acre

What d'yer think they had for dinner?
Belayin' pin soup and a squeeze thro' the wringer.

What d'yer think they had for breakfast?
The starboard side of an ole sou 'wester.

What d'yer think they had for carger?
Two hundred whores from Yokohammer

Blow today an' blow tomorrow,
Blow for this hell-ship in sorrow.

Women At Sea

Down through the ages many members of the female sex have had a strong urge to venture to sea in the guise of a seaman. And many have done just that. Of course, at different times, women went to sea, performing all sorts of shipboard duties. During the eighteenth and early nineteenth centuries they were 'powder monkeys' – 'handing up the powder from the magazine below'. And, long before Florence Nightingale, women helped to bandage and succour the wounded in sea battles. A famous painting of the Death of Nelson (not the best-known one) now hanging in the Walker Art Gallery, Liverpool, distinctly shows women aiding the wounded seamen during the famous sea fight off Cape Trafalgar. In more modern times Russian ships have had women filling all sorts of positions aboard, from cook to captain, and the Blue Funnel Line had in my time, I think, the only woman marine engineer aboard one of its ships. Of course, Chinese junks are often manned entirely by women.

But in all these cases the women were, and are, known to be *women*.

In olden times many girls followed the sea dressed as seamen and, until exposed, were believed even by their shipmates to be seamen. Some, according to the old sea-ballads, followed a seaman-lover in the garb of a mariner; others went for sheer love of adventure and a love of the sea. Some went to make a fortune by way of 'prize-money'. According to an old periodical of 1846, a great number of women enlisted aboard the Fleet, which was bound for Cape Breton. They were paid £10 each with free provisions.

Around this period many women entered as 'privateersmen'. One girl, disappointed in love, joined the privateer *'Resolution'*, calling herself Arthur Douglas. She signed as a 'landsman', going aloft to furl sail and mustered with the marines for small-arms practice. She was never sea-sick and was spoken of highly by the afterguard. During the passage from London to Liverpool, a shipmate discovered her secret. She thereupon promised him a good time in her company when they reached port; that is if he would keep his mouth closed. However, when the time came to keep this promise she left him high and dry.

Mary Johns was another 'privateersman' serving aboard the privateer *'Defiance'* during the 1750s and about ten years earlier another girl, Anne Mills, entered the frigate *'Maidstone'* as a common seaman. In sea battles she fought the French with great savagery, it is recorded, slicing heads off right and left with her cutlass. Anne Chamborlayne, a young woman of good background, was another female who dressed as a seaman and joined a fire-ship. She wound up in a six-hour battle with the French without her sex being discovered. Another woman seaman was of the prankish type, cutting down the hammocks of her 'brother' Tars as they slept. One night they retaliated and cut down her hammock discovering, during the operation, the fact that 'he' was a woman.

The famous female pirates Anne Bonney from Ireland and Mary Read fought shoulder to shoulder alongside the pirate chief Rackham, and, whereas Rackham turned yellow and hid below decks, they fought with tremendous courage until beaten by the naval boarding party from the attacking sloop. Two other women pirates were Catalona de Eranzo, who escaped from a convent, cut her

The Bosun's Locker Stan Hugill

hair, dressed as a man, shipped aboard a West-Indian bound packet and after taking part in a mutiny, became a sea-robber. The second, Ann Mills, became one of the most vicious 'Brethren of the Coast' of all time.

A young Irish girl, Hannah Whitney, served five years aboard naval ships as a marine in the 1760s. She fell into the hands of a press-gang and on imprisonment her masquerade was revealed. Around the beginning of the nineteenth century two women were bound apprentices for seven years aboard a Geordie collier brig by the husband of one and the father of the other. The older woman met her death in the bombardment of Copenhagen, while the girl, Rebecca, deserted and was eventually found destitute in the back lanes of London. About the same time, an African youth by the name of William Brown, a captain of the fore-top, with eleven years naval service and a great amount of prize money to his credit – as well as a great reputation for imbibing grog – was discovered to be a woman. She went to sea, dressed as a man, after having a row with her husband it seems. And even in the twentieth century there is a well-founded story about a certain Captain John Weed, master of several Atlantic steamers, who, on committing suicide by cutting his throat in a Sailors' Home, was found to be a woman!

But getting down to old sea-ballads based on women going to sea in the guise of seamen – some historical, some fictitious – we find that they are so numerous that we can only cite a few in this article.

One that pops up quite a lot in collections of old broadsides is the ballad called *Susan's Adventures in a Man-o'-war*. I came across it originally in a catalogue of W.S. Fortey's *'Ballads'* (Catnach Press 1813), in the Moir Collection, in the Mitchell Library, Glasgow. I've also seen it in Ashton (60).

> Young Susan was a blooming maid,
> So valiant, stout and bold,

And when her sailor went on board,
Young Susan, we are told,
Put on a jolly sailor's dress,
And daubed her hands with tar,
To cross the raging main
On board a man-o'-war.
Chorus: Oh, pretty Susan left her home,
And sailed away so far,
She brav'd the tempests, storms and gales,
Feared neither wound nor scar
And done her duty manfully,
On board a man-o'-war.

She 'faced the walls of China', and when she was slightly wounded, for the first time her seaman lover realised that she was aboard the same ship as himself. Naturally, when they reached port, wedding bells resounded.

Constance and Anthony is another fairly well-known old sea-ballad (*'Douce Ballads'*, 1, 29). Here, too, the girl follows her seaman boyfriend aboard ship becoming a worker in the ship's galley.

> In the ship 'twas her lot,
> To be the undercook,
> And at the fire hot,
> Great pains she took;
> She served everyone
> Fitting to their degree,
> And now and then alone,
> She kissed Anthony.

The ship becomes wrecked on the coast of Spain. She meets a Spanish merchant who believes her to be a boy seaman. She sails aboard his ship for two years. In the meantime Anthony has been captured by an English Barbary Coast *'runnygado'* (renegade) and made a galley slave. The ship of the Spanish merchant meets up with the English 'Turk', and after a battle, frees the slave! Constance admits to the merchant that she is a girl and that Anthony is her lover. Whereupon he sends them both to England and they marry in Westmoreland and live happily ever after.

The ballad *The Female Lieutenant*, sometimes called *Sarah Gray*, found its way on to the stage of the Theatre Royal, Covent Garden, under the title of *Billy Taylor*, and of course as *William Taylor* it has been orally transmitted down to the present day, and is often heard in folk clubs. Here the theme is that the boyfriend is pressed on his wedding day, and the frustrated bride follows him to sea dressed as a seaman with her

> Soft white hands and milk-white fingers,
> All were smeared with pitch and tar. . .

In battle her jacket flies open and her 'lily-white breast' is exposed. On the captain hearing of this he asks her why she is at sea disguised as a Tar. She tells him she has followed her husband, William Taylor. The captain informs her that William has been two-timing her. Then, in most versions she shoots her unfaithful husband and either marries the captain, or the captain promotes her to lieutenant's rank.

In the *Ship's Carpenter's Love for the Merchant's Daughter*, to give the ballad its full title, a carpenter is impressed aboard a man-o'-war on the orders of his girl's father, who is opposed to his daughter marrying a common ship's carpenter. The girl dresses herself in blue like a Tar and joins the ship her lover has been pressed aboard. She in time becomes a surgeon's mate. She takes part in the storming of Dieppe, which she comes through unscathed eventually making herself known to her lover and later, on shore, they become man and wife.

Of the older ballads *The Nobleman's Daughter*, *The Female Captain*, *Two Faithful Lovers*, *Bonnie Annie*, *The Bold Lieutenant* (slightly homosexual), *Fare-ye-well, My Dearest Dear* and *James and Flora* all deal with the oft-recurring theme of the girl 'in tarry breeches' following her lover to sea. A more modern one, *The Baltic Lovers* (given in Firth *'Naval Songs and Ballads'*) dating from the time of the Crimean War, carries the same theme. In this song a merchant's daughter (Mary of Southampton) loves a 'brisk young sailor', and follows him to the Dardanelles in the garb of a seaman. Sir Charles Napier discovers her impersonation and discharges both her and her lover so that they can get married.

For the penultimate of our examples we touch upon the sea-ballad and folk song known as *Lisbon*. In this song the sailor is bound for Lisbon and he writes to tell Nancy his sweetheart that he will be leaving her for a while. Nancy, however, has other ideas, and she says:

> I'll cut off my hair,
> Men's clothing I'll put on,
> And I'll go away along o' you
> And be your waiting man.
> And when it is your watch on deck,
> Your duty I will do,
> I'll face the worstest battle, dear,
> So that I can be with you.

The boyfriend remarks that her ...
> waist is too slender to face a cannon ball.

But she is adamant and still wants to go with him. Similar lines about the physique of a girl not being fitted to meet the rigours of the sea and sea-fights is to be found in the song variously called *Lovely Nancy* and *Nancy of Yarmouth*. Ian Campbell sings the first title on Topic record 12T110 and Bert Lloyd sings the second title on Xtra 5013. According to Bert Lloyd, the song has been widely found in the South of England and also in Ireland.

> Fare-thee well me lovely Nancy, 'tis now I must leave ye,
> All on the salt seas I am bound for to go;
> But let not my long absence be of no trouble to ye,
> For I will return in the spring o' the year.

The Bosun's Locker Stan Hugill

In the cold stormy weather, when gales are a-blowin',
My love, I'll be ready to stow the tops'ls.

Oh, your pretty little hands they can't handle our tackle,
And your dainty little feet to our top-yards can't go;
And the bitter cold weather ye will never endure dear,
I would have ye ashore when the great winds do blow.

Like a tarry little seaboy I will dress and go with ye,
In the depth o' all danger I will be your staunch friend;

We'll clew up this issue's *'Bosun's Locker'* with one of the most popular Female Tar songs of all time, one that is still going the rounds of the folk clubs. This is the *Female* (or *Handsome) Cabin Boy*. It has two or three tunes but the one I give here is the one that my father used to sing and it's the one which I most certainly prefer.

The Handsome Cabin Boy

freely

Now, 'tis of a handsome fe-e-male as you shall un-der-stand,
She had a mind for roving un to some foreign land;
Attired in sailors' clothing, she boldly did appear,
And engaged with a cap-tain to serve him for a year.

Now 'tis of a handsome female as you shall understand
She had a mind for rovin' unto some foreign land,
Attired in sailors' clothin' she boldly did appear,
And engaged with a captain to serve him for a year.

The Bosun's Locker Stan Hugill

She engaged with a captain, a cabin-boy to be,
The wind it being in favour they proudly stood to sea;
The captain's lady being on board she seemed in great joy,
To think the captain had engaged a handsome cabin-boy.

So gentle was this pretty maid, she did her duty well,
Then what followed next, me boys, the song itself will tell,
This captain and this pretty maid did oftimes kiss and toy,
For he soon found out the secret of the handsome cabin boy.

Her cheeks were like the rosebuds and her sidelocks all in curl,
The sailors often smiled and said he looks just like a girl,
Through eating cabin biscuits her colour did destroy,
And the waist did swell of pretty Nell the handsome cabin-boy.

As through the Bay of Biscay our gallant ship did plough,
One night among the sailors there was an awful row,
They tumbled from their hammocks, it did their rest destroy,
They swore it was the groaning of the handsome cabin-boy.

Oh, doctor, oh, doctor, the cabin-boy did cry,
The sailors swore by all that's good the cabin-boy would
The doctor he came runnin', a-smilin' at the fun,
To think the sailor boy would have a daughter or a son."

Now when the sailors heard the joke they all began to stare,
The child belongs to none of us, they solemnly did swear.
The lady to the, captain said, my dear, I wish you joy,
It's either you or I betrayed the female cabin-boy.

So they all took up a bumper and they drank success to trade,
And likewise to the sailor boy who was neither man nor maid,
And if the wars should rise again, our sailors to destroy,
We'll ship some other sailors like the handsome cabin-boy

The Bosun's Locker Stan Hugill

Vol. 5 No. 5
Humour At Sea

Folk song enthusiasts and readers of *'SPIN'* in general may have become slightly aware of the fact that, apart from the odd humorous couplet in a shanty or a ditty like *The Fishes*, comical songs do not appear to be numerous in the deepwater sailorman's repertoire.

Turning over in my mind the sea-songs and nautical ballads with which I am conversant, as well as a rather desultory dipping into printed nautical ballads has not produced much to remedy this state of affairs. (I've had a bout of 'Flu and am not quite up to scratch in regard to thorough research!) It would appear that songs of real humour or of exaggeration were not put together, nor sung, by the naval or merchant seamen of the days that are gone. Perhaps this is to be expected. The old-time sailor was hardly the Jolly Jack Tar of fiction and the stage. In fact his life, being a round of fighting, starving, flogging, scurvy, lack of wages and iron discipline, was hardly one from which funny songs would emanate In actual fact, it would appear to me, that with the coming of steam, cabins for sailors, ice-cream, suitcases and so on, the union-guarded deckhand of modern times produced for the first time, and in any quantity, humorous nautical songs.

One of the very few comical sailor ballads that had any sort of circulation in the early nineteenth century is *The Great Sea Snake*:

Perhaps you have, all o' you heard a yarn
Of a famous large sea-snake
And caught by Admiral Blake;
Now list not what landlubbers tell
But give to me an ear
And I'll tell you what to me befell

Chorus:
Timme right fol-low
Right fol-low
Right fol-lol-lol-lay!

The third stanza runs:

As curled up this snake did lie
Five hundred miles about
A ship by chance sailed by that way
With colonists strong and stout;
The snake they mistook for their promised lands
A grievous thing, alack!
Men, women, babies and a thousand hands
All camped on this snake's back.

These 'colonists' live for a couple of years in naive contentment on this serpent's back until one day the great snake dives deep, leaving them all, their houses, handsome church, school and possessions, floundering in its turbulent wake. Subsequent verses tell of sailors trying to get fresh beef and water from the snake believing it to be the island of Tenerife, and in the penultimate verse, a 'vessel bound for Leith' is shipwrecked on its convolute and writhing back.

Jolly nonsense songs in which all sorts of nautical terms and phrases were juxtaposed irrespective of their true meaning became rather common around the turn of the twentieth century in both sail and steam. One of the most popular, sung by apprentices in the half-deck mainly, was a version of the old transportation ditty of *Ten Thousand Miles Away*. It was *not* the parody, often seen in song books, called *The Capital Ship* but one in which the verses were made up by the men and boys themselves. We give it here as our song for this issue.

Another set of jolly nonsense rhymes, couched in similar nonsensical nautical terms to *Ten Thousand Miles Away*, is one, which we'll call for the want of a better name, *Woollamaloosh!* Captain S.C. Smith who was once an apprentice in the barque *'Inverclyde'* (1912-1917) sent me this:

It nearly broke me poor ol' mother's heart,
For I signed on with the skipper of a big four-masted clipper,
To sail round the north and foreign parts
Woollamaloosh !

Chorus:
Oh, the windy winds did blow and the rain and blinding snow,
And a devil of a hurricane did blow-o-oh!
An' it nearly knocked the stuffin' out of the good ship Ragamuffin,
As off to the tropics we did go,
Woollamaloosh !

A similar ditty ran:
The fifteenth of December, boys, it was our sailing day,
An' we sailed away from Frisco Town, an' we all felt blithe an' gay;
For the cargo it was colza-oil, bound round for Sandy Hook,
An' there wasn't a man on board the ship knew where to find the cook.

Another nonsensical ditty that may have been born in sail but more likely is a product of the Steamboat Age is the following. There are many versions of this, all, however telling a similar story with a slightly different chorus:

There was a four-wheeled craft an' her rig was fore an' aft,
And the wind blew off the skipper's wooden leg.
Then we hung the skipper out to dry,
He looked so very sick, we had to rub him with a brick,
And wash his sweaty feet with ham and egg.

Chorus: Singin' lower down the funnel, stop the ship,
An' reef the anchor chain,
Throw the maindeck overboard,
An I haul it back again,
Trice yer wash-ports up aloft,
While the stormy winds do blow,
For the ship struck a rock,
An' it burnt a sailor's sox,
Yo-ho, me lads, yo-ho!

A song of similar substance is one known around the folk song clubs as *The Irish Sea Shanty*.

In the year of our Lord eighteen hundred and six,
Oh, we sailed from the sweat-hole of Cork, etc.

Thinking over this matter, I feel pretty sure that, if modern sailing-ship men and steam deckhands could turn out this type of song, then the old sea-coneys of Chaucer's time and the mariners of the Stuart period must have been prone to similar adaptations even

The Bosun's Locker Stan Hugill

if the sons of the 'Wooden Walls' were not. But, so far as I can discover, none of this humorous stuff ever found its way into print. Steamboat men, of course, had their own material, mostly parodies on modern songs, and far too bawdy to include here. Sung to the tune of *What a Friend We Have in Jesus* they roared out 'When this bloody trip is over' and 'Roll along you hungry bastard, roll along' was sung to the air of *Covered Waggon*. Two popular brevities with steamer men, both sung to playground tunes of children, were:

> If you want to find the bosun, we know where he is,
> we know where he is, we know where he is,
> If you want to find the bosun, we know where he is,
> Down in the Cock d'Or. . .
> We've seen him, etc.

This was sung to *The Big Ship Sails Through the Alley, Alley-o*.

And the second one, using the air of *In and Out the Window* runs:

> Can I come back next trip, Sir?
> Can I come back next trip, Sir?
> Can I come back next trip, Sir?
> An' I'll work in me watch below!

I guess sailors were, and still are, children at heart!

Ten Thousand Miles Away

[Musical notation with lyrics:]

A twin-screw brig with an A.1 rig, was the good ship Bolivar, All spick 'n' span from the donkey-man, to the bilge in the capstan bar. She was bully haul'd wi' ten-foot yawl, an' a reg'lar hobo crew. An' right a-baft on the mizzen mast, the scarlet bosun flew. Then blow ye winds, an' blow, an' a rovin' I will go, I'll stay no more on England's shores to hear sweet music play-ay-ay-ay, For I'm on the move to me own true love, Ten thousand miles a-way!

We took a reef in the mizzen-top, ran out the spanker boom,
Then smartly hauled the keel on deck, to give the mainmast room;
The tiller was lashed to the starboard bow, and the bowsprit trailed behind,
Whilst all the crew, so brave and true, were three sheets in the wind.

Chorus: Then blow ye winds an' blow, etc...

The gale that came blew the pigs a'main, combed the hair of the figgerhead,
And the lookout bawled, standby for squalls, and the mate he went to bed;
They rowed her through the London Zoos they made all buntlines fast,
As they stayed the truck with an inside tuck inside the ol' foremast.

An' when they reached the port, me boys, they anchored right in town,
They dropped the harness-cask an' horse on top of Shanghai Brown;
Then running to the pump aloft the chippy slipped and fell,
The Old Man said a prayer an' coughed, an' the rest o' 'em went to Hell.

Sometimes the chorus of *The Capital Ship* was used:

For I'm off on the mornin' train, across the ragin' main,
I'm off to me love, with a boxin'-glove,
Ten thousand miles away!

The Bosun's Locker Stan Hugill

Vol. 5 No. 6
"Thar She Blows" – 'Leviathan!'
Topic 12T174 **Ballads and songs of the Whaling Trade.**

Recently I was the happy recipient of the LP *'Leviathan!'* and my lifelong interest and fascination in the hazardous trade of the old-time whaleman was kindled anew. Bert Lloyd sings the songs with Trevor Lucas and Martyn Wyndham Reade as the chorus, accompanied by Alf Edwards on the concertina and ocarina, Dave Swarbrick on the fiddle and Martin Carthy tickling the mandolin…A goodly crew! The picture on the sleeve, detail of an aquatint by Martens after Garneray, c. 1830 is, I think, the most realistic of all the numerous paintings, etchings and sketches portraying this theme – that of a sperm whale capsizing a whale-boat and trying to make a *bonne bouche* of the boat and its occupants. In the film *'Moby Dick'* the same dramatic incident was copied perfectly from a crude sketch executed by an unknown whaleman artist of the 1840s.

The booklet accompanying the LP is most informative, one section giving a description of the different types of 'leviathans' sought after by the 'blubber-butchers' and another presenting a potted history of the whaling trade. Perhaps the zoologist who gave the compiler *Megaptera boops* as the Latin name for the Humpback Whale was having a bit o' fun since all my records give *Megaptera novaeangliae* for this smooth-bellied species. The Finback Whale, so called because of a small dorsal fin on its back, is given here as Finn Whale, incorrectly I feel, as it's a spelling I have never met with. From my own many-sided nautical researches I realise that dates given are very often unreliable. The booklet gives the date of the invention of the harpoon gun as 1860, and I know for a fact that this date is also given in the Dundee Whaling Museum, which I recently visited. On the other hand I have several quite good sources giving the date as 1865. Furthermore, I have come across a very fine article which gives the year as 1845, with the statement that it was the invention of this gun which helped to stay the rot that had set in the Northern whaling industry during the 1830s, when fewer and fewer ships were going north yearly, for a brief period. According to this authority, 1820 was the peak year of whaling, and in particular of Hull whaling. Apparently, in 1822 forty ships sailed, mainly from Hull, for the Greenland Grounds, in 1823, thirty-two, and by 1834 only eight ships sailed, six of these being lost. Sven Foyn is credited with inventing the harpoon gun – one using an explosive or 'shell' harpoon. Perhaps the 1845 gun fired a non-shell harpoon?

The booklet gives 1830 as 'the most disastrous (year) in the history of British whaling'. I have come to the conclusion that one has to be wary of making such a decisive statement in regard to nautical matters. Apropos 'disastrous years', I have come across: 'The most disastrous year was 1821 when forty whalers were crushed in Arctic ice, the greatest number ever lost in one year!' Then again 1836 is given in some books as the worst year, when dozens of whalers, mainly from Hull, Leith, Peterhead, Aberdeen, Dundee, Montrose and Whitby were frozen in at Baffin Bay. The first ship to return home (in 1837) was manned by twelve survivors out of a crew of fifty. The famous whaler *'Swan'* arrived in Hull shortly afterwards. Originally she had a crew of forty-eight men, half from Hull, half from the Shetlands and elsewhere. On arrival it was learned that eleven Shetland men, seven Hull men, two Grimsby men and five from another port had all died in Baffin Bay.

The worst and most remarkable disaster in the history of American whaling occurred in 1871 when thirty-two out of a fleet of forty whalers got trapped in the ice off the north of Alaska when they were hunting for Right Whales. Their captains knew the ice was closing in but the whales were so numerous that they ignored their own knowledge and the warnings of the Eskimos and, while hoping for a nor'east gale to move the floes they became trapped in a small lagoon of water. In no time the wooden hulls became crushed and all hands had to leave their vessels. There were a number of women and children among the crews – families of the Captains. These survivors along with the men, sometimes walking over the moving ice, sometimes using the slim whaleboats, which they dragged with them, to cross expanses of water, eventually reached the open sea and the safety of the eight ships which had not become trapped. The company consisted of a thousand humans and not a soul was lost!

As to the worst disaster ever to hit the whaling fleets it is impossible to say, but a seventeenth-century event that brought into being a broadsheet ballad (probably the first whaling song of which we have any record) is the following:

On May 1st, 1630, the whaleship *'The Salutation'* of London, owned by the Worshipful Company of Muscovy Merchants, sailed from London bound for Greenland. A chap called Pelham was a member of the crew and in 1631, in a thirty-five page pamphlet, he wrote of the adventures of himself and his shipmates. They reached Greenland on June 11th, when eight men went ashore to hunt deer. They shot fourteen but during the hunt their ship was driven out to sea by fierce winds and drifting ice, leaving them marooned. They knew that another English whaler was operating from Green Harbour, but the whaler had sailed for home.

So cursing their luck, they settled down to a Robinson Crusoe existence. On May 25th 1631, two Hull ships arrived and three days later the London whaling fleet. At the end of the whaling season, August 20th, the fleet sailed for London taking the rescued men with them.

A ballad telling their story is entitled *A Wonder Beyond Expectation* using the melody of *Jasper Coningham,* and is given in Pepys, 1, 74. After the ballad's title it reads:

'In the preservation of eight men in Greenland from one season to another, the like never knowne or heard of before, which eight men are come all safely from thence in this last Fleet, 1631, whose names are these, *William Fakely*, Gunner; *Edward Pelham*, Gunner's Mate; *John Wise, Robert Goodfellow*, Seamen; *Thomas Ayers*, Whalecutter; *Henry Rett*, Cooper; *John Dawes, Richard Kellet*, Landsmen.'

In the ballad it declares that two of the men's wives got married again thinking them dead.

Their needles of Whalebone, untwisted Rope their thread,
They sow'd their clothes, and handsomely their bodies cover'd.

They killed 'sea-horses' for food, and after killing bears and boiling their flesh for food and oil, they made clothing from the skins. They are said to have been the first white men to inhabit Greenland.

But back to the booklet. Here it tells us that one of the earliest races to hunt the whale was the Basque. The whale this Biscayan people sought was the *Bahena glacialis,* or, as they called it, the 'Sardako balama' or Sardinian Whale. It is a near relation to the Right Whale. They hunted it to such a great extent that it is now believed to be more or less extinct. It is said that the word harpoon comes from the Basque root 'arpoi' meaning 'catch without delay', but

The Bosun's Locker Stan Hugill

many dictionaries give it as having been derived from the Greek root 'arp' (from which our word 'harpy' comes), 'to seize hastily, or snatch'. I rather fancy the Greek origin, since seventeenth-century references to the harpoon call it a 'harpingiron'. In *'Purchas's Progress'* (1625), however, the harpooner is called the 'harpoiner', which points more to the Basque 'arpoi'. The Basques, too, are said to be the first whalemen to 'try-out' whales – that is to boil the blubber aboard ship. Earlier it had to be done ashore, but the Basque captain François Sopite Zaburu grew tired of this lark, having to put into the beach every time he caught a whale. He built a brick furnace aboard his ship, covering it with a wooden canopy to keep the sparks from flying. Other captains scorned the idea, saying the sails would catch on fire. When, however, they realised it was successful, they all copied it and of course, very soon British and American whale men cottoned on to this shipboard 'try-work'. The British and Dutch employed these Basque whalemen in early days and then, after picking their brains, drove them off the seas. Soon after America was colonised, the Yankees started inshore whaling and then followed this with the deepwater kind, a trade well established by the time of the Boston Tea Party (1773).

Enderby's of London took out cargoes for the American colonists bringing back Nantucket whale oil, obtained by the Yankee whalemen in the South Atlantic. Unfortunately the ship that carried the famous tea at the time of the Tea Party was one of Enderby's. Thanks to this incident, Enderby lost his whale-oil cargoes. Deciding to go in for the whaling business himself, he started operations in 1785, not in the Atlantic but in the new grounds of the Pacific. Trading in the Pacific being in the hands of the East India Company, he had to obtain permission from the British government. His ship the *'Emilia'* (often wrongly called the *'Amelia'*) was the first whaler to round the Horn. She left London in 1789 returning in 1790 with a full cargo of sperm oil. His ship, the *'Eyren'* was the first to explore the Japan Grounds, and one of his captains, John Biscoe, first discovered Enderby Land, in Antarctica. His ships took convicts to Norfolk Island and his men virtually ruled New Zealand before the British government took over. These London ships virtually ruled the Pacific but going through my records I have been unable to find many Hull ships engaged in this area, even though the booklet says so.

By 1849 British whaling had reached a low level, only fourteen ships flying the Red Ensign, while the Yanks were taking home catches worth £1,250,000 yearly. Britain had again become dependent upon Yankee oil and by 1853, Enderby's Company was wound up. The Yanks who went after the Sperm Whale mainly used the Marquesas as their base, and are not to be confused with the Bowhead whalers (Yanks and others) who used Lahaina and later, Honolulu as their headquarters when returning from the Arctic. When these latter hunted in the Okhotsk and Bering Seas they called it the 'large season' and in the 'small season' they chased California Grays off the coast of Mexico. The Line Islands, the Japan Grounds and the coast of Peru were, at this time, mainly in the hands of the Yankee Southseamen.

Blow Ye Winds In The Morning

'Tis advertised in Bo-oston, New York, an' Buffa-lo, Five hundred brave A-meri-cans a-whalin' for to go-o, Singin', blow ye winds in the morn-in', Blow, ye winds, high ho! See all clear yer runnin' gear, an' blow, me bully boys, blow!

They'll send ye to New Bedford that blasted whalin' port,
They'll send ye to some land shark, boys, to board and fit yiz out

Chorus:
Singin' blow ye winds in the mornin'
Blow ye winds, High-ho !
See all clear yer runnin' gear,
An' blow, me bully boys, blow!
They'll send ye to some boarding house, there for a time to dwell,
The thieves there, boys, are thicker than the other side o' hell.

They'll tell ye of them whalers, boys, that's goin' in an' out
An' say ye'll take five hundred sperm, before yer six months out.

It's now we're off to sea, me boys, an' the wind comes on to blow,
One half the watch is sick on deck the other half below.

The skipper's on the quarter deck a-squintin' at the sails,
When up aloft the lookout sights a mighty school of whales

Now, clear away the boats, me boys, an' after him we'll travel,
But if ye git too near his flukes, he'll kick ye to the devil.

Now we've got him turned over an' we tow him alongside,
It's over wid our blubber-hooks to rob him of his hide.

Next come the stowin' down me boys, 'twill take both night and day,
Ye'll all have fifty cents a piece on the hundred and nineteeth lay.

Now we're bound for Turkeywanna, boys, an' once more in their
power,
Where a man can buy the consul up for half a barrel of flour.

An' now our ship is full, me boys, an' we don't give a damn,
We'll bend on all our stuns'ls boys, and head for Yankee-land.

NOTE: This song was probably originated among the Yankee Southseamen who hunted the Sperm Whale in the South Pacific and off the West Coast of South America

The Bosun's Locker Stan Hugill
Vol. 6 No. 1

I find it rather surprising that many of the most famous whaleships have never been mentioned in song. Glancing through the *'Leviathan!'* album well-known ships such as the *'Balaena'*, the *'Eclipse'* and the *'Terra Nova'* are well to the fore, but even more famous ships such as the Hull whalers *'Truelove'* and *'Diana'* and the *'Sarah Elizabeth'*, Enderby's London whalers the *'Emilia'* and *'Samuel Enderby'*, and the Yankee Southseamen *'Essex'* and *'Charles W. Morgan'* are entirely by-passed. I wonder why?

And now, after this long rigmarole, to the songs in the album, the words of which are given in the booklet. Bert Lloyd, as usual, sings them with gusto although I feel that one or two of them are rather high-pitched and would have sounded better if there had been a little more *basso* in the chorus work. His sleeve notes too, are most comprehensive. In his introduction he talks of sailing in the whaling ship *'Southern Empress'* from Bromborough, and mentions a crowd of Welsh singers from North Wales. I wonder if he ever met Gwyn Davies of Llanfairfechan who once sang for me a modern whaling song, part English, part Welsh, called *Farewell to South Georgia*?

The first song in the album, *The 'Balaena'* is, as most folk fans know, all about a race from Dundee to St. Johns, but in this version the whalers *'Arctic'*, *'Aurora'* and *'Eskimo'* are omitted. Most of the songs in the album are those of the Greenland trade, but the next one, *The Coast of Peru,* is an exception. The British ships in this trade were mainly Enderby's of London. The Galapagos Islands that Bert mentions were the great watering and giant-tortoise-kidnapping islands of the whalemen, where they could also post their homeward-bound mail in a barrel, which was tied to a stump in Post Office Bay. Nantucket whalers, according to my sources, were in the main, the chief habitués of these waters, and I rather think this song belongs to them and not to British whalemen.

In the note to the third song, *Greenland Bound*, reference is made to the custom of decorating the yardarms with ribbons taken from the quay girls. This custom was usually carried out in Lerwick, in the Shetlands. Here, the East Coast whalers, on their way to the North, would call to finish storing and to swell their crews with more harpooners and so on. A garland would be made of coloured scarves and ribbons swiped from the Shetland girls, and lashed to the main rigging. It fluttered here until the ship returned to Lerwick, when the first person to get aboard and climb the rigging would keep the garland as a much-coveted prize. The air used for *Greenland Bound* is a regular standby, it would seem, for both whaler and logger songs. Someone may discover one day that the crews of lumber ships calling at Miramichi heard loggers singing:

> A shantyman's life is a wearisome one
> Altho' some say it's free from care;
> It's the swinging of the axe from morning till night,
> In the forests wild and drear.

and that one of these seamen eventually became a whaler and then used the air for *Greenland Bound*. Or, of course, vice versa! I know it is very often necessary for traditional songs that are spliced into documentary films to have their words –particularly place-names – altered to suit the situation. And to anyone who has come across the Folkway record called *'Whaler out of New Bedford'*, it will be apparent that here *Greenland Bound* has words sung by Ewan MacColl to suit the Pacific and Bowhead whaling:

Greenland Bound
> Once more for Greenland we are bound
> To leave you all behind,
> Our ship is painted green
> And our blubber hooks are keen
> And we sail before the icy wind.

Whaler out of New Bedford
> And now for Alaska we are bound
> To leave you all behind,
> Though we ship it cold and green
> Still our blubber hooks are keen
> And we sail before the icy wind.

I suppose this sort of thing is bound to happen, and probably sailors in various trades did this themselves – although I doubt if any sailor singing *Rio Grande* at the capstan-head of a ship bound for Calcutta changed the chorus to 'And we bound for Cal-cut-ta!' But unless we keep track of such alterations future folk research workers may turn up some amazing half-truths!

Change occurs in the next song on the album, *The Weary Whaling Grounds*. Here instead of being as in the original (?) Yankee version:

> …home in some Dutch grocery shop,
> Eating crackers and cheese and drinking beer.

we find our whaleman wishing he was:

> … snug in a Deptford pub,
> A-drinkin' of strong beer.

Also the first line of the first verse sings of 'If I had the wings of a Gull', whereas the Yank version gives 'the wings of a goney'. A 'goney' was the sperm whalers' name for a type of albatross (a North Pacific species, possibly the Laysan Albatross), which during the Second World War nearly drove the Yankee servicemen on Midway Island crackers. They called them 'gooneys'.

The fifth item, *The Cruel Ship's Captain*, is a song which Bert Lloyd once called, and rightly so, "the briefest and most ferocious of all sea-songs". I have always felt that Bert is at his prime best when singing this song but, here again, I note he alters the weapon which kills the lad from 'tarry gasket' (what he used to sing) to a 'bloody iron bar!'

The sixth item, *Off to Sea Once More*, although here given with Liverpool as the port concerned (as I myself usually sing it) was originally, I should think, about a Bowhead or Right Whale hunter out of 'Frisco. Some versions *do* give Sperm Whale as the hunted. Fleets used to leave 'Frisco for

The Bosun's Locker Stan Hugill

Alaska to hunt the Right Whale mainly around the 70s and 80s of the nineteenth century and this I would give as the date of the song. Shanghai Brown, given in some versions, was also around about this time. The last song on this side is *The Twenty-third of March*, a ditty that can be definitely pinned down with it originating with the Arctic whalers out of London. In the *'Penguin Book of English Folk Songs'* it is called *The Whale Catchers*. Now in this song, I think rightly so, the place-name Imez has been changed to Davis Strait. Imez has never been located on a map. I myself have spent much time searching for it, even on seventeenth-century maps, but all in vain. I wouldn't be surprised if W.P. Merrick, who had it from farmer Henry Hills of Sussex, around 1900, didn't hear this place-name aright.

On the reverse side of the record we have the now well-known *Bonnie Ship the 'Diamond'* sung with gusto, and *Talcahuano Girls* (to the tune of *Spanish Ladies*). This latter song is all about the doings of British whalemen ashore on the Flaming Coast of Chile, a subject I've done much research on recently for my book *'Sailortown'*. The fourth song is *Rolling Down to Old Maui*. This song I would place at an earlier date than the booklet gives (1850). Maui was the Hawaiian island where Lahaina, the greatest 'home-port' of the Bowhead whaler was situated and whalemen were rolling down from the Arctic to this excellent sheltered haven as early as 1820. The first whaling ships recorded as having called here were the *'Belling'*, commanded by Captain Gardner, and an unknown spouter whose master was Worth (1819). As early as the 1820s castaway seamen and drunken beachcombers lived ashore here making a living as 'liaison officers' between the whalemen and the lovely island *wahines*. The melody sung here is an excellent one and sounds most thrilling but I miss the 'rolling' chorus sung in other versions.

The fifth item *The Greenland Whale Fishery* has not the most popular tune, but then again this song has been sung to a variety of airs. Steve Benbow, as well as others, has popularised *Paddy and the Whale*, but here it has lost its music-hall touch, and with its rattling chorus, rings out like a genuine whaler's ditty. Of course it is the Jonah story, and folk fans may be interested to know that it has a basis of truth. In the year 1895 the American whaler *'Star of Peace'* was hunting the Cachalot or Sperm Whale in the South Pacific. One was sighted and the chase was on. The whaleboat, however capsized and one whaler, Jim Bradley, disappeared in the turbulent waters. Hours later, when cutting the intestines in search of ambergris (a valuable commodity which is the basis of many scents and often found in a sperm whale's intestines) an unusual lump was noticed by one of the men. On cutting through the huge tube, the astonished whalemen discovered Jim Bradley – alive!

Although a little light-headed for several months, Jim recovered and lived to a ripe old age in New Bedford. But his skin, which had changed to a ghastly blotting-paper white during his sojourn in the whale's belly, never again regained its natural colour.

Of the penultimate song *The Whaleman's Lament*, I'm afraid I know but little, apart from the fact that the text is given in Gale Huntingdon's book *'Songs the Whalemen Sang'*. The final item *The 'Eclipse'* is sung to one of the many tunes of *Blow Ye Winds in the Morning* and tells the tale of the poor whaling season of 1887 when the *'Eclipse'* and others came back from the North to Peterhead with very little to show for their trouble.

Altogether *'Leviathan!'* is a fascinating and interesting social document of the tough and hazardous, yet at times romantic, trade of the seamen who once ploughed the Seven Seas in sail and steam auxiliaries, seeking the elusive Greasy Luck.

Go To Sea No More

When first I landed in Fri-is-co-o, I went up on the spree, Me hard-earn cash, I spent it fast, Got drunk as drunk could be, An' when me money wuz all gone, 'Twas then I wanted more, But a man must be blind for to make up his mind, for to go-o to sea once more.

That night I slept wid Angeline, too drunk to roll in bed,
Me watch was new and me money wuz too, next morn wid them she'd fled;
An' as I wuz rollin' down the street the gals they all did roar,
"Oh, there goes Jack Ratcliffe, poor sailor boy, who must go to sea once more".

The first chap I run foul of wuz Mister Shanghai Brown,
I axed him neat for to stand treat, but he looked at me wid a frown;
Sez he, "Last time you wuz paid off wid me you chalked up no score,
But I'll give ye a chance an' I'll take yer advance an I'll send ye to sea once more".

Oh, he shipped me aboard of a whaling ship, bound for the Arctic Seas,
Where the cold winds blow, an' the ice and the snow, and Jamaicy Rum do freeze;
I can't stay here, I have no gear, me cash spent on a whore,
Oh, 'twas then that I said that I wished I was dead so I'd go to sea no more.

Some days we caught our whales, me boys, so days we did catch none,
Wid a twenty-foot oar stuck in yer paw, we pulled the whole day long,
An' when the mornin' came at last an' ye rest upon yer oar,
Oh, yer back's so weak, ye never could seek, a berth at sea no more.

Come all ye bold seafarin' men, and listen to me song,
When ye comes off them damned long trips, I'll tell ye what goes wrong,
Take my advice don't drink strong drink, nor go sleepin' wid a whore,
But git married lads, an have all night in, an' go to sea no more.

NOTE: Most probably this song was the property of the Alaska Right Whale hunters out of 'Frisco.

The Bosun's Locker Stan Hugill
Vol. 6 No. 2

In this issue of *'SPIN'*, my Bosun's Locker I'm afraid, will have to be short and sweet. Plus the fact that I'm taking a holiday within a few days, I am at present engaged in proofreading and indexing my new book, *'Shanties and Sailor's Songs'*, to be published, I believe, in the autumn. Apparently it has already been referred to in many folk song catalogues and I've had letters of inquiry for over a year asking whether or not it is on sale. I suppose pre-publishing publicity is a good thing but it can be a little wearing to the writer!

Perhaps at this stage I may be permitted to say something about the contents of the book. Of interest to all shanty fans, this book was commissioned by Herbert Jenkins and Co., as the first of a series representative of English folk song in all its varied fields. The well-known researcher and writer, Leslie Shepard (of ballad fame), suggested myself as the chap to execute the volume on the songs of the sea, and Routledge, my normal publisher, let me off the hook for this one.

At first, I was rather inclined to believe that it couldn't be done but, on going into the matter, by doing further research, pinching a little from previous *'Bosun's Lockers'*, and tackling the items from a new angle, I have managed to produce an instructive book on the subject, a volume with a fair amount of new material and one certainly complementary to my earlier *'Shanties From the Seven Seas'*.

In the text there is much about naval songs and ballads that I have not touched on before, with related yarns concerning the Mutiny at the Nore, flogging and other naval punishments, slavery, piracy, the press-gang and so on, with representative ballads and songs on these rather grim topics. To balance these there are some songs of humour and love. Also I have delved into the songs of the coasting trade, of the shipyards and other trades directly or indirectly connected with the sea. Much of this material has not been in print before, with a few songs also new to print.

Those shanty and sea-song fans who wish to know something of the background from whence sprang these inimitable songs of the sea, I invite to read my recent book, *'Sailortown'*. Here, in all their sordid glamour, one will find the sailor streets mentioned in shanty and forebitter: Ratcliffe Highway, Paradise Street, San Pauli, Park Lane, the Barbary Coast and so on. The streets, their buildings and the predatory inhabitants are described in detail and at all periods. The 'girls' too, famous names like Madame Gashee, Serafina, Maggie May and other round-the-corner Sallies are all described and the varied ways of carrying out the ever-perennial sailor-robbing techniques in which they excelled are fully documented. Stanzas of shanties and forebitters head their relevant chapters. If you can't afford this book then your library will be bound to have a copy.

With these brief and rather self-advertising paragraphs, I will say 'goodbye fare ye-well' until the next, and I hope, more expansive *'Bosun's Locker'*.

The Bosun's Locker Stan Hugill

The Ebeneezer

I shipp'd on board of the "Ebenezer", Every day 'twas scrub 'n' grease 'er, Send us aloft to scrape 'er down, An' if we growled they'd blow us down, Oh, git-a-long, boys, git-a-long do, Handy, me boys, so, handy! Git-a-long, boys, git-a-long, do, Handy, me boys, so handy!

The Old Man wuz a drunken geazer,
Couldn't sail the Ebenezer;
Learnt his trade on a Chinese junk,
He spent most time, sir, in his bunk.

Chorus:
Oh, git-a-long, boys,
Git-a-long do,
Handy me boys, so handy!
Git-a-long boys, git-a-long do,
Handy me boys, so handy!
The Chief Mate's name wuz Dickie Green, sir,
The dirtiest beggar ye've ever seen, sir,
Walkin' his poop wid a bucko roll,
May the sharks have his body an' the divi! have his soul.

A Boston buck wuz Second Greaser,
He used to ship in Lime Juice ships, sir,
The Limey packets got too hot,
He jumped 'em an' he cursed the lot.

The Bosun came from Tennessee, sir,
He always wore a Blackball cheeser,
He had a gal in every port,
At least that's what his Missus thought.

The Ebenezer wuz so old, sir,
She knew Columbus as a boy, sir, '
Twas pump fer bullies, night a day,
To help fer git to Liverpool Bay.

Wet hash it wuz our only grub, sir,
For breakfast, dinner and for supper,
Our bread wuz tough as any brass,
An' the meat wuz as salt as Lot's wife's ass.

We sailed away before a breezer,
Bound away for Valliparayser,
Off the Horn she lost her sticks,
The molly-hawks picked up the bits.

141

The Bosun's Locker Stan Hugill

Vol. 6 No. 3
Songs of The Ratcliffe Highway

Since first I became interested in sailor song (many, many years ago) of all the districts frequented by the seafarer when ashore and sung of in their shanties, forebitters and ballads, that of Wapping and its Ratcliffe Highway have fascinated me more than any other.

Ancient shipmates, lounging in the lee of the foresail, had often recounted their long-winded yarns and sung their 'fire-ship' songs about its Rabelaisian delights – delights which by my time had, more or less, petered out. But, even so, I often roamed around its salt-saturated highways and byways, reconstructing, in imagination, its one-time maritime pleasures.

It was, as they used to say, a fine place in which to spend a pound. When I was engaged in research work for my recent book *'Sailortown'* I spent some time tramping around the cobbled streets that margin the London and St. Katharine docks, finding, to my delight, some of the pubs mentioned in sailor song still existing. On the whole, however, the area is now devoid of any glamour or romance, even of the tawdry kind. The aftermath of war with its bombing, and during this century, the wholesale movement of merchant ships to the newer east-end docks of London River, have left behind a rather dilapidated area of deserted dwellings, ugly warehouses and scantily peopled streets. In Cable Street dubious Maltese cafes and the odd broken-down brothel exist. At night, the pavements are the home of the meth-drinkers and other social outcasts. The mariner, however, is noticeably absent, and yet, over a hundred years ago, continuing until the 1870s, this was London's Sailortown.

Ratcliffe Highway – 1840s.

During the early part and middle of the nineteenth century the labyrinthine maze of narrow streets, cobbled lanes, alleyways and courts of Stepney and Wapping, and in particular those neighbouring the Ratcliffe Highway, were peopled with a most colourful populace. Sunburnt Flying-Fish sailors from the East Indiamen, Scandinavian vikings from the timber-droghers, soldiers from the Tower garrisons, West Indian 'sambos' and bland Orientals rubbed shoulders with dock labourers, gaugers, ballast-getters, watermen, coal-whippers, Negro street singers, sellers of broadsides, 'chaunters' or fiddle-players, dog-dirt collectors, shell sellers, mudlarks, dance-hostesses and Irish and German prostitutes. (See my *'Sailortown'* for a fuller description of these types). Street stalls abounded everywhere, selling everything from a needle to an anchor, the gutters being strewn with their refuse, and many side streets were famed for their old-clothes stalls. Gin-palaces and dance-halls would be chock-a-block with the motley habitués of the Highway. The 'Prussian Eagle' was jammed between a row of German and Scandinavian boarding houses. In Wellclose Square stood the romantic old 'Mahogany Bar', where the clipper-ship men laid bets as to the expected winner of a tea race. 'Paddy's Goose', along Shadwell High, was another focal point of the Flying-Fish sailors.

This London Sailortown comprised the three parishes of St. George's, Wapping and Shadwell, known to the police as H Division, and in its heyday was generally referred to by sailormen as 'Ratcliffe Highway' or 'Tiger Bay'. Actually, both Ratcliffe Highway and Tiger Bay are definite locations, the former running parallel to London Docks, the latter an adjacent square (Wellclose Square). A rough outline of the district as referred to in sailor song and yarn would appear to be (see map) Leman Street, Royal Mint Street, Dock and Well Streets and East Smithfield (shouldering St. Katharine's Docks) on the west, Cable Street on the north, Ratcliffe Highway and Pennington Street on the south, and Shadwell High to the east, with Wellclose Square with its Ship Alley and North-East Passage at its heart. Some of these thoroughfares have changed their names during the years; Royal Mint Street once being Rosemary Lane, and the Ratcliffe Highway has been called St. George's Street and is nowadays merely The Highway according to the nameplate adorning its entrance, which I recently noted. Not far away, on the south side of London Docks, among the warehouses and overlooking the Thames stands the now very popular Wapping pub of ancient vintage 'Prospect of Whitby', and close by along Wapping Wall can be seen the site of the infamous Execution Dock. Wapping Old Stairs, cut into Wapping Wall, and mentioned by Dibdin in a song of the same name, are still with us, but the Pelican Stairs, once the tying-up site of ferries and small boats that conveyed seamen ashore from the Wooden Walls and the early East Indiamen, and, naturally, the gathering place of Ratcliffe prostitutes awaiting the paid-off pigtailed seamen, are no longer with us, being smothered in the building of the London Docks.

Pubs harking back to the Sailortown days of Wapping still around are the 'Czar's Head' (where Peter the Great of All the Russias once had a dram), the 'Tiger' (recently demolished in the re-planning of the Tower area), the 'Norwegian Flags' (Shadwell), 'Sir Sydney Smith' (Dock St.), the 'Blue Anchor' (Dock St.), and the 'Brown Bear' (Leman St.). The latter two are given in the halyard shanty:

I hailed her in English, she answered me clear,
Way, hay, blow the man down!
I'm from the Blue Anchor bound to the Brown Bear,
Gimme some time to blow the man down!

Older versions give the 'Black Arrow' and the 'Shakespeare' as the pubs concerned, but these are no longer with us. From around the end of the eighteenth until the middle of the nineteenth century many infamous taverns and dives existed in this area. In New Gravel Lane stood the 'King William', with the 'Angel', a taproom of fame, in Bluecoat Fields. The 'Three Crowns' and the 'Grapes' were

The Bosun's Locker Stan Hugill

well-known taverns of Shadwell High, and the 'Three Jolly Sailors', as well as the 'Jolly Tar' (there were three of these) were found in the Highway and Shadwell. The 'Lamb and Flag', often mentioned in song, and the 'Old Rose' ranked with the 'Britannia' and the 'Barley Mow' as popular sailor pubs.

In Dock Street stood the already mentioned 'Blue Anchor' and nearby, the 'Hole-in-the-Wall'. Farther north in Whitechapel was the 'Angel and Crown'. A notorious concert-hall plus tavern called the 'British Queen' stood in Commercial Road, and 'Wilson's Music Hall' was to be found in Wellclose Square (Tiger Bay).

Most, if not all, of the foregoing drinking, singing and dancing dives are to be found in sailor song, and it is also a well-known fact that the great maritime artist Turner, during odd week-ends would patronise most of these places, where he would sketch and paint the Ratcliffe harpies. These pictures are said to be in the inner recesses of the British Museum.

Before the building of the London Docks prior to 1805, (the year of Trafalgar) this area of Wapping was prevented from river erosion by the Wapping Wall, and it was alongside here that smaller boats moored, the larger ones laying at anchor in the stream. Judging by our first 'Highway' song the district must have been slightly more salubrious at the end of the eighteenth century, even, I should think semi-rural.

> Upon one Summer's morning I carelessly did stray,
> Down by the Walls of Wapping where I met a sailor gay
> Conversing with a bouncing lass, who seemed to be in pain,
> Saying, 'William, when you go, I fear, you will ne'er return again!'
>
> His hair it does in ringlets hang, his eye's as black as sloes,

May happiness attend him, wherever he goes,
From Tower Hill down to Blackwall, I will wander, weep and moan,
All for my jolly sailor bold, until he does return.

My father is a merchant – the truth I now will tell,
And in great London city in opulence does dwell;
His fortune doth exceed three hundred thousand pounds in gold
And he frowns upon his daughter, 'cause she loves a sailor bold.

A fig for his riches, his merchandise and gold,
True love is grafted in my heart; give me my sailor bold,
Should he return in poverty, from o'er the ocean far,
To my tender bosom, I'll fondly press my jolly tar.

My sailor is as smiling as the pleasant month of May,
And oft we have wandered through Ratcliffe Highway,
Where many a pretty blooming girl we happy did behold,
Reclining on the bosom of her jolly sailor bold.

Come all you pretty fair maids, whoever you may be,
Who love a jolly sailor bold that ploughs the raging sea,
While up aloft, in storm and gale, from me his absence mourn,
And firmly pray, arrive the day, he home will safe return.

My name it is Maria, a merchant's daughter fair,
And I have left my parents and three

144

thousand pounds a year,
My heart is pierced by Cupid, I disdain all glittering gold,
There is nothing can console me but my jolly sailor bold.

This song is a broadside of which, unfortunately, the tune is lost. Whether it was popular among the seamen who frequented the Ratcliffe Highway it is difficult to say. Seamen did not always accept shore turned-out ballads with nautical themes, but this one has something about it, which may have given it a certain limited circulation among eighteenth-century seafarers.

Another early broadside referring to the Highway is *Beautiful Nancy*, given by Ashton (*'Real Sailor Songs'*, 1891). It is one of a class of songs known as 'token songs', and starts:

As beautiful Nancy was walking one day,
She met a young sailor, all on the Highway,
He stepped up beside her and to her did say,
Ho, where are you going to my pretty maid?

Nancy does not recognise her sailor bold but by verse six he reveals his true identity and a wedding results. Another eighteenth century ballad, entitled *The Seaman's Adieu to his Pritty Betty Living near Wapping*, tells of the sailor boy being drowned and 'pritty' Betty as a result dying of grief. Not all these early girls of Wapping were as lovable and true as the foregoing; some were 'deceivers ever'. *The Sailor Deceived*, a broadside given by Ashton (p. 56) is a 'tearjerker' about a sailor returning to Wapping to find his love married to a miser. Naturally he hastens off to sea again in an attempt to drown his sorrows. And sometimes the Wapping girls were out-and-out shrews and viragos. The one in the following ditty *Doll of Wapping* follows her Jack around the watery world – and he wishes she hadn't!

'Twas at Stepney church I was spliced to Doll,
Pull away, pull away, together:
In wedlock you'll often meet with a squall,
But I found it all foul weather
Such a curious clapper-hung tongue had she,
Doll's music there was no stopping.
So, in less than a week I put off to sea,
Pull away, pull away, say
What a devil of a Doll of Wapping:

I sailed for Jamaica to give her the slip,
But, soon finding my latitude Doll took a trip, etc.

In verse 3 he heads for Calcutta but she catches up with him, so he has her shipped out to Botany Bay. The final stanza finds our hero well hidden from his 'Wapping Doll' on an islet in the Philippines where he camps down with a 'tight young squaw' and lives happily ever after.

Many of the early Wapping and Highway songs came into being during the Napoleonic War period, and are all guns and powder barrels. But, as I have pointed out elsewhere, it is very difficult to ascertain whether the songs are those of naval or merchant seamen. Gunnery terms, as well as orders used in working ship are sprinkled throughout many of these ballads, and in the later ones much *double entendre* covering sexual actions is to be found. But such nautical phrases were common to both naval and merchant seamen. Many of the songs that are supposedly naval I have strong reason to believe are more likely to have been the monopoly of merchant seamen from the East Indiamen. In the great wall-sided East Indiamen – in the eighteenth century moored regularly abreast of Wapping – topmen, midshipmen, gunners and so on were to be found carrying out their duties in a Royal Naval fashion. Gun-drill was a daily routine;

The Bosun's Locker Stan Hugill

the side was 'piped' when the master came aboard; cutlass drill and the rigging of boarding nets were routine, and in nautical phraseology that of the East Indiaman could not be distinguished from that of the naval seaman.

The same was true of the later Blackwall 'frigates' and the 'Blackwallers' as their seamen were known. Naval ships *did* lie in the Thames, but from literature, it would appear that their seamen were not as frequently found in the purlieus of Wapping as they were in the sailor taverns of Chatham, Portsmouth and Plymouth. In fact, the Ratcliffe Highway seems to have been the property of the merchant seaman. The following song is one of a type, which, on account of its phraseology, may be thought naval, but, more like as not, was a ballad of the East Indiamen. Of course the older a song the more likely it would be that the phrases have a naval ring; the reason being that the distinction between naval and merchant vessels at one time hardly existed as merchant ships fought French, Spaniard and Hollander alongside of naval ships, and naval ships often engaged in trade.

Rattling Jack (Ashton, p. 50)

> Avast, no flat you'll find in me, I'm
> Rattling Jack just come from sea,
> The shiners I now flash, and down
> Wapping cut a dash,
> All ripe for fun and jollity;
> Now merrily I push about the grog
> And treat the girls like a jolly dog,
> Or Poll I take in tow,
> And to the Royalty we go,
> For Rattling Jack's on shore, d'ye see?
>
> My cash I'll freely spend on shore, for damme I can fight no more,
> Ram shot, or sponge the gun, till the fore they fight or run,
> For a battle's glorious fun, d'ye see?

> On deck, ordered up aloft,
> I take my duty hard or soft
> Whatever winds may blow,
> I'll work and sing, yo ho!
> For Rattling Jack's at home at sea.
>
> With Poll, when I'm under way, down Wapping or Ratcliffe Highway,
> So stylish I declare, we make the people stare,
> None does it like my Poll and me
> Then while the reckoning I can pay,
> The grog shall flow, the fiddle play
> Hornpipe, jig or reel,
> I'll come it, toe and heel,
> For Rattling Jack's on shore, d'ye see?

The 'Royalty' in this song was a music hall of the period. The first song of these early Wapping days that mentions a *dock* is called *Bonny Shadwell Dock* (Ashton p. 51). Shadwell Dock was one of the first in the area, being built about 1805.

> When I come back to bonny Shadwell Dock,
> *Chorus: Fol de rol, lol de ra ra, fol de rolla!*
> How the girls will stare at their friend Jack *Block,
> *Chorus: With his chip chow cherry chow, Fol de liddle, la de do, fol,lol, la!*

(*See my new book *'Shanties and Sailor's Songs'* for explanation of this name (pp 18, 19.))

> When with Poll I suck the grog at the Anchor so blue,
> Says she, 'Jack, you beat hell,' says I, 'Here's to you!'
>
> The purser at me looked very big,
> But the rumbo I sluiced o'er his white chizzled wig.

'Ask my pardon,' says he, then damn it how he swears,
Says I, 'With all my heart,' so I kicked him downstairs.

'Then,' says Poll, 'Let us go to our box at play,'
'I like a box,' says I, so we tripped it away.

Oh, the gen'men and the ladies clapped and encored,
'Silence,' says I, and I bawled and I roared.

The link-boy he lighted us clean in the mud,
'Will your honour take care' – O, damn his little blood!

Let us drink a health to little England,
May our seamen always the ocean command.

Ashton explains 'rumbo' as 'rope stolen from the dockyard', but how one could *sluice* rope over a chap's wig I wouldn't know. In fact I believe the word is just a naval slang term for rum, or rather grog (watered rum). There's something a bit mysterious I fancy about 'link-boy'. Whether the eighteenth-century link-boy was still around at the time of Shadwell Dock I have my doubts, surely oil lamps (whale or otherwise) lit the streets of London by this time, even if it were a little too early for gas.

But, of course, the type of song most common to the shore roisterers of Wapping was that known as the 'fire-ship' ballad – all powder barrels, jet flames and fire-bombs. This metaphor for a song about the fiery and explosive Ratcliffe harpies was, of course, derived from the type of ship all schoolchildren associate with the destruction of the Spanish Armada. At the time of the Armada any old wagon was stuffed with combustibles and used as a fire-ship, but by the seventeenth and eighteenth centuries a fire-ship was a specially constructed vessel. They were usually square-rigged on two masts with a triangular lateen on the mizzen. The 'tween-decks, from slightly abaft the mainmast to the foremast, were strengthened by means of hefty oak walls or bulkheads so as to contain the fire for a while, because this section between the two walls was the danger point of a fire-ship. Here were wooden tubes or troughs leading to specially constructed ports; like gun ports but without guns. In battle the troughs were filled with inflammable liquids, and bombs placed near the ports. When lit the flaming liquid ran out through the ports exploding the bombs en route. On the upper deck above this section stood four giant barrels, also filled with a similar liquid, with spouts pointing upwards and slightly outwards. The liquid when ignited would jet up through these spouts and set fire to the sails and rigging of the enemy ship alongside, while the flaming liquid from the 'tween-decks would gush out through the ports and ignite the bulwarks and so on of the same ship. What a terrifying sight these ships must have been scattered between the lines of, and grapnelled to the sides of, French, Spanish, or Dutch frigates! When awaiting a war (and they didn't have to wait long!) the fire-ships were used as guard-ships and so on around the ports. Latterly old, worn-out ships were adapted for this kamikaze chore.

The first of our 'fire-ship' songs is one that has caught on in the clubs. First we give its broadsheet form, called *Jack's Disaster*.

Come all you roaring boys, that delight in roaring noise,
I compare it to nothing but laughter,
When a sailor comes on shore, with his gold and silver store,
There's no one can get rid of it faster.

The Bosun's Locker Stan Hugill

The first thing Jack craves, is a chamber fine and clean,
With good liquor of every sort,
With a pretty girl likewise, with her black and rolling eyes,
Then Jack Tar he is pleased to the heart.

And so the game goes on, till his money's spent and gone,
When his landlady begins to frown,
With her nasty, leering eye, and her nose turned all awry,
Crying 'Sailor, it's high time to be gone!'

This strange and sudden check, puts Jack's headsails all aback,
Not knowing to what shore for to steer,
Resolving for revenge, and himself for to defend,
Swore the deck, fore and aft, should be clear.

'No quarter!' did he cry, candlesticks at him did fly,
Then Jack he began to engage,
The old girl in a fright, called the watchman of the night,
Crying, 'Bundle him away to the cage!'

Then Jack understands there's a ship wants to be manned,
And to the East Indies she is bound,
With a sweet and pleasant gale, she spreads a swelling sail,
Bids adieu unto England's fair ground.

So all you sailors bold, pray be careful of your gold,
You will find that to be your best friend,
Take some honest, sober wife, then you'll ne'er be deceived,
But on her you may always depend.

The forebitter version handed down orally by seamen differs somewhat from the above. Peter Kennedy collected a version of this called *Jack Tar Ashore* from Harry Cox of Norfolk, but here the East Anglian coasting influence is apparent. Of course both Cox's and my version appear more modern than the ballad one. The main differences seem to be: Cox's version has a verse similar to that of verse 5 in the ballad (not found in mine) in which bottles instead of candlesticks are the ammunition used:

> Now Jack in all his rage he threw bottles at her head,
> And likewise all the glasses he let fly,
> And the poor girl in a fright called the watchman of the night,
> Saying take this young sailor-lad away.

and Cox's last verse (my fifth, which doesn't appears in *Jack's Disaster*) runs:

> Then he laid her on a tack like a cutter or a smack,
> And she rolled from the lee to the weather,
> And he laid her full and by, as close to the wind as she would lie,
> We are bound for Blackwall in stormy weather.

This use of nauticalism to cover rather bawdy material, according to Admiral Cyprian A.G. Bridge, did not come about until the third decade of the nineteenth century:
'It took a good many years and the complete extinction of the old sea-dogs of King Billy's reign, or of Queen Victoria's earlier years before the *double entendres*, or worse, of the music-halls obtained toleration on the forecastles of British men-of-war.'

Flash Gals of The Town
Transcribed by Miss A.R. Wilkinson.

Now come all you ladies gay, what rob sailors of their pay, And list while I sing this tar-ry tune — When Jack Tar he comes ashore, with his gold and silver shore, There's no one can get rid o' it so soon.

Now, the first thing he demands is a fiddler to his hand,
A bottle of Nelson's Blood so stout and warm,
And a pretty gal likewise with two dark an' rollin' eyes,
An' he'll drop his anchor an' never more will roam.

Then the landlady she comes in with her brand new crinoline,
She looks like some bright an' flashin' star,
An' she's ready to wait on him, if his pockets are lined with tin,.
An' to chalk his score on the board behind the bar.

Then she calls a pretty maid, right-handed and soft-laid,
And up aloft they rolled without much bother,
And she shortened in her sail for a-weatherin' of the gale,
An' soon in the tiers they were moored right close together.

Then he shifted her main tack and her caught her flat aback,
They rolled from the lee to the weather,
An' he laid her close 'longside, oh, closehauled as she would lie,
'Twas tack an' tack through hell an' stormy weather

But his money soon was gone, an' his flash gal soon had flown,
She roamed along the Highway for another,
An' the landlady she cried, pay yer score and git outside,
Yer cargo's gone an' you've met stormy weather.

Then poor ol' Jack must understand that there's ships a-wantin' hands,
And to the Shadwell Basin he went down,.
And he shipped away forelorn on a passage round the Horn,
Goodbye to the boys and the flash gals of the Town.

The Bosun's Locker *Stan Hugill*

Vol. 6 No. 4
Songs of
The Ratcliffe Highway II

Before we get down to the Fire-ship Songs proper (those rollicking, nautical, most certainly sailor-made efforts, full of *double entendres* and singing of the Highway Harlots) let us examine similar songs based on another street in the area – Rosemary Lane. Rosemary Lane was the old name for the short street running from Leman Street down towards the Tower, and now known as Royal Mint Street (see map in *'SPIN'*, Vol. 6 No.3). In the early nineteenth century it was a dangerous and dirty thoroughfare of broken-down tenement houses, the ground floors of which were mainly cheap-jack shops, with stalls in the gutters on both sides of the lane. Everything from a needle to an anchor was sold here; in fact it was a veritable thieves' market. Secondhand hand-me-downs, rusty household culinary equipment rubbed shoulders with chinaware and broken toys. Barrowmen sold all the denizens of the deep from their scruffy barrows – fish, eels and shellfish. In the tenements dwelt dockside watermen, ballast-getters, coal-whippers, lumpers, and dredgermen. And they, too, frequented the so-called 'gin-palaces', where the Irish brogue out-blared the local Cockney voice. In the evening oil-lamps lit the stalls and the raucous singing of bawdy songs

> Oh, me name is Sammy Hall, Sammy Hall, Sammy Hall,
> Oh, me name is Sammy Hall, Sammy Hall…

would rend the night air. Where Rosemary Lane abutted the Minories there was a meeting ground known as 'Sparrows Corner'. Here the local Phrynes congregated, awaiting custom from the Tower garrison and the St. Katharine's Dock sailormen.

In the eighteenth century, or earlier, this district must have berthed slightly more respectable citizens – tenants who could afford servants, if we are to believe the earliest versions of the song now known as *Bellbottomed Trousers*. This song was originally called *Rosemary Lane,* and both the words and tune varied according to locale and period. The first verse of the earlier versions runs:

> I lived in service in Rosemary Lane,
> I keep the goodwill of my master and dame,
> Till one night a sailor came in from the sea,
> And that was the beginning of my misery.

or

> When first I was in service in Rosemary Lane,
> I gained the goodwill of my master and dame;
> Then came a young sailor just home from the sea,
> And that was the beginning of my miserie.

The second verse usually is the start of the seduction by the sailor of the rather naive servant girl.

> He asked for a candle to light him to bed,
> And likewise a (silk) hankerchief to wrap (roll, tie) round his head
> To roll (wrap, tie) round his head as sailors always do,
> Saying, I Pretty Polly (Maggie) will you come to bed, too'.

Then the girl 'jumps into bed to keep the

sailor warm', because she thought 'there was no harm' in it. After the play all versions have the sailor paying the girl 'for the damage he had done' either in gold or (in later versions) notes. The penultimate verse invariably includes:

> If he be a boy he shall fight for his King,
> And if it be a girl she shall wear a gold(en) ring;
> She shall wear a gold ring like a maiden so true,
> In fond memory of your sailor true blue.

or something of the kind. In the less refined versions, it's something after this fashion:

> And if it be a girl ye can bounce her on your knee,
> And if it be a son then send him off to sea,
> In his tarpaulin hat and his little jacket blue,
> He shall walk the quarterdeck like his daddy used to do.

The final verse always (or nearly always) has a warning to all young maidens or servant girls, never to allow a sailor to go 'too far'. Of course, down through the years, being a song of this nature, one that begs for coarseness, naturally, the coarseness came. The result being that most versions extant nowadays are bawdy to a degree. At some time or other *Rosemary Lane* became entangled with the North Country ballad *The Oak and the Ash*, the rousing chorus of the latter being added to the former.

> It's home, boys, home, oh, it's home I want to be.
> Home far away in my own counterie;
> Where the oak and the ash and the bonnie ivy (rowan) tree,
> Are all a-growing green in the North Counterie.

[Music: A North countree maid up to London once stray'd]

Of course, the opening of this song, with its lovely tune dating back to the seventeenth century, had nothing to do, originally, with Rosemary Lane, but all the later versions of *Rosemary Lane* adopted the 'tree chorus'. W.E. Henley, I believe, changed the usual locale of Amble in older versions of *The Oak and the Ash* to Falmouth. American seamen sang of Baltimore. Sometimes instead of the ivy or rowan tree, the birch or birchen tree is used. In fact, a proper coverage of this song, with its many ramifications, would make a lengthy article. The main divisions appear to be:

The oldest form: *Rosemary Lane* (both 'clean' and suggestive).
Later form: *Home, Boys, Home* and *Hame, Boys, Hame* (Northern version), (clean and rather bawdy).
Modern form: *Bellbottomed Trousers* (usually bawdy or even filthy).

There is a version of the latter, without the 'tree chorus', with its 'childish' tune, that has passed orally through every school playground for several generations. I learnt it in the playground of Christ Church School, Bootle! I often think Gershon Legman was right when he said that most dirty versions of songs are learnt at school, taken by collectors and put into expensive books, which books children are forbidden to buy or read! The folk process?

We have wandered a little from our Wapping locale, but our next version will bring us back. The sailing ship sailor's forebitter and homeward-bound song that follows puts the girl on the Ratcliffe Highway. I've had to delete a verse and the second

The Bosun's Locker Stan Hugill

couplets of verses 3, 5 and 6 have been camouflaged.

The alternative ways of singing *Home, Home, Home* are:

There once was a servant gal in Sackville Street did dwell,
Well in with the missus and the master as well,
Early one morning, oh, a sailor came from sea,
And that was the beginning of all her sweet misery.

He axed for a candle for to light him up to bed,
He axed for a handkerchief to wrap around his head.

(This couplet is to be found in the song *The Wexford Girl*.)

… girl from Dublin town.

Early next mornin' I the sailor awoke,
Put his hand in his pocket and pulled out a note.

Now if it be a daughter bounce her on your knee,
If it be a son pack the bastard off to sea.

A topical version of this, with an Irish touch, is that in which two stamps of the foot are given after the first 'Home, boys, home!' The Irish folk group The Dubliners has sung it.

The expression 'fire-ship' to mean a harlot was not confined, apparently, to the London Sailortown area only. It is to be found in seventeenth-century literature in regard to the masked 'ladies' who infested the popular music-halls and theatres of the day. The masks worn were called 'vizard-masks' and although respectable ladies wore them – not wishing to be seen and recognised in such places – they were really the badge of the fire-ship girls. There exists a satire of 1691, *'The Fire-ships'*, describing a Restoration playhouse and such women:

The Play-house is their place of Traffick, where
Nightly they sit, to sell their Rotten Ware.

Actually, Nell Gwynne was a 'vizard mask'd fire-ship' at one time in her career, and of course her habitat, Old Drury, was a haunt of vice in these days. One version of the previous song has the servant girl living in Drury, and not Rosemary, Lane.

Our next song dates back to the seventeenth century and has turned up in fairly recent years as a pop-song under the title *Dark and Rolling Eye*. Its old name was *The Fire Ship*. In the new version there is a line about the sailor buying his girlfriend 'fish and chips', an anachronism I should say! Sailors sang this at the pumps and, making one verse of this do two, it was adapted and sung as *Can't Ye Dance the Polka*, a capstan song.

In an older version instead of her hair hanging down in ringlets, her hair hung down like 'glow-worms'. And the last line of the chorus was sometimes sung:

A rare sort, a rakish sort, she's one for a fire-ship's crew.

In the above version two verses have been omitted between five and six, and the second couplet of the last verse has been camouflaged. In the next issue I hope to deal with two songs that include a sort of catalogue of the pubs and taverns of the Ratcliffe Highway.

Home, Home, Home

[Musical notation with lyrics:]
There once was a fair young maid, on the Highway she did dwell. She had no lovin' parents, oh, as far as I could tell. One day a fine big clipper ship came into London town, an' with them bully sailor boys, her sorrow she did drown, Singin' home, home, home I wanner be, Singin' home, home, in me only counteree, For the pine an' the ash, an' the bonnie ellum tree, Are all a-growin' green in sweet Nort' Ameri — Kee!

She took her fine young sailorman and axed him in to tea,
And for a while the pair did dine and sing quite merrily;
And then he brought his rum-flask out and offered her a dram,
And from that moment onwards, oh, her troubles they began.

Chorus:
Singing home, home, home I wanner be,
Singing home, home in me only counteree;
For the pine and the ash and the bonnie ellum tree,
They're all a-growin' green in sweet Nort' Amerikee!

She had no lovin' husband for to save her from his spell,
She had no kind young sister did our sorry little Nell;
But very soon she'd furled her sail, and struck her colours down,
And then he left that fair young maid, that gal from London town.

The very next day he sailed away, but before he went aboard,
He gave her a silver dollar for to pay her for his board;
And as she waved the last farewell, our little Nell she knew,
She'd never see that lad again, that darlin' o' the crew.

He said to her before he sail'd 'Now, when our babe do come,
You will make a sailor of him, if he do be a son,
With his tarpaulin hat an' his coat O' navy blue,
Oh, let him climb the rigging like his daddy used to do'

Now, all ye young servant gals, a warnin' take from me,
Never let a sailor give you drinks too fast or free,
For I trusted one and he deceived me,
And now he's gone and left me with a daughter on me knee.

The Bosun's Locker Stan Hugill

The Fireship

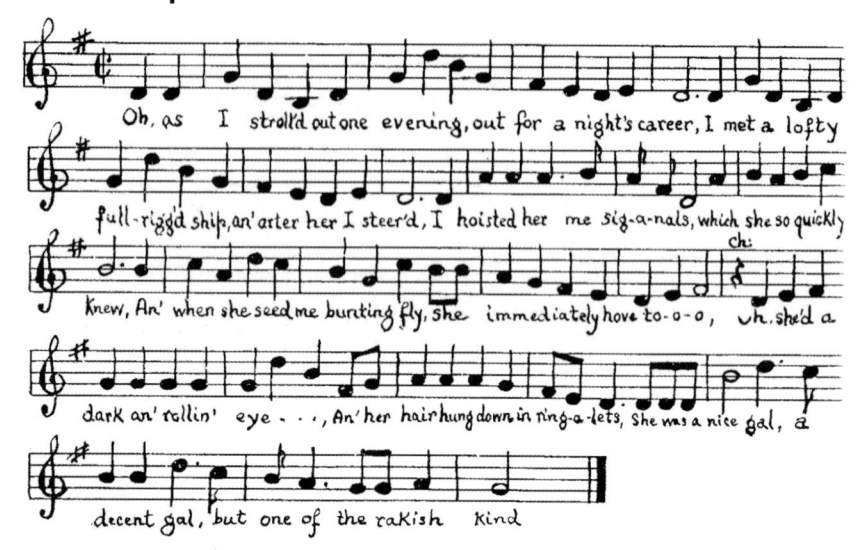

[musical notation with lyrics:] Oh, as I stroll'd out one evening, out for a night's career, I met a lofty full-rigg'd ship, an' arter her I steer'd, I hoisted her me sig-a-nals, which she so quickly knew, An' when she seed me bunting fly, she immediately hove to-o-o, Oh, she'd a dark an' rollin' eye..., An' her hair hung down in ring-a-lets, She was a nice gal, a decent gal, but one of the rakish kind.

Kind sir, ye must excuse me for being out so late,
For if me parents knew o' it, then sad would be me fate;
Me father he's a minister, a true and honest man,
Me mother she's a Methodist (dancing gal), I do the best I can.

Chorus:
She'd a dark an' rollin' eye-eye-eye,
An' her hair hung down in ring-a-lets,
She was a nice gal, a decent gal,
But one of the rakish kind.

I eyed that wench full warily, for talk like this I knew,
She seemed a little overbold, she lied for all I knew;
But still she was a comely lass, her lips a ruby red,
Her bosom full, her lips so slim, she coyly hung her head.

I took her to a tavern, an' treated her to wine,

Little did I think that she belonged to the rakish kind;
I handled her, I dangled her, an' found to my surprise,
She was nothin' but a fireship, rigg'd up in a disguise.

And so I deemed her company for a sailorman like me,
I kiss'd her once, I kiss'd her twice, she said' Be nice to me',
I fondl'd her, I cuddl'd her, I bounced her on me lmee,
She wept, and sighed, an' then she cried' Jack will ye stay with me

Now'all ye jolly sailormen that sail the Western Sea,
An' all lje jolly 'prentice lads, a warning take from me,
Steer clear of lofty fireships, for me they left well spent,
For one burnt all me money up an' left me broke an' bent.

154

Songs of The Ratcliffe Highway III

Vol. 6 No. 5

Both the Highway songs I have chosen for this issue of *'SPIN'* are of fair vintage.

From the terms, people's names and so-on, included in the verses we can judge them both to be late eighteenth century; the time when the Highway existed as a waterfront 'drag' as yet without docks. Around this period Voltaire's idea of the 'noble savage' had fastened itself on the minds of Europeans. Captain Cook had brought back a Polynesian, a brown-skinned native who acquired western etiquette with amazing speed engulfing all the upper crust of England with her charm, personifying in the minds of everyone, the theme of the 'noble savage'. Oberea, Queen of Tahiti, or Otaheite as the island was then called, had become a symbol of South Sea beauty, although actually obese, hence the reference in verse 2, of our first ditty, *The Rigs of Ratcliffe Highway*, to the 'Dowager Queen of Otaheite'. Hawksworth, a recorder on Captain Cook's South Sea voyages, refers constantly to the beauty of the islanders, and also describes the public sex relations of the South Sea Islanders that occurred during their great feasts. All this, of course, tended to bring the Pacific and its wonderful islanders very much before the common man; sailors in the main, being the spinners of these tales of 'Island Nights'. The East too, was very much 'in the news'.

Bungo, mentioned in verse 2 of *The Rigs of Ratcliffe Highway*, was one of the earliest ports of Japan open to Western trade. Japan was a mysterious country, closed to the West until Commodore Perry came knocking on its portals in 1852. The only ports that Western seamen ever managed to set foot ashore in being Bunga and Deshima (Nagasaki). These

Tahitian Girl
(after a drawing by one of Capt. Cook's artists)

were the days of the wall-sided East Indiamen ploughing the China and Indian Seas, bringing home that priceless commodity, tea, and of the tough ships of the circumnavigators such as Wallis, Vancouver and Cook, nearly one hundred years before the tea clippers arrived on the scene.

However, such seamen, after experiencing the delights of the languorous South Seas and the enchanting East, still had a warm spot in their hearts at the end of their journeyings for the delights of London's Ratcliffe Highway.

According to the various dictionaries I

The Bosun's Locker Stan Hugill

have consulted the etymology of the word 'rig' is doubtful. As a noun it can mean: 'a swindling scheme', 'a trick,' 'a dodge' or 'a frolic or prank', but its older meaning is 'a strumpet', and by extension, 'a brothel'. As a transitive verb it means, to 'hoax or trick', but as a verb intransitive it implies 'to play the strumpet'. It is, of course, in these 'strumpet' connotations that the word makes sense in our first song.

The Rigs of Ratcliffe Highway

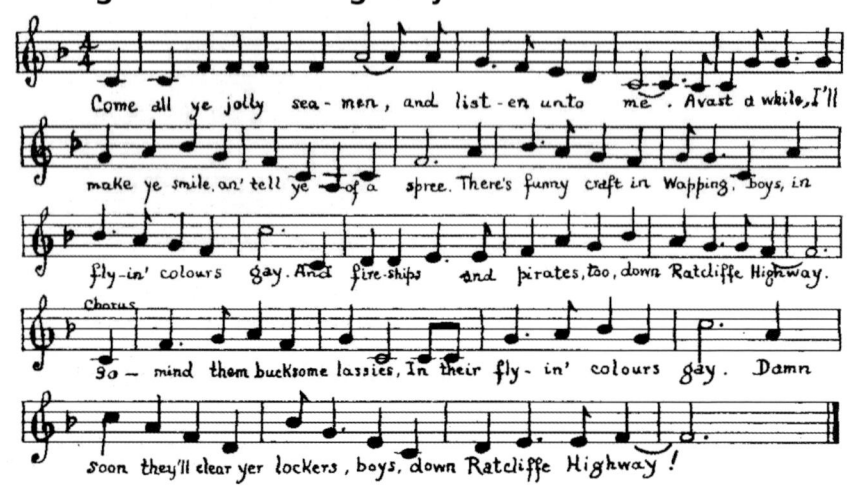

Come all ye jolly seamen, and listen unto me. Avast a while, I'll make ye smile, an' tell ye of a spree. There's funny craft in Wapping, boys, in flyin' colours gay. And fire-ships and pirates, too, down Ratcliffe Highway.

Chorus: So — mind them bucksome lassies, In their flyin' colours gay. Damn soon they'll clear yer lockers, boys, down Ratcliffe Highway!

I've sailed, me boys, right round the world,
But never before me flag unfurled;
In India, China, Bungo Bay,
What a hell of a spot is the Highway:

Chorus:
Stand clear ye sailors gay,
From the rigs of Ratcliffe Highway:

Some gals there, boys, are smart and neat,
As the Dowager Queen of Otaheite
Oh, there's gals there boys, of every hue,
White, yellow and brown, boys, black an' blue.

Some of them gals had faces red,
Eatin' trotters an' boiled pigs heads;
Dancing a jig, them gals did sing,
Drinkin' beer an' pints o' gin.

I went one night to have a reel,
At the Angel Tap in Blue Coat Fields;
I drank and capered, all night long,

An' then turned in wid Lucy Long

There's shrimps for sale and oysters, too,
And coves a-selling fried eels too;
There's ugly Bet and Poyy Jane,
At the King William in Gravel Lane.

One big, fat gal, she did me drag,
To have a spree at the Lamb and Flag;
We got blind drunk an' started a row,
An' got chucked out of the Barley Mow.

One gal I met, she looked quite queer,
Her belly big wid pots of beer;
She tossed up her skirts an' played the deuce,
An' broke her nose in Paddy's Goose.

You jolly sailors one and all,
If at the Port O' London call,
See Ratcliffe Highway, them damsels loose,
The William, the Bear and Paddy's Goose.

A broadside version is called *Ratcliffe Highway in 1842* – a rather limiting title I fancy. This date of 1842 appears to me unusually late. It is fairly obvious that the song, from internal evidence, must have been around several years before this. After giving the oral version which I obtained (along with the second song) many years ago from a West Country naval friend of my father's, I will give several verses from the broadside that differ from mine.

All the public houses and taverns named in the songs are known to have existed, in actual fact, many of them were quite famous (or notorious!) and are referred to in various eighteenth and early nineteenth-century London records. Also, many of the infamous prostitutes mentioned once were flesh and blood, although I am inclined to believe that their names, particularly in the oral examples, have come down through the course of years slightly altered. Anyone who read the extracts from Ronald Pearsall's new book *'The Worm in the Bud'* in the *People* (March 2nd), will have noted the curious names these 'legger's motts', or sailors' women of the Ratcliffe Highway possessed: Lushing Loo, Cocoa Bet, Salmon-faced Mary Ann, China Emma – names very similar to those in our songs.

Incidentally, Gravel Lane mentioned in verse 6 still exists. It takes its name from the fact that in olden times the part of the Thames that used to wash its lower end was where the Geordie collier brigs discharged and loaded their gravel ballast. These vessels were known as 'cats' and the 'cat' owned by Dick Whittington was actually one of these coal brigs. It made him a fortune on a voyage or two to the Barbary Coast The well-known pub near Gravel Lane called 'The Prospect of Whitby' takes its name from one of these colliers.

Those stanzas in the broadside which differ from those of the traditional version are:

2) Some lassies their heads will toss,
   With bustles as big as a brewer's hoss,
   Some wear a cabbage net called a veil,
   And a boa just like a buffalo's tail.

(3) I married a lass with her face so red,
    She eat three salt herrings and a bullock's head,
    She danced a jig, then began to sing,
    Drank a gallon of beer and a pint of gin.

(5) There's eels and shrimps as black as fleas,
    And a covey a-selling blue, grey peas,
    There's Ugly Bet and Dandy Jane,
    At the King William in Gravel Lane.

(6) I fell in with a lady so modest and meek,
    She eat thirteen faggots and nine pigs feet,
    Three pounds of beef, and, to finish the meal,
    Eat eight pounds of tripe and a large cowheel.

(Ashton – *'Real Sailor Songs'*)

The remaining verses are much the same as those of the oral form.

Our first song is obviously an advert for all the Highway pubs, and their women, the flash packets, fire-ships, or 'rigs'. Our second could be likened to a modern television

The Bosun's Locker Stan Hugill

Down Ratcliffe Highway

You jolly sailors list to me, I've bin a fortnight home from sea. Which time I've travelled night an' day, among th' rigs of the High-way.

Chorus: *Stand clear ye sailors gay! — From th' rigs o' Ratcliffe High-way!*

Oh, the Old Three Crowns I anchored in had such a jolly crew,
There's rough an' tough from every clime, an' copper coloured too;
The lassies there beyond compare, with hair both grey an' red,
Some with no nose, an' some no teeth, an' damag'd figgerhead.
Chorus:
So mind the buxom lassies, in their flyin' colours gay,
Damn soon they'll clear yer lockers boys, Down Ratcliffe Highway.

To the Blue Anchor I next did go an' a frigate took in tow,
She ran me aground, me cargo lost, I found that I must go;
So I sail'd into another port an' there by the next day,
Me hulk well rigg'd an' watertight lay in Ratcliffe Highway.

In the old Three Jolly Sailors bad rum there is galore,
The lassies muster twenty, or mayb_ ten times more;
They foot it there so neatly, but mind without a doubt,
They're sure to cut your cable, so keep a good lookout.

In the Old Rose an' Britannia there's frigates close at hand,
There's Crooked Loo, an' Squintin' Sue an' bandy Mary Ann;
There's Skinny Nell, the yellar gal, and flash Maria neat,
There's Randy Het an' Poxy Bet who's bin all thro' the fleet.

And in the famed King William, that's in New Gravel Lane,
There's Taffy Jones, a bag 0' bones, an' knock-kneed Mary Jane;
There's thick-lipped Kit, as black as jet, with a bustle such a size,
An' Snufflin' Liz, with such a phiz, an' Sukie gravy-eyes.

An' in the good 01' Barley Mow, I hailed a frigate tight,
We steered away without delay, I boarded her that night;
She took me watch and earrings as well as all me pay,
Two bullies came an' chucked me out into Ratcliffe Highway.

158

advertisement – 'our product is better than theirs' type of thing. After telling one all about the infamous pubs and women of the Highway, and warning the rantin', rovin' seaman to by-pass them, if he wants a good, clean night ashore without being bumped off and robbed, in the last stanza it advises Jack Tar to visit 'Paddy's Goose' only.

'Paddy's Goose' or 'Paddy's Grey Goose' was the sailor name for a public house called correctly the 'White Swan'. The landlord, at one period, had another brainwave relating to advertising his wares. He had a small paddle-boat, with flags a-flying and music playing, loaded to the gunnels with whores, plying up and down the Thames abreast the Wapping area. It is reported also that during the Crimean War he enlisted so many men as soldiers that the authorities rewarded him for his patriotism. The impressment of seamen – although officially still extant – by this time had died a natural death, therefore it would seem that these recruits took the King's Shilling voluntarily. Or did they? Paddy's gin, one must remember, was extremely potent!

The broadside of this second song bears the title of *The Sailors Frolic*, or *Life in the East*, the 'East' of course, being the East End of London. It differs from the oral version a little. The latter we now give under the title of *Down Ratcliffe Highway*.

In our next issue we will tackle more Fire-ship Songs and go into the matter of *double entendre* often found in such ballads.

The Bosun's Locker Stan Hugill

Vol. 6 No. 6
Songs of The Ratcliffe Highway IV

The Ratcliffe Highway song most commonly heard in folk clubs – and, in the past, the one most popular with the Jack Tars – is that usually referred to as *Ratcliffe Highway*, *The Fire-ship* or *Rattle Me Rigging Down Ratcliffe Highway*. It harks back to the days of Pepys, and has had as many titles, tunes and stanzas as the years of its existence.

Fragmentary forms have appeared in nautical yarns and reminiscences down through the ages, but very rarely has a full set of words appeared in print. It is the daddy of all *double entendre* sea-ballads, and uses nautical terminology to the full, to explain the spicy adventures of Jack in the purlieus of the Highway, and his fiery encounter with a Ratcliffe harpy or fire-ship. To the uninitiated it appears to be a fairly innocuous ditty; to the Seaman of the Sail it was as bawdy as they come. In theme it starts much the same in all versions, but part way through the hero is either robbed or cheated of his change while imbibing, or, alternatively, receives a memento of his, as Bone so aptly puts it, 'voyage to Cytherea'. However, there is no fixed rule as to which set of words went to which set of music. As in all sailor singing, the preference was up to the singer. Couplets from all the versions were used by the Western Ocean Packet Rats in the tops'l halyard shanty *Blow the Man Down*, usually prefaced by:

I'm a Flying Fish sailor just home from Hong Kong,
Chorus:
Timme way, hay, blow the man down!

If ye give me some whiskey, I'll sing ye a song,
Chorus:
Gimme some time to blow the man down!

This pattern, in turn, was used in later versions of the Highway song as the introductory verse, and by this time, the song came to be known as *The Blackballer*.

Come all ye bold seamen and listen to me,
I'll sing ye a song all about the high sea;
It ain't very short, nor it ain't very long,
'Tis of a Flying Fish sailor just home from Hong Kong.

The Highway, of course, was a promenade of seamen from the East Indiamen and the later Blackwallers and tea clippers – in other words the Flying Fish sailors. This alteration of themes, locations and heroes is, of course, what is known as the folk process, but how exactly this famous Highway song got around to Norfolk it is difficult to explain and appears to me to be stretching the folk process more than a little:

Strolling through Norfolk one day on the spree,
I met a fair packet, her sails blowin' free.

A similar version is the one called *Cruisin Round Yarmouth*. In both versions the sailor is found on the Highway, although how he got there from Yarmouth or Norfolk in general takes a bit of explaining. We have versions of this from two famous traditional singers, Harry Cox and Sam Larner.

The song continues, as in all the others under review, with the sailor and his Highway moll heading for a pub, the sailorman, later, paying for his night out in the manner of all sailors in all Highway ballads.

My friend, the most prolific shanty and sea-going collector in the New World, Bill Doerflinger, had a version, called *As I Went A-walkin' Down Ratcliffe Highway*, from Captain Tayluer (one time mate of the 'shipentine' *'Shenandoah'*) with a similar fol-de-lol refrain, also using the introductory verse already mentioned:

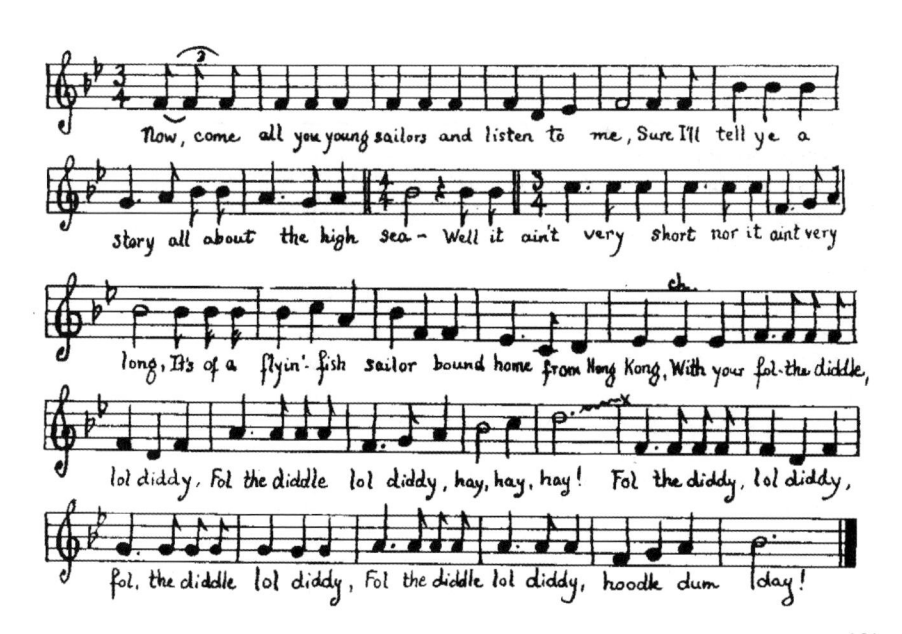

The Bosun's Locker Stan Hugill

A version I have often sung, called wrongly on my record *The Flash Packet*, which I had from an old Irish seaman Paddy Delaney, and which I gave in an earlier edition of *'SPIN'*, is the following:

[musical notation]

Now, as I wuz a-walkin' down Ratcliffe Highway, A flash lookin' packet I chanct for to see, Of the port that she hail'd from I cannot say much, But by her appearance I took her for Dutch, Singin' too-relye-addie, too-relye-addie, Singin' too-relye-addie, Aye, too-relye-ay!

Up to the sailor arriving and staying in the flash packet's 'lily-white room', the verses are the same as those given later in my final Highway song. These are also to be found in *'SPIN'*, vol. 3 No. 1. The final verses are a little different:

She clewed up her courses, we had much sea-room,
I raked her from for'ard wid a shot from me gun;
I manned me stern-chaser and caught her at large,
Fired into the stern gallery a hefty discharge.

We closed alongside, boys, I hauled in me slack,
I busted me bobstay and then changed me tack;
Me shot locker's empty, me powder's all spent,
Me gun needs repairin', it's choked at the vent.

She then dropped her courses, I lashed up and stowed,
I gave her some shillings 'fore I left her abode,
But it warn't enough, boys, she wanted some more,
She cursed me and called me a son-o-a-whore.

She blazed like a frigate, at me she let fire,
But nothing could stem, boys, that Irish tart's ire;
She kicked me and bellowed, she spat in me jaw,
An' I beat retreat thro' her open back door.

I've fought with the Rooshians, the Prussians also,
I've fought with the Dutch and with Johnny Crapaud;
But of all the fine fights that I ever did see,
She beats all the sights of the heathen Chinee.

Now all ye young seamen take a warnin' I say,
Take it aisy, me boys, when yer down that Highway;
Steer clear o' them flash gals, on the Highway do dwell,
They'll take up yer flipper an' yer soon bound to hell.

Another version, telling a similar tale, which I also had from Paddy Delaney now follows:

As I wuz a-rovin' round London, Thro' Wapping, down Ratcliffe Highway, Oh I chanc't for to drop in an ale-house, For to spend a long night an' long day, long day, long day, long day, For to spend a long night and long day.

A young doxy came up to me
And she axed if I'd money to sport,
When I gave her a guinea for a bottle,
She sez, 'Damn me eyes, you're the sort.'

Chorus:
The sort, the sort, the sort,
She sez, 'Damn me eyes, you're the sort.'

The bottle wuz put on the table,
Likewise glasses for everyone,
When I axed for the change of me guinea,
She tipped me a stave of her song.

This doxy she flew in a passion,
Put her hands on both of her hips,
'Young man, don't ye know our fashion,
D'yer think yer on board of yer ship?'

A gold watch hung over the mantel,
For me guinea I'll take it as change,
And down the back steps I ran quickly,
Sayin', damn me, but 'tis fair exchange.

Now the night being dark in me favour,
To the waterfront then I did slip,
And I got me a boat bound for Deptford,
And soon got back on board me ship.

So all ye young fellas that wander,
Especially down Ratcliffe Highway,

If ye chance for to drop in an alehouse,
Be careful how long ye do stay.

For their songs and their wines will beguile you,
Till your mind it'll sure feel deranged,
When you give 'em a guinea for a bottle,
Ye can go to the devil for change

Peter Kennedy points out that Vaughan Williams collected a tune very similar to this, but the repetitive refrain is omitted. A Mrs Howard of King's Lynn, Norfolk sang it to him in 1905. The lady's text was supplemented from an unpublished version collected in Sussex in 1954 (given by Bob Copper) and from a broadside by Catnach. This latter is called *Rolling Down the Wapping*, (British Museum 11661 dd20 p.20). Frank Purslow, the noted folk song collector and singer, apparently rediscovered this broadside. Jim Baldry of Woodbridge, Suffolk, sang a slightly different version to Peter Kennedy in 1956. A couplet about the doxy throwing bottles at the sailor is not in my version, and Baldry gives 'Devon' as the place the escape boat takes him to.

In all the foregoing Highway ballads the ending is one in which Deepwater Johnny is either robbed or cheated of his change. The following songs belong to the type in which

The Bosun's Locker Stan Hugill

he suffers from a clinical outcome as the result of sleeping with a tarnished and syphilitic Highway harridan.

The first one I give is a version as sung by Cyril Tawney, one having many naval references, some fairly modern, with Portsmouth as the port concerned, and not London. But, here again, the London Highway is sung of in the chorus – another geographical error, apparently! Of course, in the days of the 'Wooden Walls' it was recorded that a battalion of prostitutes, nearly a thousand strong, marched across the southern English countryside from London to Portsmouth, to await the arrival of the Fleet, in effect bringing together the Ratcliffe Highway and Point Beach, Portsmouth!

Oh, as Jack was a-walkin' Point Beach up'n'down, He met with pretty Polly of merry Portsmouth town, As soon as Jack seed her most beautiful face, He hoisted three tops'ls, an' to her gave chase, To my riggin' grey, Come rattle my riggin' down, Come rattle my riggin' down Ratcliffe Highway!

All the following verses are much the same as those in our final 'Rattle me rigging' song, but the last verse is different:

Now Jack he's reached home to Portsmouth at last,
He lies on the lower deck among the low class;
He lies on his back, and he cries out, 'Oh, Lord!
'Wasn't that a stiff breeze when I sprung me mainyard!'

The last verse appears to me as a more modern offering. And now here is, in my opinion, the best, and worst, and most comprehensive 'Rattle' song:

And to wind up this issue I feel I can't do any better than to cite a verse or two of a fairly modern child of these Highway ballads that I picked up by way of a friend from America, who learnt it from a shipmate of his:-

The tune of this ditty is that of the cowboy song *Strawberry Roan*.

And so folks until next time in our final Ratcliffe Highway songs.

Rattled Me Rigging

As I wuz a-rollin' down th' Highway one morn, I spied a flash packet from old Wapping town, As soon as I seed her I slack'd me main brace, An' I hoisted me stuns'ls an' to her gave chase, Oh me riggin's slack, Oh, me rattlin's are frayed, I've rattl'd me riggin' down Ratcliffe Highway.

Her flag. wuz three colours, her masthead wuz low,
She wuz round at the counter, an' bluff at the bow;
From larboard to starboard an' so rolled she,
She wuz sailin' at large, she wuz runnin' free.

Chorus:
Oh, me riggin's slack, oh, me rattlin's frayed,
I've rattl'd me riggin' down Ratcliffe Highway!

I fired me bow-chaser, the signal she knew,
She backed her main tops'l an' for me hove to;
I lowered down me jolly-boat, an' rowed alongside,
An' I found Madam's gangway wuz open an' wide

I hailed her in English, she answered me clear,
I'm from the Black Arrow, bound to the Shakespeare ';
So I wore ship wid a what d 'yer know,
An' I passed her me hawser an' took her in tow.

I tipped her me flipper, me tow-rope an' all,
She then let her hand on me reef-tackle fall;
She then took me up to her lily-white room,
An' with her main rigging I fouled me jibboom.

I entered her little cubby-hole, and said, 'Damn her eyes! '
She wuz nothin' but a fire-ship rigg'd up in disguise;
She had a foul bottom from stern-post to fore,
Tween the wind and the water she ran me ashore.

She set fire to me riggin', likewise to me hull,
And away to the lazareet I had to scull;
Wid me helm hard-a-starboard as I rolled along,
Me shipmates all cried, 'Jack, yer mainyard is sprung! '

Now I'm safe in harbour, me moorings all fast,
I'll lay here quite snug, boys, till all danger is past;
Wid me mainyard all served, boys, an'

The Bosun's Locker Stan Hugill

parcelled and tarred,
Wasn't that a stiff breeze, boys, that sprung me mainyard ?

Here's a health to the packet with the black curly locks,
Here's a health tothe fireship that ran me on the rocks;
Here's a health to the quack, boys, that freed me from pain,
If I meet that flash packet I'll board her again.

And to wind up this issue I feel I can't do any better than to cite a verse or two of.a fairly mpdern child of these Highway ballads that I picked up by way of a friend from America, who learnt it from a shipmate of his:

I was sailing up Broadway one fine summer's day,
When a trim looking craft I spied coming my way;
I gave .her a hail as she came alongside,
'I'm a Chinatown bum goin' out wid the tide

So I passed'her me hawser and took her in tow.
Straight up the Channel the compass did show,
We sailed up an alley that wasn't quite sweet'
An' moored fore' n ' aft at the end of the street.,
Ten days after this when me fores'l was hung,
An' the doctor said' Sailor, your mainmast is sprung',
As I looked at me bent spar an' me ragged fore course,
I swore off that day from all Chinatown whores.

The tune of this ditty is that of the cowboy song *Strawberry Roan*.

And so folks until next time in our final Ratcliffe Highway songs.

166

The Bosun's Locker Stan Hugill

Vol. 7 No. 1
Songs of The Ratcliffe Highway

We now come to the last pair of our Highway songs. The first of these has rarely made print. There is a fragment in Gale Huntingdon's *'Songs the Whalemen Sang'* culled from the pages of the journal of a whaleman who sailed in the ship *'Cortes'* out of New Bedford in 1847. Here it is called *Down Wapping*. The air given by Huntingdon bears little resemblance to mine, but then again, as he points out, the songs in these whalemen's journals were without tunes. In most cases he has remedied this deficiency, sometimes giving the text a recognisable air, sometimes one he felt suitable. Some of the lines of the text differ from mine and it also lacks the chorus I give.

Down Wapping

Oh, an honest Jack Tar was a-cruisin' ashore, A-rollin' round Wapping fell in with a whore, She call'd him her love an' her own sweet dear, Sayin' 'Look here, me boy, can't yer raise us some beer!'

chorus
Yo....! ho...! the stormy winds blow! Sayin' 'Look here, me boy, can't yer raise us some beer!'

The Bosun's Locker Stan Hugill

Down Wapping

Oh, yes, my dear love, my own heart's delight,
But please can you find me a lodging tonight?
Oh, no, my dear Jack, you shall sleep in my arms,
For I am a guard-ship that'll guard you from harm.

Chorus: Yo, ho, the stormy winds blow!
For I am a guard-ship that'll guard you from harm!

So away the pair went with their stuns'ls hauled out,
They stopped at an alehouse and drank ale and stout;
Jack knocked on the counter an' axed what's to pay?
Three shillings an' sixpence the barman did say.

Jack pulled out his purse an' he paid like a man,
Sez Poll to herself, oh, now this 'ere's me plan;
When 'e's fast asleep, oh, I'll lighten his load,
So it won't be heavy when 'e's on the road.

So away our brave Jack an' his sweetheart did go,
A-whistlin I gee-up an' a-whistlin' gee wo!
Then thro' a dark alley they chanc'd for to steer,
 But Jack was a boy who no colours did fear

They then hove to in a tough boarding house,
Jack staggerin' a bit an' feeling half-soused;
But after a frolic an' a strop an' a block,
As soon as he slept, boys, she went fast to work.

An' while he slept taut, she went deep through his breeks,
An' soon robbed the purse of its fat, bloated cheeks;
Her bucko came in and he hauled Jack away,
Dumped him in the gutter an' bade him good-day.

When Jack woke next morn, his head fat an' sore,
At all Wapping bawds, oh, he cursed and he swore;
And back to his ship, sure he staggered along,
And this is the end of a rattlin' good song.

A ubiquitous tune of the eighteenth century is *The Vicar of Bray*. Many contemporary ballads use this air, one for example, being about the naval mutineer Parker and the Nore Mutiny and called *A New Song on Parker the Delegate*:

I will not sing in Parker's praise, disgraceful is the story,
Nor yet to seamen tune my lays, eclips'd now in their glory, etc.

The tune of the sailor song called variously *The Rambling Sailor* and *The Trimrigged Doxie*, in some forms, also reminds us of the good old *Vicar of Bray*. In particular the version in Miss C. Fox-Smith's *'A Book of Shanties'* (Methuen and Co. Ltd., London 1927):

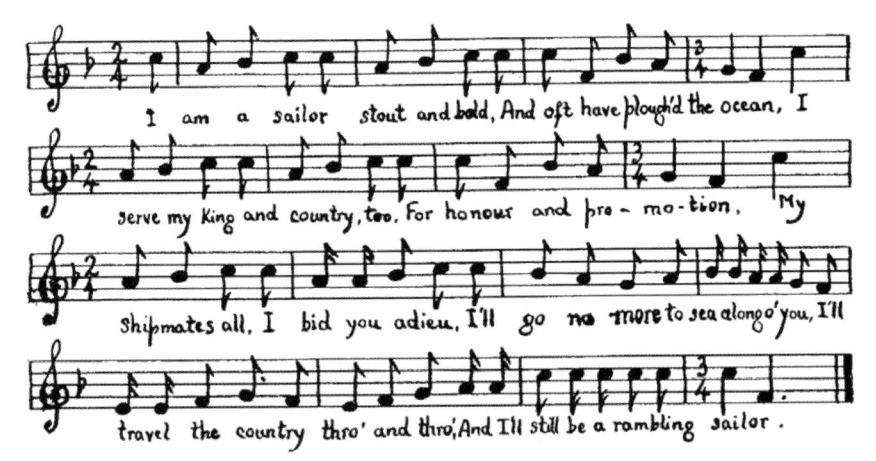

I am a sailor stout and bold, And oft have plough'd the ocean, I serve my King and country, too, For honour and pro-mo-tion. My shipmates all, I bid you adieu, I'll go no more to sea along o' you, I'll travel the country thro' and thro', And I'll still be a rambling sailor.

Miss Fox-Smith learnt this from her father, and she mentions that Cecil Sharp also collected a version. The sailor in her version rambles around Portsmouth in search of his female prey, and the impression given is that the song has been bowdlerised. A.L. Lloyd sings a more unexpurgated version on *'A Sailor's Garland'* (Transatlantic Records, XTRA 5013), the tune of which, that of a West Country hornpipe, still bears a faint resemblance to our *Vicar of Bray*. It bears the title *The Trimrig Ducksie*. Lloyd mentions on the sleeve that the Rev. Baring-Gould and Hammond, as well as Sharp, collected versions but 'suppressed most of the text as unfit for polite ears.' He also believes that the song started life as *The Rambling Soldier* (18th century) and states that in 1818 John Catnach, the broadsheet publisher, turned out the first 'sailor' version. However, in my version, which I obtained in the West Country (my parents' home), the sailor hangs around Wapping, which makes it fit and proper to be included in our Highway songs. The air, too, although different from either Fox-Smith's or A.L. Lloyd's, leans towards our *Vicar of Bray* tune.

This song has two or three nautical *double entendre* phrases and two or three lines I have admittedly purloined from Bert's version, as being rather better (or worse?) than mine. One must not think that it was in songs and ballads only that these nautical two-edged phrases were used. Literature of the time has many examples. For instance the description of a coloured 'mott', Black Sarah of Bluegate Fields, runs: 'she was a Dutch-built piratical schooner carrying a free-trade under the black flag, and many and many a stout and lusty lugger has borne down upon, and hoisted the British standard over our sable privateer, Black Sall.' (*The Town*, 1837.) Expressions such as 'holed atween wind and water by an enemy privateer' to mean sexual assault were common enough on the lips of the habitués of the Highway.

The songs we have dealt with in this series have all been related to the doings of merchant seamen – the East Indiamen, Blackwallers, and later, the clipper-ship men, the 'Flying Fish Sailors' as they were known, with an occasional reference to naval seamen. In regard to the latter, I've pointed out elsewhere, that although many of the Highway songs may belong to naval seamen, it is more likely that they were the compositions of the armed and semi-naval East Indiamen. In fact, it would appear that the Navy was fairly absent around the Highway during the late eighteenth and early nineteenth centuries. It would be naval seamen that would be seen at the various

The Bosun's Locker Stan Hugill

'steps' and 'stairs' of the River Thames, mostly on duty and rarely free to wander. Naval ships-of-the-line came no nearer London than Gravesend, Greenwich, the Nore and the Downs, except for an occasional rig down at the Deptford dockyard and victualling yard. However naval cutters, barges and all kinds of small tenders arrived at and departed from such places as Wapping Old Stairs and Cherry Garden Stairs in the line of duty. Press-gangs had their headquarters around Wapping 'village' in the days of Captain Cook, who joined the Royal Navy here as a volunteer. Once the press-gang had got its full complement aboard the Wooden Walls down at the Nore there was little chance of the men getting ashore again.

This of course was one of the reasons why bumboats full of rum, 'bumbo', 'swipes', arrack, tobacco, fruit, and women were allowed to go down the Thames from Wapping and elsewhere to the anchored Fleet moored at the booms, and trade aboard with the Jack Tars who were virtually prisoners in the 'tween-decks until the Fleet sailed. Here aboard ship, the tumble-home sides of which would be decorated with crimson ropes, her gun-ports a-flutter with the scarlet petticoats of former ship-visiting prostitutes, the naval Jacks, with their rum and women, their singing and their dancing and whoring, had their playground between the guns. Broadly speaking, the Highway was not for them.

As well as the naval press-gangs, the Army, of course, had its recruiting parties working the Highway area, and a few songs relating to their forceful recruiting methods such as *The New Deserter*, have been collected. As the Tower and its barracks were only a stone's throw from Ratcliffe Highway, soldiers of course wandered through its purlieus, and some 'leatherneck' ditties and broadsides relating to their amatory and fisticuff experiences with the Highway harpies and pimps do exist. However, these are outside the scope of this article.

In more modern times imitations of these Highway songs have circulated in fair number. One I can call to mind, collected by my friend John Brune, seems to be mixed with *Maggie May* and other sailor-robbing songs from various seaports. This is called *Mary Grey*, the first verse of which runs:

> I walked by Surrey Dock, when I ran into Mary Grey,
> She was cruising up and down in search of prey;
> Said she, 'My Jolly Tar, I can see you're fresh ashore,
> To the Mermaid Tavern we had better stray.'

> *Chorus:* Better stray, to the Mermaid Tavern we had better stray.

So we will say goodbye to the bonneted, bustled and 'lastic-side booted harpies of other days – Crooked Loo, Skinny Nell, the Yarmouth Bloater, Lushing Loo, Randy Het, Black Mott and China Emma – doxies who once figured largely in the daydreams of many an old-time tar as he handled a bucking wheel down in the Roaring Forties. And goodbye to the Highway, Frederick Street, Tiger Bay, the North East Passage, Jamaica Place, Shadwell High, St. Katharine's Way, Rosemary Lane, Dock Street, Leman Street, and to the pubs of the area: the 'Blue Boar', 'Half Moon', 'Rose and Britannia', 'Shakespeare's Head', 'Brown Bear', 'Three Jolly Sailors', 'Ship and Shears', 'Norwegian Flags', 'Seven Stars', 'Paddy's Goose' and 'Duke O' York'.

Yes, we will now leave the area, its surviving pubs and cafes, to the Maltese restaurant owners, to the meth-drinkers, the teenage good-time girls, the hemp addict, the odd docker and the few respectable old inhabitants, who, in spite of the dilapidated, tatty and war-scarred buildings around them, still have a soft spot for the place in which they were born.

The Rambling Sailor

Transcribed by Theresa Craven

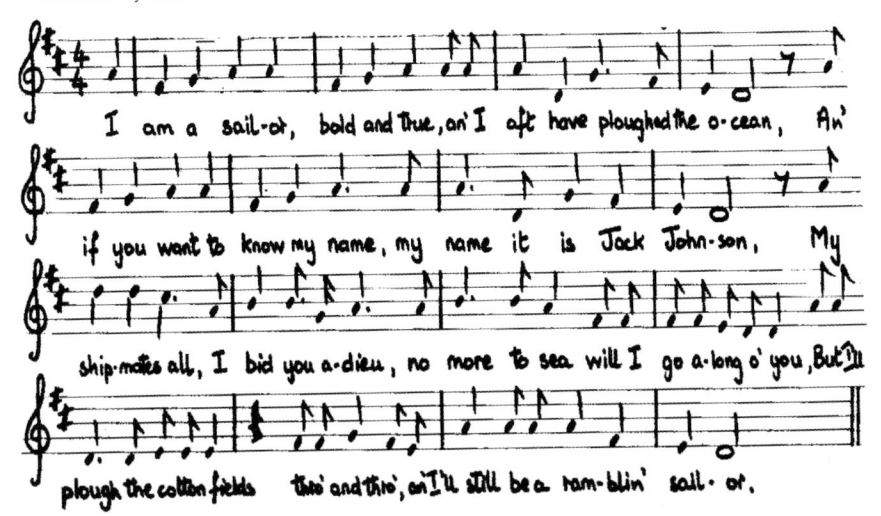

*I am a sailor, bold and true, an' I aft have ploughed the ocean,
An' if you want to know my name, my name it is Jack Johnson,
My shipmates all, I bid you adieu, no more to sea will I go along o' you,
But I'll plough the cotton fields thro' and thro', an' I'll still be a ramblin' sailor.*

As I was rollin' out one day, down by the London River,
A Wapping gal I chanct to spy, we rolled along together;
Her cheeks were like the rosebuds red, she'd a Greenaway bonnet on her head,
I axed her for a favour but she said she was a maid,
That saucy little trim-rigged doxie.

I can't and I won't go along o' you, you saucy rambling sailor,
My perents they would not consent, I'm promised to a tailor;
I was right damn eager to savour her charms, a guinea sez I for a roll in yer arms
We came to an agreement, cos I promised her no harm,
I was only a rambling sailor.

She clewed up her courses an' let her stays'ls fall, yardarm to yardarm touchin',
Me shot all gone, a short caulk came, an' she soon fell a-robbin';
She emptied me breeks o' everything I had, she pinched me boots from underneath the bed,
She even stole me watch from underneath me head,
That robbin' little false-rigged doxie.

When I awoke an' found her gone, I started to roar like thunder,
Me gold watch an' me money too, she'd bore away as plunder;
Oh, it 'twarn't for me watch, nor me money too, them as I vallee, but I tell ee true.
That saucy little fireship she burnt me bobstay through,
'Twas the end of a rambling sailor.

The Bosun's Locker Stan Hugill

Vol. 7 No. 2
Some more songs of Jack ashore

My recent series of articles on Songs of the Ratcliffe Highway having come to an end, I dallied with the idea of doing an article on other notorious streets that had mention in sailor song and shanty. However, working through my own material I came to the conclusion that sailor songs linked with, say, Liverpool's Paradise Street, or New York's Bowery, and so on, are too well known to repeat here – e.g. *Blow the Man Down*, *Can't Ye Dance the Polka?* etc. So, I searched for rarer songs, songs in the Highway mode, in which the sailor gets done down 'brown' by a sailor-robbing harpy, ones that have not as yet been over-aired. It wasn't too easy the task I set myself, and the first one I came across was a Liverpool ditty only picked up within recent years.

In my *'Shanties from the Seven Seas'* I mentioned the fact that true Welsh shanties were, as far as I could see, non-existent, with the exception of one sent me by an old-timer from Amlwch. This is called *Rownd yr Horn*, and during the last ten years Welsh school choruses and glee clubs have often given it over the air. It always appeared to me to be a shore-composed song of fairly recent birth, and even Welshmen told me they didn't think the tune sounded Welsh. For those who can read Welsh the first verse and chorus runs:

> Daeth diwrnod i ffarwelio, Ag annwyl wlad y Cymro,
> Gan sefyll am hen dir y Werddon fras;
> Fe gododd y gwynt yn nerthol, Y mor a'i donnau 'n rhuthro
> Gan olchi dros ein llestr annwyllas.
>
> *Chorus:*
> Dewch Gymry glan, I wrando ar fy nghan,
> Fel bu y fordaith rownd yr Horn, rownd yr Horn!
> Sef y trydydd dydd o'r wythnos,
> Y chydig cyn y cyfnos
> Gan basio ger glan greigiau glannau Mon.

Then, in my researches I came across a book called *'Sailor in Steam'* by J. Murray Lindsay, an ex-sailing ship Scot now living in Australia. He relates that when aboard the barque *'Killoran'*, during the First World War, he heard an old clipper ship seaman named Andrew Johnson singing a forebitter called *The Oyster Girl* (not to be confounded with the more usual *Oyster Girl* of folk song books).

Johnson said it was very popular in the seventies aboard the famous tea-clipper *'Leander'*. On examining the tune I found it to be that of the so-called 'genuine' Welsh shanty *Rownd yr Horn*. The old sailor's song obviously being of Liverpool origin, caused me to look nearer home for someone who knew it. Luckily, an old Whitehaven sea captain who I meet regularly in Aberdeen, stirred the links in his chain-locker of memory, and brought it back to life. He produced the following with its rousing chorus in much the same vein as that in Lindsay's book. (See *The Oyster Girl*.)

Another song of a sailor's downfall is *Jack-all-alone* or *The Shirt and the Apron*. I give this in full on p.376 of *'Shanties from the Seven Seas'*. As it was never used as a shanty I did not give its tune, the sole reason for its inclusion in that book being the fact that many of its stanzas were slightly altered and often fitted to versions of the capstan shanty *Can't Ye Dance the Polka?* or *The New York Gals*.

The Oyster Girl

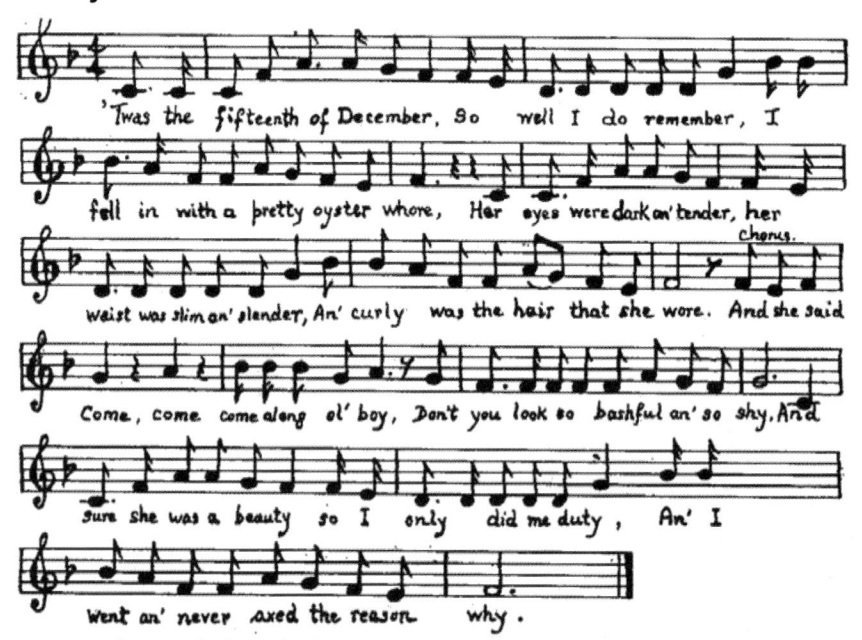

'Twas the fifteenth of December, So well I do remember, I fell in with a pretty oyster whore, Her eyes were dark an' tender, her waist was slim an' slender, An' curly was the hair that she wore.

Chorus:
And she said Come, come, come along ol' boy, Don't you look so bashful an' so shy, And sure she was a beauty so I only did me duty, An' I went an' never axed the reason why.

So, I gave her 'lots of brandy, it made her neat and handy,
And guzzled down some oysters, p'rhaps a score;
And then I drank a dozen, and she then brought her cousin,
And said now give 'im half a dozen more.
And she said, 'Come, come, etc.
Chorus:

Her cousin then came' to me, intent on to sail through me,
A-sayin 'Sailor boy be on yer way:
I answered with a stutter, he threw me in the gutter,
An' with her cousin the lady walked away.

'Twas early in the mornin', just as t_e day was dawnin',
Two policemen came and hauled me right away,
They dragged me from the gutter; they put me on a shutter,
Dumped me in Walton Gaol there for to stay.

Final Chorus: And they said' Come, come, come along ol' boy,
Don't ye look so bashful an' so shy;
You've bin cheated by yer beauty, but we have. to do our duty.,
Or the Magistrate will know the reason why!

The Bosun's Locker Stan Hugill

I had this one from an old Irish sailor Paddy Cunningham. There is, if I remember rightly, a version in *'Ballads and Sea-songs from Newfoundland'* (Greensleaf and Mansfield), with a tune different from the one I give here. I give a full description of the 'panel-game' which the sailor in the song falls victim to, in *'Shanties from the Seven Seas'*, so here I will merely say that in many seamen's brothels, apart from the bed, the only item of furniture was a chair which stood near the head of the former, on which the sailor victim naturally placed his jacket and trousers and so on. In the night a panel in the wall would open and the silly sailor's clothes with the contents of their pockets, would disappear through the aperture into the hands of the harlot's 'bludger' later to be divided between the artful pair. Here is the song:

Jack All Alone

Ye 'pren-tice lads and sea-men bold, come lis-ten to me song—, An' I'll tell ye how I met me fate, when I was ve-ry young—; 'Twas on the day I came from sea, a flash gal I did meet—, An' she kind-ly axed me to a dance, 'twas up on Bleek-er Street,

CHORUS: *She kind-ly axed me to a dance, 'twas up on Bleek-er Street.*

To take us to a barroom boys, the distance warn't too far;
Some gals passed by the other side, these words to me did say,
Oh, you young chap, 'll lose yer cap, if you do steer that way.

Chorus: Oh, you young chap, 'll lose yer cap, if you do steer that way.

Now, when we reached the barroom, boys, the liquor was brought in,
And every man waltzed round the room as the dancing did begin;
Me and my love waltzed round the room, danced to a merry tune,
Sez she, , My dear, now we'll repair to a chamber all alone. '
Chorus: (Repeat last line)

When the dancing it was over, we straight to be bed did go,'
' Twas little did I ever think she'd prove me overt'row; .
Me watch and clothes and eighty puns wid me fancy gal had fled,
An' there was I, Jack-all-alone, stark naked in the bed.

Chorus: (Repeat last line)

When I came to me senses, oh, nothing could I spy,
But a woman's shirt an' apron there upon the bed did lie;
I wrung me hands, I tore me hair, I yelled, 'What shall I do?'
And said 'Farewell, oh, my home town, I'll never more see you!'
Chorus: (Repeat last line)

Oh, everywhere was silent, the hour was twelve o'clock,
I put the shirt and apron on, and hauled out for the dock;
Me shipmates saw me come aboard, these words to me did say,
'Well, well, ol' chap, you've lost yer cap, since last ye went away.'
Chorus: (Repeat last line)

'Is this the new spring fashion the ladies wear on shore?
Where is the shop that's sellin' it, have they got any more?'
The Ol' Man cried, 'Why, Jack, my boy, to Boston I thought ye'd gone,
A better suit I sure could buy than that for eighty pun!
Chorus: (Repeat last line)

'Sure I could get a better suit if I'd only had the chance,
But I met a gal on Bleeker Street and she sure led me a dance;
I danced to my destruction, got stripped from head to feet,
So I swore an oath I'd go no more to a dance on Bleeker Street.
Chorus: (Repeat last line)

Come all ye lads and seamen bold, a warnin' take by me,
Be sure ye choose good company when ye go on the spree;
Steer clear of all the flash gals, there, or else ye'll rue the day,
With a woman's shirt and apron, boys, they'll fit ye out for sea!
Chorus: (Repeat last line)

Thinking there may be a song of the type we are discussing among the older broadsheets, I browsed and rummaged for a while, but came up with one only – *The Sailor's Return.* Ashton gives this in his *'Real Sailor Songs'* (1891). It has many of the components of *Jack-all-alone* and *The Flash Gals of the Town* (Ratcliffe Highway Series), but instead of being the adventures of an individual couched in the first person, this ballad is both an admonishment and severe warning from an onlooker as to what happens to feckless and money-squandering seamen when they come ashore at the end of a voyage.

The Bosun's Locker Stan Hugill

Maggie May

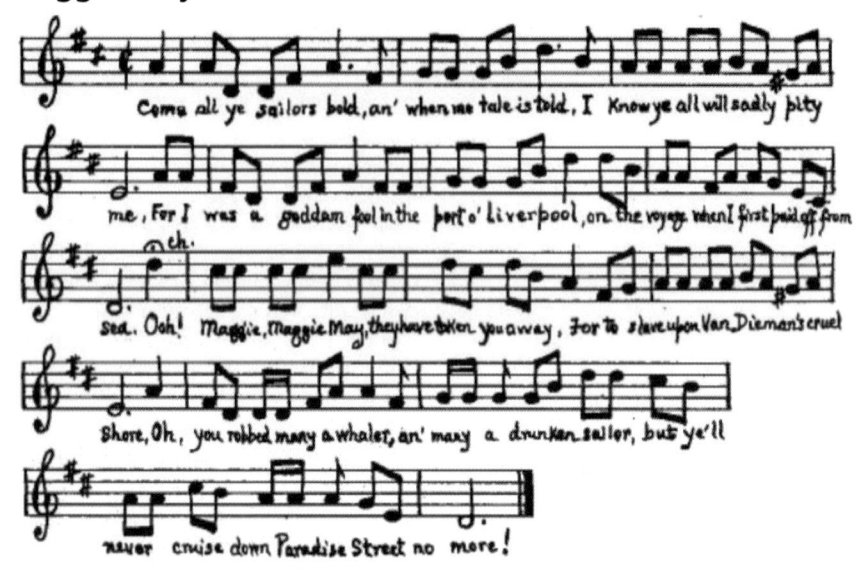

Come all ye sailors bold, an' when me tale is told, I know ye all will sadly pity me, For I was a goddam fool in the port o' Liverpool, on the voyage when I first paid off from sea. Ooh! Maggie, Maggie May, they have taken you away, For to slave upon Van Dieman's cruel shore, Oh, you robbed many a whaler, an' many a drunken sailor, but ye'll never cruise down Paradise Street no more!

I paid off at the Home, after a voyage from Sierra Leone,
Two pound ten a month it was my pay;
As I jingled in my tin, I was sadly taken in,
By a lady of the name of Maggie May.
Oh, Maggie, Maggie May etc.

When I ran into her I hadn't got a care,
I was cruisin' up and down ol' Canning Place;
She was dressed in a gown so fine, like a frigate of the line,
An' I being a sailorman gave chase.

She gave me a saucy nod, and I like a farmer's clod,
Let her take me line abreast in tow;
And under all plain sail, we ran before the gale,
And to the Crow's Nest tavern we did go.

When I got full of beer, to her lodgings we did steer,
She charged me fifteen shillings- for the fight:
I was so ruddy drunk when I landed in her bunk

I never knew what happened in the night.
Next mornin' when I woke, I found that I wuz broke,
I hadn't got a penny to me name;
So I had to pop me suit, me John Ls an_ me boots,
Down i' the pawn shop, Number Nine. Park Lane.

Oh, you robbin' Maggie May, you robbed me of my pay,
When I slept wid you last night ashore;
Guilty the jury found her for the robbin' of a homeward bounder,
An' she'll never cruise down Park Lane any more.

She wuz chained an' sent away, from Liverpool one day,
The lads they cheered as she rolled down the Bay;
And every sailor lad he only was too glad,
They'd sent the ol' whore out to Botany Bay.

176

Vol. 7 No. 3
Shipboard music and dancing

In our previous articles we have discussed all angles of sailor singing, but what of his accompaniments, if any? of his music? of his dances and so on?

Well, in the nautical journals and log-books which I have perused, the paucity of any reference to such items is markedly noticeable. Taking musical instruments first, the earliest, I suppose, was the drum. Aboard the Greek triremes the drum kept the beat by which freemen pulled the oars. Aboard the Roman galleys and the Xebecs of the Sallee Rovers it likewise measured the in-and-out of the prisoners-of-war and slave rowers who manned such vessels. The Viking oarsmen, free men all, did not use this percussion instrument as far as we know. The conch shell was more likely to have been their favourite, and some historians seem to think that aboard many Greek and Roman galleys the flute or whistle was used in preference to the drum.

Down through the years the drum beat the crews of great carracks, galleons, galleasses and wooden walls to quarters when a sea fight was anticipated;

> The drums they beat to quarters and cannons did loudly roar.
> Strike up ye lusty gallants with musick and sound of drum,
> For we have descryed a Rover upon the sea has come.
> (*Captain Ward and the 'Rainbow'*)

It played the *Rogue's March* when some poor devil was flogged through the Fleet during the hectic years of the eighteenth century.

In some ships, in particular, the great East Indiamen, the Chinese gong often replaced the drum, and was used both for duty and pleasure. In some ships it replaced the bell – the writer having struck one for hours on end, in a heavy fog, on the poop of a Blue Funnel ship, while on the foc's'lehead the bell rang in dismal answer. Pilots and fishermen on the British coasts for many years favoured the conch shell for signalling in fog, and the latter even used a cow-horn.

In early days tambourines were in evidence at foc's'le dances. We all are familiar with the antics of little Pip and the tambourine, with which he accompanied his singing and dancing, in that marvellous whaling epic *'Moby Dick'*.

One of the most interesting of early writers on nautical matters is a 'man of the cloth' called Teonge. He made a voyage to the Mediterranean in 1675 aboard a ship called the *'Bristol'*. He writes in his *'Diary'*: 'When the ship left the Downs our trumpets sound *'Maids, where are your hearts'*, which must have filled the hearts of the poor matlows with nostalgia. The harp, too, was a shipboard instrument in the seventeenth century. Pepys, in his *'Journal'*, written during a passage to Tangiers in 1683, remarks 'Saw the seamen dance to the harp and sing.'

In early days Admirals carried their own personal band, which they sometimes 'loaned' to the lower deck, and some of the Grand Captains of the East Indiamen also carried such luxury. In later years the Marines took over this job of being the ship's band. Actually, up to World War One, 14 Marines mainly manned gangways and played in the band. Such unsailor-like duties earned them the opprobrium of being 'Neither flesh, nor fowl, nor good red herring'. When the anchor was being hove such a band, on a foreign station, would play *Rolling Home* or some such suitable tune. In earlier days, however, the drum, fife and fiddle were the only instruments used at the capstan-head.

Fifes were always a favourite in naval vessels. The Marine Society, which is still with us, in the days of the Wooden Walls, would take into its bosom orphan and destitute children of seamen from off the streets of London and elsewhere and turn them into 'fifers' for naval use. In *'Landsman Hay'*, edited by M.D. Hay, there is a. reference to H.M.S. *'Culloden'* sailing for the West Indies in 1804. The men are at the capstan heaving the anchor and the fifer starts up a dismal tune, which the officer in charge considers too slow. He demands the fifer to strike up something more lively like *Off She Goes* or *Drops of Brandy*. The fiddle, too, about this period, was a popular instrument at the ritual of anchor-heaving aboard naval vessels. The acorn ornament at the centre of the drumhead or top of the capstan would be removed and the fiddler ensconced thereon would strike up a lively dance tune to help the men in their arduous task. He may have got a little light-headed in the merry old roundabout that ensued, but he'd still keep fiddling. I think I have pointed out elsewhere that the ship's fiddler was entered aboard as a member of the sick bay, being a sort of anti-scorbutic to prevent scurvy in the days when they believed, falsely, that movement such as dancing kept the red corpuscles romping through one's veins, thereby preventing scurvy.

But, in the seventeenth century, the hornpipe was the instrument that accompanied shipboard dancing, the dance called the Hornpipe taking its name from this instrument. This pipe was, originally, an old Welsh instrument, made of wood with holes in it, and a ram's horn at each end, one to collect the wind blown into it, the other to carry off the sounds as modulated by the performer. A different instrument again, the shipboard pipe or bosun's call, according to Commander Beckett, is first mentioned in print in 1248, in a Crusader's log, when reference is made to Crossbowmen being piped to come on deck and engage the enemy. Both Shakespeare and Samuel Pepys mention this pipe in their plays and diaries. The 'side was piped' for royalty, commanding officers and so on, and the corpse of a naval officer was 'piped over the side'. Its call is still used aboard ship but many of the different tunes once played to 'call men to the capstan, tail on the topsail halyards or the jeers, to haul on boats, falls or hawsers', are no longer in use. In the seventeenth and eighteenth centuries, however, no pipe was allowed to sound after sunset. Pirates infested the seven seas so that after dark silence was the rule, and all lights were extinguished.

Aboard nearly every merchant ship in the days of sail a 'fufu' band would be found. This usually consisted of a mouth organ, melodeon, jew's harp and fiddle. A drum would sometimes be added if the 'doc' or cook could be bribed to produce a pig's bladder, which would be stretched over a small cask or a metal paint drum. Sometimes a piece of soaked sailcloth stretched over a flour barrel would be incorporated, and even the skin of an albatross would be used for the drumhead. I have seen men in the West Indian trade make quite respectable fiddles from Havana cigar boxes. If a coloured West Indian was one of the crowd then a banjo would be in evidence, but guitars, in my opinion, never made the fo'c'sle until the days of steam. In many ships the concertina would be heard as well as the humble penny whistle. Tissue-paper and comb, naturally, were employed in these fo'c'sle 'banyans'.

On the old East Indiamen passengers had to carry all their furniture, even a cot, with them *en passage* to India. It is recorded that a 'pianoforte' was often included in the paraphernalia of such passengers, and 'musical instruments for ladies' can be seen listed in the passenger baggage forms of these old East Indiamen. The calling of passengers to dinner by bugle is a long established custom at sea, and the tune the bugler plays, *The Roast Beef of Old England*, is one of great antiquity.

I have already mentioned the Hornpipe as an instrument. As a dance it was the one *par excellence* indulged in by the Jolly Tars. However the present gentle form executed by groups of village school children has little connection with the rough and tumble steps of the shipboard hornpipe of the seventeenth century, say. It was one of the oldest dances performed by barefooted matlows, but it wasn't the only terpsichorean antic performed by them. Around the sixteenth and seventeenth centuries a wild Moorish dance, probably learnt by British seamen who had been slaves in the *souks* and galleys of the Barbary Coast, called the Saraband was immensely popular on shipboard. A milder form of it was also danced ashore by ladies and gentlemen in ballrooms, but the sailors' form had all the abandonment of the gyrations of a howling Dervish. Perhaps danced *more* often ashore in Sailortown than at sea was a step called Jack's Alive. It was a great favourite down the Ratcliffe Highway. Nowadays the word 'shindy' means a bit of a row, but long ago sailors used to perform a rowdy dance in the dogwatch with this name. Apparently the word comes from *Sheen,* meaning 'clamour' in Old Erse. Which brings us to Irish and Scottish sailors. Like Scandinavian and German seafarers who were famous for performing their native dances aboard ship, the Celts, too, would trip a nifty jig or reel on the fo'c's'lehead on a warm tropic evening in the trades. I remember once a bunch of Irish seamen performing jigs on the deck to an appreciative audience of Portuguese peasants bound out to Brazil, the latter following this exhibition by a charming performance of Jotas of their native land.

And aboard the Scottish whalers out of Dundee, Peterhead, Arbroath and so on, many an anchor was hove up and many a tops'l set to the wailing skirl of shipboard bagpipes.

Trying to find some shanty, or sea-song referring to musical instruments to go with this article I searched and sook (past tense of seek!) but with no success. And then I found this: *The Ol' Moke Pickin' On the Banjo*. It is obviously of mixed Negro-Irish origin and it is one of the many railroad work songs that grew up in Young America and was taken over by seamen to use as a capstan shanty. Sharp gives a version and he thinks it, like many another shanty, is a variant of the Irish folk song *Shule Agra*. Try it in the clubs!

The Bosun's Locker Stan Hugill

Old Moke Pickin' on a Banjo

He-bang, she-bang, daddy shot a bear, Shot it in the stern m'boys an' niver turn'd a hair
We're all from the railroad, too-rer-loo, An' the ol' moke pickin' on the banjo. Hooraw!
What th' hell's th' row? We're all from th' railroad, too-rer-loo, We're all from th' railroad,
too-rer-loo, Oh, th' ol' moke pickin' on the banjo!

Paddy get back, take in yer "slack, heave away, me boys,
Heave away, me bully boys, why don't ye make some noise?

Chorus
We're all from the railroad, too-rer-loo,
An' th' Ol' Moke's pickin' on the banjo:

Full Chorus
Hooraw! What the hell's the row?
We're all from the railroad - too-rer-loo,
We're all from the railroad - too-rer-loo,
Oh: The Ol' Moke's pickin' on the banjo:

Roll her, boys, bowl her, boys, give 'er flamin' gip,
Heave the bloomin' anchor up, an' let the barstard rip.

Rock-a-block, chock-a-block, heave the caps'n round,
Fish the flamin' anchor up, for we are outward bound.

Whisky-O: Johnny-O: the anchor is in sight,
It's a hell-ov-a-way to the gals that wait, an' th' Ol' Nantucket Light.

Vol. 7 No. 4

Fisticuffs, I suppose, have always dominated fo'c'sle life. Listening to the yarns of old-timers, or delving into literary reminiscences of old mariners, produces many references to fights – and to the 'cock-o'-the-fo'c'sle'. In the narrow, enclosed world of sailor life, shut off for months, and in times further back, for years, from shore and womanly influences, the law of the jungle manifested itself daily. The strongest man ruled the roost, and was cock on his own dunghill. At certain periods of the sailing ship's history, this tough fisticuff attitude to life dominated the poop as well as the fo'c'sle. We all know about the bucko mate …

> He's a man that's shipped for fighting, cos his fists is ironbound;
> And generally speaking you'd find his wind is sound;
> He's a dandy with a sling-shot, and you'd have to travel far,
> Before you'd find his equal with a heavy capstan bar.
> (C. Fox-Smith)

… who ruled the quarterdecks of Yankee blood-boats in the forties, fifties and sixties of the nineteenth century. We have heard or read, of 'belayin'-pin soup' and 'handspike hash' as being the main dishes of such fliers. However, perhaps these clipper-ship seamen were not as tough as their predecessors, the Irish Packet Rats of the Western Ocean packet ships.

These ships, the forerunners of the modern Atlantic liners, ran to schedule, the first ships in the world to do so. To keep monthly dates meant speed, and speed meant the carrying of sail, and the carrying of sail meant a tough afterguard. It naturally follows, of course, that the fo'c'sle hands had to be equally tough. Mainly Irish seamen from County this or that, or New York or Liverpool Paddies, they were famous for their aggressive nature as their descendents still are. Since the masters and mates were such a hardcase gang, the men, although excellent seamen, were naturally turbulent and soon formed themselves into tight communities of mariners determined to break these Lords of the Poop. One of the most notorious of these groups was known as the 'Bloody Forty'. These forty seamen had one adamant decision – to break the 'belayin'-pin' discipline of these iron-willed bullies who lorded over them. They would ship as a gang, but when signing on before the shipping master they would deny any knowledge of each other. Once at sea they would proceed to shave the whiskers of the afterguard, and it is true that mates and masters alike dreaded them, since, in many cases, they did tame such brutes. However, the Bloody Forty once shipped with the redoubtable Captain Samuels of the Blood-boat of the Atlantic – the *'Dreadnought'* – who, in turn, flattened a mutiny they attempted, and turned them ashore in New York, a completely tamed and repentant lot.

According to Basil Lubbock, who, in his *'Western Ocean Packets'* describes in detail the happenings aboard such ships, there existed an unwritten rule known as the 'Western Ocean Packet Law'. Before I describe this law, let me say that mates in many windjammers knew nothing of navigation, and weren't expected to; the Old Man was the only navigator.

The Bosun's Locker Stan Hugill

Bold MacCarteney (or The City of Baltimore)

[Musical notation with lyrics:]
Come all ye bold seafarin' men, an' listen to me tale, Concernin' bold MacCarteney in Liverpool town did dwell; Down by the Salthouse Docks one day, as he did chance for to stray, On board a West-bound packet ship, he stowed himself a-way.

As down the Mersey we set sail, to New York we wuz bound,
This poor young lad began to think of his friends he'd left behind;
This poor young lad began to think of his friends and his native shore,
And he cursed the day he'd stowed away in the City of Baltimore.

When he came out of his hiding place the Mate to him did say,
What made you stow aboard this ship, come tell to me, I pray;
Among these wild Irish packet rats you'd have wished ye'd have stayed ashore,
An' ye'll curse the day you sailed away in the City of Baltimore.

'Twas early every mornin' the Mate he turned us to,
'Twas early every mornin he came to kick us through;
Where is that Irish stowaway? the Mate I heard him say,
I'm here, sez bold macCarteney, what do yer want of me?

Now the Mate he wuz a cowardly dog, for MacCarteney he did go,
An' wid an iron belayin'-pin he tried to lay him low;
But MacCarteney being a smart young chap as he often proven ashore,
He laid the Mate upon his back in the City of Baltimore.

The second mate and bosun came to the Mate's relief,
But wid an heavy capstan bar he made 'em both retreat,
His Irish blood wuz boilin' p.ow, an' then we heard him roar,
Oh, skin an' hair will fly this day on the City of Baltimore

I know I am an Irish lad, these words I won't deny,
But before I'll be cowed down by the likes O' you, I'll fight until I die;
If you'wil.l only give me fair play, like'I often been given ashore,
I'll fight any man that walks fore 'n' aft on the City of Baltimore.

The cap'n a Nova Scotiaman, MacDonnell wuz his name,
An' when he heard this fight, me boys, right for'ard then he came;
Sez he, me bold MacCarteney, you're a regular son-o-a-whore,
I'll make ye Bosun of my ship, the City of Baltimore.

The law went like this: If you fancied your chance you could take on the fo'c'sle bully, and, having laid him low and taken his place over the men, you could next proceed to have a go at the bosun. If he fell to your mighty left, then you automatically became the bosun. Perhaps you would be dissatisfied and want to set your sights higher. O.K. The next move would be to trim the whiskers of the 'blower' or second mate, usually an extremely tough guy. Of course, you need not stop here; why not have a bash at the chief mate? On laying this mighty figure low, you were now the Lord and Master of the Poop and Fo'c'sle, with the Captain only as your boss. You could go no further. However there is a recorded case of a shanghaier chap reaching the captain's position, mainly by means of Western Ocean Law. The true story is about a British Admiral, in charge of the Fleet at Esquimault, being shanghaied in 'Frisco on a Cape Horner, finishing up in New York as her master.

Morley Roberts, that wonderful writer of nautical yarns, took the true story and made an even more exciting yarn about the incident in two parts. The first part he called *'The Promotion of the Admiral'*, the second, *'The Settlement with Shanghai Smith'*. Both yarns are to be found in Roberts' book *'Salt of the Sea'*. The story runs thus: The Admiral, Sir Richard Dunn, fifteen years before the story opens, when he was captain of H.M.S. *'Warrior'*, had fallen foul of Shanghai Smith on the pier in Sandridge, out in Australia. The naval officer gives Smith the only licking he'd ever had before or since, and Smith lived only for the day of reckoning. The story opens with the Admiral visiting 'Frisco. Smith and his runner Bill, seizing their opportunity, sandbag 'Dicky Dunn' as the sailors called the Admiral, and, in retribution, dump him aboard a hell-ship called the *'California'*, which is about to sail. At sea Admiral 'Dicky' orders the master to put him ashore. Instead of agreeing to his preposterous demand, the hell-ship master,

Captain Blaker, orders him into the fo'c'sle. Here, 'Dicky soon tangles with the "cock" and knocks him out.' An old mariner then informs Dicky that Captain Blaker, who was once a Western Ocean packet ship seaman, allows the packet law aboard the *'California'*. The end sequence sees Dicky smash the mate to a pulp and take over his position on the poop.

Like many another isolated sailing shipmaster, Captain Blaker is a secret drinker; in fact he is a real alcoholic. Also, religious dementia is slowly developing within his rum-sodden mind.

In the middle of a rising gale he orders 'all halyards, who are aloft, down on deck' to listen to his ranting religious sermon. Admiral 'Dicky' goes into a huddle with the second mate. They decide the Old Man is not fit to sail the ship, so 'Dicky' takes command. The Admiral brings her into New York, where he is met by eager reporters, to whom he admits the fact that he does not know who shanghaied him. In the second part, back in 'Frisco, he does a little detective work, learning that it was Shanghai Smith who sent him for a ride round the Horn. With the aid of

The Bosun's Locker Stan Hugill

some of his matlows he proceeds forthwith to shanghai Smith himself on a hell-ship voyage aboard the blood-boat *'Harvester'*.

I advise every *'SPIN'* fan to try and get a copy of this little book of Morley Roberts', now unfortunately out of print, and read fully this engaging yarn of the shanghaiing of an Admiral.

I have given some space here to this Western Ocean Packet Law because the song we present in this issue of the *'Bosun's Locker'* is the only one, so far as I know, which has this law as its theme. This forebitter, *Bold MacCarteney* or *The City of Baltimore* is only given in print by Doerflinger. His version is just slightly different from mine, which I learnt many years ago from a Liverpool seaman Spike Sennit. Doerflinger has tried to find out whether the ship referred to was factual or not, and he has come to the conclusion that she was a sail-carrying steamer of the Inman Line of Liverpool. It is quite true that, as he writes, many of the Packet Rats joined these early steamers, but I am fairly certain that this song is a true sailing packet-ship forebitter, and, more than likely, the name of the ship is purely the figment of some Irish matlow's imagination, some mariner who probably 'made the song up from out of his head' while sitting on the edge of his bunk, or at the wheel, or on the look-out during a Western Ocean passage. Of course it is too late now to get to the truth.

Nevertheless, it is a good song with the true hallmark of a real deepwater forebitter.

For some years now I have corresponded with a member of the Dutch Cape Horn Society, and I must say I have profited greatly in consequence. Recently he sent me the copy of a story by one of the members of the club, a certain Captain Oranje, as to how the 'fish' version of *A Long Time Ago* originated. The claim made in the yarn, that Paddy was the originator of these couplets, is incorrect as most folk enthusiasts will know. Nevertheless, it does show the method by which many folk songs have come into being. I have left the translation more or less as I received it; to make it into 'good English' would, I feel, spoil the flavour. Here is the yarn:

'The Origin of a Sea-Shanty'
From the diary of C.L. Oranje

The *'Beeswing'* had been a good living ship up till now, but it became lower when we arrived at Valparaiso on the shore of Chile after about eight months. The reasons why we were degraded from a good living ship to a 'starvation barque' (a term of the second mate) were: low freight, expensive provisions not fit to eat, decline of equipage, etc.

More and more the grub grew less. We were six months at anchor at the port of Caleta Colosa, which had just opened (on departure we were amidships fettered on our own refuse-heap). *

(This means refuse thrown overboard for six months had formed a mound under the ship. S.H.)

Then we got orders to peddle back to Australia, in ballast, Sydney Heads for orders. There was a dilemma. We only had a skeleton crew. And provisions? These were sorrowful too. Replenishment had not been possible according to the opinion of the shore skipper.

But our Captain, a real limejuice master a long time ago, had foreseen this. Already for some weeks he had all the people catching herring which were swimming in the Bay, and later he had them salted in the already salt-beef barrels. As was evident later on, this fish was to replace the salt horse and salt pork. The second mate considered it a wretched substitute.

The captain also had a solution for the crew. A few days before departure we sailed up to Antofagasta, which is situated six miles higher up the coast, in the ship's boat, and from that place we took away some dagos and beachcombers via a Danish boarding master with which we filled up the equipage partly. (*Equipage means 'crew'. S.H.*)

Soon after departure we were regaled with the fish-dish. The cook did not know better than to put a quantity of the herring into a casserole and cook them. Everyone had a royal spoonful of this herring-pulp for breakfast. The spirit was not big. *(They weren't happy about it. S.H.)* But the menu was the same at dinner – some potatoes with skin and a quantity of herring. Supper was still plainer; tea and biscuits with or without herring-pulp – all washed down with the never-missing limejuice.

Soon, from high to low, there came a big dislike for these herring banquets. Everyone agreed it was food for swine!

The captain to keep down the rebellious atmosphere portended that we should call at Pitcairn for provisions. This happened on the 31st of December, 1905. We heaved to at Pitcairn from morning till evening, where we could play, to our heart's content, chinky for chinky *('changey for changey' S.H.)* with the frank inhabitants. Some pigs and a number of hens, which walked around on the ballast,

The Bosun's Locker Stan Hugill

together with fruit, and some baskets with citrons – to replenish the limejuice stock – were taken on board. We sailed unwearyingly westwards again, one and all satisfied.

After a fortnight the salt herring entered anew on the menu. With this grub the humour of the crew went down. Now it was Paddy, an Irishman who signed on at the West Coast, that saved the situation. Paddy had only one eye. He had a melancholy impression when you looked at his face where the eye was missing and only a fissure was remaining. From the other side the vitality and humour shined from his face. Well then, it was Paddy, who already was looking for the beer-cellars of Australia, who pulled everybody out of bad humour, when, hoisting the topgallant sails after a squall on good day, introduced the next song. From this time it was known as the *Herring Shanty*.

Paddy: Of all the fishes in the sea
All hands: Away - ay - ay - oh,
Paddy: O, herring is the king for me!
All hands: A long time ago!

> I once was wind bound in Milford Bay!
> Away - ay - ay - oh,
> We had herrings for breakfast and dinner and tea,
> A long time ago!.
>
> So what did we do with the herring's head?
> We made it into loafs of bread.
>
> So what did we do with the herring's tail?
> We made it into pints of ale
>
> So what did we do with the herring's back?
> We made it a lad and we called him Jack.
>
> And what did we do with the herring's belly?
> We made it a lass and we called her Nelly.
>
> Of all the fishes in the sea,
> Oh, herring is the king for me!

Belay that:

We sang that song with every hoisting occasion. The cook came out of his caboose and so did the steward – the captain's brother. Only the Old Man was sitting on the poop with an acid face. I think this was because of his dignity he could not sing. He too must have groaned with herrings for breakfast and dinner and tea: too bad!

On the 9th of February we arrived in front of the coast of Australia. Our orders were: Newcastle, N.S.W. and coals for Coquimbo. When the tug was fastened and we passed the Nobbies the remainder of the bloody stuff was thrown overboard, and Paddy, till the end the pacesetter, changed his shanty to as follows:

Of all the fishes in the sea!
No more bloody herring for me!

The tug brought us under the coal tip immediately. We took 200 ton of stiffening, and then unloaded the ballast up river, in the bush. This we had to do by ourselves. The Captain came and promised everybody two bottles of ale if the ballast was unloaded by Saturday night. And that happened, of course and we took our turn under the tip. Saturday afternoon, I had to help serving out the beer in the cabin. All the seamen passed through – Peter, Scotty, Louis, Pedro, Taft, and of course Paddy. Paddy received his two bottles of ale and kept them in his breast. He was standing before the Old Man, one eye crying, even a tear, the other gaily laughing. He said: "Captain, you are a gentleman. I hope you have a long life."

That was the last time I saw Paddy. Monday morning, during shifting, he wasn't there. Perhaps he was in the hands of another land shark. On shore Paddy would not have been enjoyable. On board he was, as the second mate said, "a real white man".

I feel this story forcibly shows what is known as the folk process. And now I will give you the commoner version of *A Long Time Ago*.

Vol. 8 No. 1

Blood Red Roses

This edition of *'SPIN'* published a repeat of Vol.1, No. 4 with the addition of the following song:

Our boots and clothes is all in pawn
Go down you blood red roses, Go down.

Its mighty draughty round Cape Horn
Go down you blood red roses, Go down.

Oh you pinks and posies,
Go down you blood red roses, Go down.

Oh, myoid mother she wrote to me,
Go down you blood red roses, Go down.

My dearest son, come home from sea,
Go down you blood red roses, Go down.

But round Old Shipp we all must go,
Go down you blood red roses, Go down.

For that is where the whalefish blow,
Go down you blood red roses, Go down.

It's growl you may but go you must,
Go down you blood red roses, Go down.

If you growl too much your head they'll bust,
Go down you blood red roses, Go down.

Just one more pull and that'll do,
Go down you blood red roses, Go down.

For we're the boys to kick her through,
Go down you blood red roses, Go down.

The Limejuice Act

Among British seamen salt meat and the inevitable sea biscuit were the main staff of life which kept them going. Aboard Scandinavian ships stockfish of various kinds was the chief daily diet, whilst Latins went in for fish and varieties of macaroni or spaghetti.

The 'Law of Oleron', which I think I've referred to in earlier *'SPIN'*s, was the savage code which governed the mariner life while at sea – a system which was common to both Northern and Mediterranean seamen. Both the type of food and the laws, however, were interpreted by each master in his own way, the result being some seamen had good food and fair treatment whilst others were virtually starved and punished savagely for minor delinquencies.

So, by the early nineteenth century, following hard on the heels of the Industrial Revolution, and with a state of peace for the first time for years between us and the French, and our American colonists, and of course, the Dutch, Spaniards and Portuguese, with whom we had been at loggerheads for generations, there grew a rather more humane interest in the treatment of the sailor in general.

The Navy was probably the first service in adopting this new attitude towards the men

The Bosun's Locker Stan Hugill

of the lower deck. But, by the 1840s merchant seamen, too, began to receive, in general, a little more humane treatment. Some readers, those who are familiar with the raw forebitters of this period and the yarns prevalent of the Yankee blood-boats, packet ships and whalers, may think this statement to be somewhat untrue. However, if the conditions under which the mariners of the seventeenth and eighteenth centuries existed were to be studied by the readers they would have to agree that there was a vast gulf between the tough treatment of the nineteenth century seaman and the really vile and inhuman acts awarded to hapless mariners of these earlier centuries.

However, along with various social movements ashore, which around this time were beginning to sprout up as small organisations for the betterment of the lot of the low caste and ill-treated working man, nautical bodies got together and formed in 1845, for more or less the first time, (in the fifteenth century some codes for the treatment of the sailor and regulations relating to his food *did* exist) a code governing food, punishment, etc. for the merchant seaman under the title of *The Merchant Shipping. Act*.

It was enlarged and revised in 1894, and again in 1906, the year in which I was born. And, in my time, this ochre-coloured list of regulations commonly referred to as *The Articles* was hung on the bulkhead of every British ship, for one to gaze on while eating one's salt beef and Liverpool pantiles. From time to time white slips of paper (alterations, additions or revisions) were stuck to this 'vellum sheet', usually stuck on with 'connyonny' i. e. condensed milk.

This *Merchant Shipping Act* was the main bone of contention in the seaman's strike of recent years, and, although I'm not conversant with its present position, I feel sure that the Articles are still displayed with more revisions and so on, on the bulkheads of modern British supertankers.

Let us take a looksee at a couple of its archaic paragraphs – *ad verbatim*:

> When potatoes are not so issued, an equal amount of yams, or vegetables preserved in tins, or equivalent amount of dried or compressed vegetables in the proportion of 1lb. to 6 1bs. of fresh potatoes, must be issued in their place.
>
> Taking on board and keeping possession of any fire-arms, knuckledusters, loaded cane, slug shot, sword stick, bowie knife, dagger or any other offensive instrument without the concurrence of the Master, for every day during which a seaman retains such weapon or instrument... 5s.0d. fine.

Very appropriate for the old Packet Rat but hardly relevant to modern times.

According to this Act, in the early 1900s, a week's allowance of food, per man, ran somewhat like this:

> 16 ozs. of sugar, less 2 ozs. for the sweetening of the limejuice,
> with molasses issued in lieu of 5 ozs. of margarine (later changed to butter).
> 11 ozs. of marmalade.
> Salt pork one day, salt beef the next, with salt-fish on Fridays.

Sunday was a 'banyan day'. Rice and molasses was a Sunday treat, and a Harricot Lane or tinned meat (so called from a girl murdered in 1874 in Whitechapel, London) made into a sea pie, plus 'duff', was the menu on Sunday as well. Tea and coffee were the main drinks. This 'whacking out of the grub' was known as one's 'pound 'n pint' and was strictly adhered to in most ships, although some skippers allowed what was known as 'plenty without waste'. When a British ship, towards the end of a voyage, reached an order port in the British Isles,

The Bosun's Locker Stan Hugill

fresh food – vegetables and so on – would be allowed from shore for a few days. But after several days it was usual to return to 'sea grub'.

Fresh water, of course, was scarce aboard windbags, and 'According to the Act' each man was allotted four quarts of fresh water per day – two quarts going to the galley, the remainder being used for drinking and washing clothes and the body.

The *Merchant Shipping Act* of 1894 introduced the anti-scurvy clause, which ordered that limejuice must be issued to each seaman after ten days at sea. This caused the Yanks who had no such ruling to dub British seamen 'Limeys'.

The Act became known as 'The Limejuice Act' throughout the seafaring world. Sailors, always quick on the draw, soon turned out a forebitter both singing of, and poking fun at this Act. They called the song *The Limejuice Ship* or *According to the Act*.

The Limejuice Ship or According to the Act

Now, if ye want a merchant ship to sail the seas at large, Ye'll not have any trouble if ye have a good discharge, Signed by the Board o' Trade an' everything except. For there's nothing done in a Limejuice Ship contrary to the Act – So haul, boys, yer weather mainbrace an' ease away yer lee – Hoist jibs 'n' tops'ls, 'lade an' let the ship go free – Hurrah, boys, hurrah! We'll sing this Jubilee – Damn 'n' bugger the Navy, boys, A merchant ship for me!

(b) an alternative way of singing this chorus is:

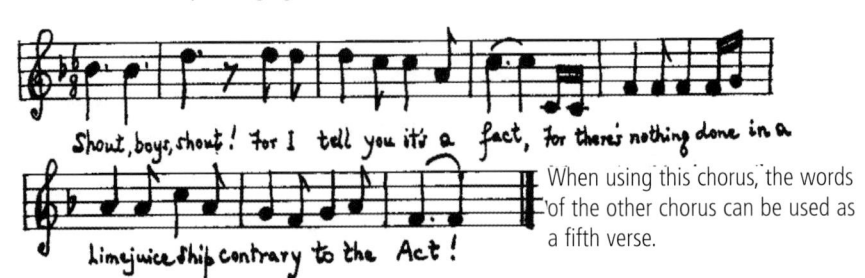

Shout, boys, shout! For I tell you it's a fact, For there's nothing done in a Limejuice Ship contrary to the Act!

When using this chorus, the words of the other chorus can be used as a fifth verse.

The Bosun's Locker — Stan Hugill

The first thing that they do to you,
You hear your Articles read;
They tell ye of yer beef and port, yer butter and yer bread;
Yer sugar, tea, and coffee, boys, yer peas and beans exact,
Yer limejuice and vinegar, boys,
According to the Act.

Chorus:
Soo! haul boys yer weather main brace, an' ease away yer lee,
Hoist jibs an' tops 'ls, lads, an' let the ship go free,
Hurrah boys, hurrah, we'll sing this JubHee,
Damn and bugger the Navy, boys, a merchant ship for me.

Oh, watch an' watch th_ first day out's
Contrary to the Act
Ten days out we all lay aft, to get our limejuice whack,
Fetch out yer handy billy, boys, an' clap it on the tack,
For we're going to set that mains'l, oh,
According to the Act.

It's up the deck, me bully boys,
With many a curse we go;
Waiting to hear eight bells struck, that we may go below,
The watch is called, eight bells is struck, the log is hove exact,
Relieve the wheel an' go below,
According to the Act.

The Bosun's Locker Stan Hugill
Vol. 8 No. 3

Seeing that nowadays I have become more or less, an armchair collector (who hasn't!). The days when I garnered orally from shipmates the inimitable songs of the sea have long since departed, with my instructors either beneath the turf or beneath the salt sea. I, along with hundreds of other folk singers, have had to dip into the pages of other people's works. Not that this demerits the results in any way; collectors have been doing this – although they would not like their chelas to discover this – for many, many years; in fact, I feel right in saying that probably the only song to come down in a perfect, unbroken line to almost the present day, handed down orally, is the sailor shanty. In almost every other form of folk song the tradition has been broken and revived artificially. Perhaps in parts of Ireland, in Northumberland and in the western part of Scotland and other out-of-the-way places the oral tradition has survived, but nowhere, I feel certain has it had such an unbroken, full-blooded continuance as at sea.

Having then to search through literature I am always awake to the possibilities of finding some titbit I have not come across previously in *all* and *every* type of literature and in all European languages. I have picked up an unusual verse or rare chorus in a children's book, in a stuffy Victorian romance and in an unexciting MS of Edwardian politics.

Of course the curse of copyright always rears its ugly head when a chap contemplates any comparative study of folk song. You find a 'new' version of an old song in someone else's work and you must either defy the existing law and copy and be damned, or pay the publisher his blood money for reproduction, or else ruin your genealogical treatise on the song in question. All of which makes the life of a fervent collector doubly hard.

Some years ago, having a couple of free days in 'No Mean City' – Glasgow – I descended on the Mitchell Library and was kindly allowed to wade through the Moir Collection of Victorian and Edwardian ballads, 'parlour songs'. It contained music-hall ditties, and folk songs. Much of this was sheet material, some true broadsheets, others just common-or-garden printed foolscap, some in dusty envelopes, some in binders marked Vol.1, 2, and so on, up to 10, or even more. The collection had every type of song imaginable within its scope; but I was only interested in weeding out sea-songs, real, pseudo or just plain phoney. The songs were without tunes and repetition common throughout the collection.

In Vol.1 I came across *Outward Bound* – 'To the Liverpool docks we'll bid adieu.' – and a Negro ditty *Sally Come Up* with the couplet:

She's clipper-built from toe to heel,
She's got a heart as stout as steel.

and a song called *The Clipper Yankee Girl*, neither of which were sea-songs.

A catalogue of W.S. Fortey's *'Ballads'* (Catnach Press, Est. 1813) contained *Paul Jones, Sailor's Will, The Mariner's Grave, The Poor Worn-out Sailor, Joan's Ale was New* (sailors had their version of this!), *Susan's Adventures in a Man-o'-war, The Bonnie Blue Jacket, I'm a Tough True-hearted Sailor, Pirates of the Isles, The Storm* (*Come Rude Boreas*), *Tom Bowling, Fair Phoebe and Her Dark-Eyed Sailor, Bold 'Princess Royal',*

Anchor's Weighed, *'Shannon' and 'Chesapeake'*, *Wappin' Old Stairs*, and *Jack Williams the Boatswain*.

Several more folios contained little of interest to me, then on sheet 5 I came across *High Germany*, *Ten Thousand Miles Away*, *Bold William Taylor*, *The Wonderful Crocodile*, *Young Edwin in the Lowlands Low*, *Ward the Pirate* and an interesting privateer song called *Paul Jones*:

An American frigate called *'Rachel'* by name,
Mounted guns forty-four, from New York she came ...

Other sheets produced: *The White Squall*, *The Banks of Claudy*, *Tarry Trousers*, *I'm a Tough, True-hearted Sailor*, *A Sailor and his Lass*, and a most comical ditty called *The Adventures of a Cork Leg amongst The Cannibals*.

Vol. 2 contained *The Rambling Sailor*, and *The Saucy Sailor Boy*. A song called *The Bonnie Blue Jacket* is described as being 'In Memory of 300 Young British Sailors, the crew of H.M. Training Ship *'Atlanta'* which is supposed to be Lost at Sea.'

Two songsters appear within this folder; *'The Naval Songster'* and *'The Nigger Songster'*, this latter having a Negro version of *A Long Time Ago*:

As I was going down Shinbone Al,
Long Time Ago,
To buy a bonnet for Miss Sally,
Long Time Ago.

On other sheets are: *Tobacco is an Indian Weed*, *Will Watch* (Printer, Harkness, Preston), *Lowlands of Holland*, *God Bless the Earl of Shaftesbury* (about the founder of the Ragged Schools, many of whose lads went to sea as fifers), and *Jimmy and Nancy of Yarmouth*, a long ballad in four parts, printed by Cadmon of Manchester.

Vol. 3 contains *Jack at the Opera* and *Little Mary the Sailor's Bride*. Other sheets offer *The Pilot*, *Heaving the Lead* and *Black-eyed Susan*, with many repetitions such as *The Pirate of the Isles* and *Fair Phoebe*. There was also a folder *'The Nigger Melodist'* containing songs with couplets much the same as those found in shantying.

In Vol. 4. there is a broadsheet called *The Harp without the Crown,* but it is not the shanty I sing, the chorus being:

So, Hurrah, boys, for Ireland, etc...

as well as versions of *Ben Block*, *The Female Captains*, *Sailor's Farewell*, *Dance' De Boatman* and *Larboard Watch*.

Vol. 5 has *The Tar's Farewell*, one I used to sing:

When forced to bid farewell to Loo,
Pull away, me boys, pull away
I did not know what I should do,
Pull away, pull away.

as well as *The Cruel Ship's Carpenter*, *Franklin Ballad* (printed by Such), *The Man at the Nore* and *The Midshipmate*.

The four volumes of *'The Poet's Box'* (80 London Street, Glasgow) were alphabetically listed and contained many repetitions of the songs already mentioned, and also a version of the *Bleacher Lass of Kelvinhaugh*. In a musty envelope I found a collection of English, Scottish and Irish ballads, among them *Jack and the Bearskin*, *Henry and Mary Anne* and an interesting song *The Spanish Snow* (a 'snow' being a type of brig) which starts:

'Twas on the fourteenth of November . . .

All the remaining volumes up to Vol. 10, which I examined, contained repeats in profusion, but before I leave off writing about this collection I must mention a song I found which I had forgotten down through the

The Bosun's Locker Stan Hugill

years – a song extremely popular years ago with sailors and fishermen of both England and America. My reminder was in Vol. 5 where it is called *The Grimsby Fisherman*. It starts off:

> I'm a rarem, tarem fisherman that sails from Grimsby town.

with a chorus:

> Then watch her, twig us, we're a popular juba jue,
> Give her sheet and let her rip, we're the boys to put her through!

Although I believe this ditty probably started life among the North Sea fishermen as the above, it certainly moved smartly across the Atlantic to the Great Lake schooner men. Miss Colcord in her *'Roll and Go'* gives us a version, calling it *The Cruise of the 'Bigler'*:

> Oh, watch her, and catch her, jump up on her Juba Ju,
> Oh, give her sheet and let her rip,
> We're the boys to put her through!
> You ought to've see her howling, when the wind was blowing free,
> On our passage down to Buffalo from Milwaukee!

The version of this nonsense ditty as sung deepwater, and of the one I know also by that fine nautical writer of the twenties, Bill Adams – is as follows:

> Oh, watch her, aye catch her, 'tis up the Juba Ju,
> We'll give her sheet and let her rip,
> We're the boys to put her through,
> You ought to have seen her howling,
> With her tops'ls blowin' free,
> On that passage round the Horn, me boys,
> To Old Shanghee.

That's all for this issue shipmates. Keep your weather eye lifting for 'new' and old ditties and cheerio!

Sacramento

O – around Cape Horn we are bound for to go, Timme hoodah, Timme hoodah! Around Cape Horn thro' the sleet an' the snow, Timme hoodah, hoodah day! Blow, boys – blow! For Californ- eye- O! There's plenty o' gold, so I've bin told, On the banks of the Sacta-men-to!

The Bosun's Locker Stan Hugill

I've given this capstan shanty an airing because I feel that it has been by-passed by folk singers. At sea it was one of the most popular of shanties. Perhaps the reason the Folk don't sing it is because it smells of Stephen Foster's *Camptown Races*. However, as I have already pointed out elsewhere, there is some doubt which came first, *Camptown Races* or the sailor shanty, since seamen were singing their shanty as early as 1849, and Foster didn't copyright his song until 1850 and didn't publish it until 1856. It is too late in the day, to settle this tantalising query, but the fact still remains it WAS a shanty, and a good one, too.

Oh, around Cape Horn in the month of May,
Chorus: Timme hoodah, timme hoodah
Oh, around Cape Horn is a bloody long way,
Chorus: Timme hoodah, hoodah day;

Full chorus:
Blow, boys, blow!
For Californi-O,
There's plenty of gold so I've bin told,
On the banks of the Sacramento

Oh, around Cape Horn wid a main skys'l set,
Around Cape Stiff an' er're all wringin' wet.

To the Sacramento we're bound away,
For there the gold's more bright than day.

Round Cape Horn an' up to the Line,
We're the buckos for to make 'er shine.

We're the buck os for to make 'er go,
All the way to the Sacramento.

Breast yer bars an' bend yer backs,
Heave, an' make yer spare ribs crack

Ninety days to Frisco Bay,
Ninety days for to make our pay!

The Bosun's Locker   Stan Hugill
Vol. 8 No. 4

When I started to write articles about nautical songs, ballads and shanties, under the heading of *'The Bosun's Locker'*, I made some sort of statement to the effect that I did not think I would be able to keep the series going for more than a few months owing to lack of material. However, after ten years or so, I am still pushing ink and, thanks mainly to the increasing growth of those whom I call my 'pen-pals', people who furnish me with songs and material they come across in odd corners and rare books, I am still receiving 'new' items. Of course, as is my bounden duty, I always present such material to the readers of *'SPIN'*, along with unusual bits and pieces I myself have collected in recent years. Taking the last sentence first, within the year that has gone, with my little eye, I have singled out two or three interesting items, as yet unmentioned in my books or previous *'SPIN'*s.

Reading through a rather rare book by Commander C.N. Robinson called *'The British Tar in Fact and Fiction'* (1909), I came across a reference to early shantying. He writes: 'Luiz de Camoens, in his *'Lusiades'*, originally published in 1572, tells us, in his description of Vasco de Gama's voyage to India, that it was the custom, when getting the ship under way, or making sail, for the mariners to sing songs and catches to lighten their work.'

This statement is rather important in the history of shantydom, since it is the consensus of opinion among shanty collectors that, from the year 1549 when a book called the *'Complaynte of Scotland'* was published (a book containing several ancient anchor and hauling songs used when a certain ship was getting under way in the Firth of Forth) until the early 19th century, it has been impossible to find any reference to sailors singing at work. There is perhaps one exception to this in print, a case I mentioned in an earlier *'SPIN'*, in which the crew of an American galley *'Mary'*, whilst working the ship out of Gloucester harbour in 1665, were working to the singing of the *British Grenadiers* although this song could hardly be called a *shanty*. There is also a reference in Morison, *'Admiral of the Ocean Sea'*, Vol. 1, p.229, to an early Spanish shanty (supposedly) from the days of Columbus.

In regard to the common belief that shanties were 'taboo' in the British Navy, Commander Robinson is of the opinion that they *were* sung in naval ships prior to 1815 when the 'silent system' became the rule in the Navy. This is something new to the writer. I agree that in small naval vessels, where discipline was more relaxed, some shanties – particularly 'stamp 'n' go' ones – were sung. On this matter Robinson quotes the evidence of a naval officer in the *'United Service Journal'* for January 1834, describing seamen's work aboard a revenue cruiser.

'On board a well-disciplined man-of-war no person except the officers is allowed to speak during the performance of the various evolutions. When a great many men are employed together, a fifer or a fiddler usually plays some of their favourite tunes; and it is quite delightful to see the glee with which Jack will 'stamp and go' keeping exact time to *Jack's the Lad* or *The College Hornpipe*. On board a revenue cruiser, for want of music, it is customary for one of the men to give them a song, which makes the crew unite their strength and pull together.'

He then gives a specimen of the shanty *Cheerily Man*.

Gascoigne, who commanded the Marines aboard the frigate *'Melpomene'* in 1805, when describing the manoeuvre of beating to windward, writes: 'Now with a song the bowlines well they haul.' This, however, was probably no more than a *sing-out,* as cited by Smyth in his *'Sailor's Word Book'* (1867): 'ONE, TWO, THREE! – The song with which the seamen bowse out the bowlines; the last haul being completed by "Belay O!"'
He also has another entry under 'SONG: The call of the soundings by the leadsman in the channels. Songs are also used to aid the men in keeping time when pulling on a rope, where a fife is not available. The whalers have an improvised song when cutting docks in the ice in Arctic seas.'
Robinson (p.347) endeavours to prove that 'forebitters and chanties were common in the 18th century in both mess rooms and forecastles of men-of-war and merchant ships,' a suggestion with which I don't agree, and he gives a verse of the naval ballad called *The Boatswain's Whistle* to 'prove' his point:

Hark the crew with sun-burnt faces
Chanting Black-eyed Susan's graces.

I mentioned on p.428 of *'Shanties from the Seven Seas'*, in reference to the Crimean War shanty *Sebastapol* the old tune called *Loth-to-depart*. Teonge, the famous naval chaplain writes in his *Journal*, that, when dropping down the Thames aboard the *'Assistance'* in 1675, with drunken tars and their women around the decks, the 'song *Loath-to-depart* was sung by the men.' Whether this was sung at the capstan or windlass is not recorded. Smyth also remarks in his *'Word Book'*, under the entry 'Yeo-Heave-Yeoing' that this is a 'chant or noise made at the windlass and

Fun Ashore in the Colonies

purchase falls in a merchantman, to cheer and lighten the labour, but not permitted in a man-of-war'. It has been suggested in some quarters that the 'Yo-ho' of a seaman was a derivative of the Hebrew word Jehovah, and goes back to the work chants of the Israelite slave labour when building the pyramids. This attempt, however, at going into the misty past in order to prove the origin and age of shantying is, I feel, labouring the point rather heavily.

Having studied the subject of shanties and forebitters for nearly a lifetime, I'm always pleased when I come across, in print, some new angle on an old theme.

Naturally, it's always been my belief that the shanty *A-rovin'* ('In Amsterdam there lived a maid') is based on a sailor's shore adventures in Holland. Recently, however, in an old copy of *'Shipping Wonders of the World'*, I came across a remark, which gave me cause to wonder. It said:
'The earliest shanty of which we have any definite record is *Amsterdam* or *I'll go no more a-rovin'*. This can be traced back to the first part of the 17th century, (I doubt this!) when the Dutch port of Amsterdam was closed to British seamen. There were, however, two well-known seamen's taverns named 'The Amsterdam', one on the riverfront at Gravesend and the other one in St.George's-in-the-East. That the words of the song refer to crimping and to the company which these taverns supported make it probable that this was one of the shanties that originated on the London River.'

Although it is usually stated in most shanty-books that sailors never sang these songs except at work, according to old sailors' journals, they were often sung in unusual places. It was commonplace apparently, in sailors' homes in the Colonies to hoist the fattest apprentice up to the roof to the accompaniment of a shanty as a sort of 'show-off' to the Australian ladies who laid on 'tea and tabnabs' for the men from the ships in port.

In Geraldton and other small ports it was the custom, also, to shanty up the curtain at the beginning of a theatrical performance.

Recently, a 'pen-acquaintance' of mine, the nautical researcher Dr John Lyman of America, sent me 'photostat' copies of some unusual shanty material he found in the Library of the University of North Carolina. Thanks to him, I have been able to present some 'new' shanties to *'SPIN'* readers. At this late date to come across anything new in the way of shanties is a miracle. The first specimen, without music, is a Negro shanty and comes from an article in the *'Journal of American Folklore'* called *'Sailors, Chanties'*, by Percy Adams Hutchison, dated 1906, the year of my birth.

Ol' Joe, bully ol' Joe,
Hi pretty yaller gal!
Kicking up behind, ol' Joe,
Ol' Joe's got some very fine clo's,
Whar he get 'em nobody knows
Hi pretty yaller gal,
Kicking up behind, ol' Joe!

In this article the writer gives a solo of *Poor Old Man* I have not seen previously.

As I was going to Rig-a-ma-row,
I say so and I hope so.

The geographical location of Rig-a-ma-row is beyond me. The author spent part of his time 'cruising on merchant sailing ships' so he is obviously a good source.

The second interesting photostat is that of the *'Atlantic Monthly'* of April 1892, and the article is called *'American Sea-songs'* by Alfred M. Williams. He gives the words of many sea-songs popular with American seamen years ago, also a few well-known shanties and he also refers to several French matlows' songs. His version of *Blow the Man Down* he calls a 'bowline chant' and it is the third example I have discovered (the other two being those of Briggs and of Cecil Sharp, which have often been doubted) of the *Knock a man down* refrain:

> I wish I was in Mobile Bay.
> Way-hay, knock a man down,
> A-rolling cotton, night and day
> This is the time to knock a man down.

Briggs in his book *'Around Cape Horn to Honolulu in the barque 'Amy Turner''* gives a similar version, which probably comes from the Southern States Hoosiers or cotton stowers.

The third photostat is also from the *'Journal of American Folklore'*, No.44 (1931) and this has the words and music of a slightly different version of the pumping song and my old favourite *Strike the Bell,* collected by May Folwell Hoisington and transcribed from her singing by Helen H. Roberts.

The fourth article is called *'Some Nineteenth Century Shanties'* by James Taft Hadfield which is in the *'Journal of American Folklore'*, No. 59 (1946) and this to me is the most interesting of all the four photostats. Hatfield in 1886 undertook an 84 days crossing of the Atlantic from Pensacola to Nice in the three-masted barque *'Ahkera'* of 548 tons. Her foremast hands consisted of eight strapping Jamaican Negroes, and when the shout came to "Sing up a scrap!" these chaps apparently had a right good repertoire. As well as the common shanties such as *Rio Grande*, *Blow the Man Down*, *Ranzo*, *Whiskey Johnny* and so on, they also sang unusual versions of *Johnny Come Down to Hilo* (*Johnny come along too ma high-low*) and *We're All Bound To Go*:

> Heave away John Brown,
> A-a-a-a-ay!
> Three pretty girls bound for Baltimore City
> Heave away my bonny boys, we're all bound to go!

Their *Fire Down Below*, too, is slightly different from the usual:

> Easy, easy John Brown,
> Too ma ha-a-a-ay, ho!
> Easy John Brown, why don't you come along?
> O, fire down below!

Ranzo, too has two stanzas unknown to me:

> O whiskey for the Irishman,
> And limejuice for the Englishman.
>
> And stockfish for the Norwegian
> And baked beans for the Yankees.

And I wonder if their *South Australia* is the key to a Shantydom mystery. The 'ruler king' has always mystified me. Theories put forward are:
(1) It is a mis-quote for 'rolling king' ('Roll' being Negro for 'work').
(2) 'Ruler king' is a corruption of 'Zulu king' (see p. 426 of *'Shanties from the Seven Seas'*).
    I rather feel, however, that the matter is clarified once and forever in the version these Jamaican 'boyos' sang:

> Hooray, you're a lanky!
> Heave away, haul away!
> Hooray, you're a lanky!
> I'm bound for South Australia!
> What makes you call me a ruler and king?
> Heave away! haul away
> 'Cause I'm married to an Indian queen,
> I'm bound for South Australia!

The third verse has:

> 'Cause I wear a diamond ring.

Professor Hatfield is long since deceased, but before he died his daughter took down the

The Bosun's Locker Stan Hugill

words and melodies of the shanties he heard on this passage. He had previously made a personal record of them, faithfully copying every note and word of his Negro tutors, and it is thanks to his retentive memory and the labour of love of his daughter who transcribed them that we have, amongst those already mentioned, three 'new' shanties. These are *Shiny-O, Nancy Rhee*, and *Way Down Low*.

Before we continue let me point out that Hatfield's version of *South Australia* is not only different in melody from the usual, but also has no 'grand chorus'. Neither has his *Rio Grande* nor *Johnny Come Down to Hilo* (called *Shake Her Up*) and since he writes: 'If the vessel. . . . leaked like a basket . . . it was almost continuous sessions at the pump; prevailing head-winds called for very frequent tacking; hauling the yards (as well as pumping) and was always done to the rhythm of these songs.' I am sure all of his shanties can be taken to be the very earliest forms of 'four-liners', without the latter-day 'grand chorus', which once, I believe, was the form of every shanty. There is an article by me in an earlier *'SPIN'* regarding these 'four-liners'. In fact he does not mention once that any were used at the capstan or windlass, hence the true form of the real hauling song of the sea; solo, refrain, solo, refrain.

For these 'new' shanties to have been unearthed in this year of our Lord 1972, shanties which would have lain embalmed in the halls of greater learning possibly for ever but for the eagle eye of Dr John Lyman, is to me a real milestone in the history of Shantydom.

Shiny-O

Captain, captain, you love your brandy. A-a-a-a-a-ay, shiny O!
Captain, captain, I love your daughter. A-a-a-ay. Shiny O!

O ferryman, ferryman, Won't you ferry me over?
Won't you ferry me from Queenstown across to Dover?

O from Queenstown to Dover's a hundred miles or over,
From Queenstown to Dover's a hundred miles or over.

Captain, captain, how deep is the water?
She measures one inch, six feet and a quarter.

The Hen and the Chickens were all flying over,
When she pitches, she pitches into Dover.

O captain, captain, what is the matter?
I lose my wife and my pretty little daughter.

O rivers, rivers, rivers are rolling,
Rivers are rolling, and I can't get over!

Nancy Rhee

Nancy Rhe - e, O Na-an-cy Rhe-e-e-e, My gallant Nancy Rhee! O, why don't you come a-long? My gallant Nancy Rhee!

Way Down Low

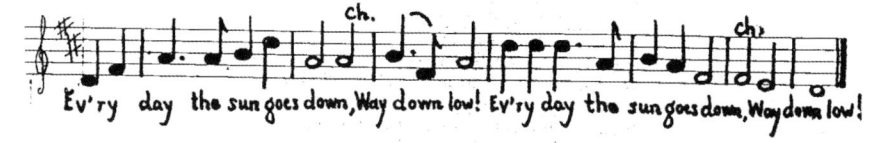

Ev'ry day the sun goes down, Way down low! Ev'ry day the sun goes down, Way down low!

The Bosun's Locker Stan Hugill
Vol. 9 No. 1

To say that my books have caused a mild furore in odd corners of the shanty world and have even altered the lives of one or two people, may sound somewhat of an exaggeration. But in actual fact this has already happened.

In past *'SPINS'* I have already referred to the fact that my statement that the Dutch had no shanties started a search by the Dutch section of the International Folk Society and the Dutch Cape Horn Society to disprove this, the result being that one or two unknown shanties were unearthed. Several other statements in my works have also caused other nationals to search more diligently for long-lost shanties – and this I think is great. However, one of my greatest triumphs, I feel, is that an ex-British coasting schooner man, who for twenty-five years or more, followed the occupation of selling Hoovers or such machines in the States, on reading my first book suddenly became fired with an enthusiasm to return to nautical surroundings, packed in his job, headed for the splendid, resuscitated whaling port of Mystic and got himself a job re-rigging the old New Bedford whaler *'Charles W. Morgan'*. I constantly receive mail from overseas telling me of instances like the foregoing and this thrills me no end.

At the recent Keele Folk Festival I was informed that the song *Fiddler's Green* with its tune reminiscent of *Wrap Me Up In My Tarpaulin Jacket* – was the outcome by the composer of his having read my *'Sailortown'*; he was so intrigued with the old-time yarns therein and, in particular, those of Fiddler's Green, that he went straight 'into seclusion' and produced this splendid little song.

This is all marvellous and shows that folk is something more than club nights, although the latter of course are also very important.

In the case of these 'modern' sea-songs such as *Fiddler's Green, Marco Polo* and several others, we must set the record straight and be careful that some future research worker does not include them in his opus in the same category as genuine sea-songs and shanties. The bare bones of many a good old sea-song or shanty, also, have been furnished with a tune by modern composers in a case where the original tune has been lost. This of course, I quite agree with. Songs are not made to lie undisturbed in the mouldering pages of old tomes. Drag them out into the light by all means! However, in most cases, the fact that such a song has been given a tune where one originally didn't exist, is not recorded on sleeves and so on, and this, to my way of thinking, is bad. One excellent old shanty (actually a 'chant'), which has been given this treatment, is the Young Tradition's *Fire Marengo*. I think the resultant song is excellent and probably very near to what the cotton Hoosiers sang, but, as far as

I can see, the fact that its tune is 'mod' has not been recorded. The words of the song as I stated in my *'Shanties From The Seven Seas'*, come from p.40 of Charles Nordhoff's book *'The Merchant Vessel – A Sailor Boy's Voyages'*, published in New York, in 1884.

And while I have a 'moan' on, let me continue with one more grievance. For years I have been rather annoyed that the rousing, and at sea ubiquitous, halyard shanty *Roll the Cotton Down* has been, apparently, pushed aside in favour of *The 'Alabama'*, which bears the same tune. I don't know of any disc bearing this shanty with the exception of a German one. I never really discovered how this mix-up occurred, but I believe it came about owing to Miss Colcord in her book *'Roll and Go'* writing of the shanty *The 'Alabama'*: 'From the days of the Civil War comes a beautiful and spirited version of *Roll the Cotton Down*.' Someone, somewhere, took this for granted, and without using her tune for the latter song, which now I am glad to say has been recorded by the Critics Group, and others, put the words of *The 'Alabama'* to the tune of *Roll the Cotton Down*, and established the result firmly in the clubs. Naturally *Roll the Cotton Down* suffered.

This latter song was originally a chant of the cotton Hoosiers of Mobile Bay, as was *Fire Maringo, Fire Away*.

Originally the job of screwing cotton into the holds of the cotton droghers in the ports of the Southern States was in the hands of Negroes. However, white seamen, particularly those of the Western Ocean packets began to desert their ships in New York, and by fair means or foul, travelled down to the Gulf Ports and offered their services as cotton 'Hoosiers'. In time there were even more whites than coloureds engaged in this tough job. In order to get the maximum amount of cotton bales down into the holds of these cotton carriers, great jack-screws were employed to force the bales, particularly the last ones, under the beams of the deck. The men would heave these screws around to chants very similar to the sailing shipman's shanty; in fact many of these chants became shanties, when the erstwhile white cotton Hoosiers returned to sea, taking with them the ditties they had learnt while screwing cotton. Nordhoff writes:

'The chants as may be supposed have more rhyme than reason in them. The tunes are generally plaintive and monotonous, as are most of the capstan tunes of sailors, but resounding over the still waters of the bay, they had a fine effect. There was one in which figured that mythical personage, 'Old Stormy', the rising and falling cadences of which, as they swept over the Bay, on the breeze, I was never tired of listening to.'

This Stormy chant was the one now popular in the clubs, often referred to as *General Taylor*. Another one, without a tune, he gives is:

Hurrah, Bee-man, Do
Oh, we work for a Yankee dollar,
Hurrah, see-man-do!

And he also gives *Bonnie Laddie, Highland Laddie*.

Of the cotton Hoosiers he writes: 'The men who yearly resort to Mobile Bay to screw cotton are, as may be imagined, a rough set: They are mostly English and Irish sailors, who, leaving their vessels here, remain until they have saved a hundred or two dollars, then ship for Liverpool, London, or whatever port may be their favourite, there to spree it all away, and return to work out another supply. Screwing cotton is, I think, fairly entitled to be called the most exhausting labour that is done on shipboard. Cooped up in the dark and confined in the hold of a vessel, the gangs tug from morning till night at the screws, the perspiration running off them like water, every muscle strained to its utmost. But the men who

The Bosun's Locker Stan Hugill

follow it prefer it to going to sea. They have better pay, better living, and, above all, are not liable to be called out at any minute in the night, to fight the storm, or, worse yet, to work the ship against a head wind. Their pay is two dollars per day, and their provisions furnished. They sleep upon the cotton bales in the hold, but few of them bringing beds aboard with them. Those we had on board drank more liquor and chewed more tobacco than any set of men I ever saw elsewhere, the severe labour seeming to require an additional stimulus. Although, I thought theirs a rough life, not at all to be envied them!' For this month's issue of *'SPIN'* I have decided to bring *Roll the Cotton Down* out of its obscurity. Have fun with it!

Roll the Cotton Down

Oh, away down south around Cape Horn,
Chorus: Roll the cotton down!
Oh, we wish to Christ that we'd never bin born
Chorus: We'll roll the cotton down!

We're bound away to Mobile Bay,
We're bound away at the break of da;y.

Oh, around Cape Stiff we're bound to go,
Round Cape Stiff through the ice and snow.

So stretch it aft and start a song,
A bloody fine song and it won't take long.

Oh, stretch yer backs and haul away:
And make yer port and take yer pay.

Oh, rock an' shake her is the cry,
The bloody topmast sheave is dry.

Oh, I wish Jack Salt would keep his luff,
The Squarehead thinks we've hauled enough.

Oh, sweat that yard the Mate do say.
Give one more pull, lads, then belay:

204

The Bosun's Locker Stan Hugill

Vol. 9 No. 2
Fresh finds in shanty research

Three issues ago I gave the sailor capstan song *Sacramento* or *Hoodah Day*, remarking on the fact that it would appear to be by-passed by shanty collectors and singers on the grounds that it was not a 'genuine' shanty; in fact it is usually considered to be, by those 'in the know', a pseudo-Negro ditty called *Camptown Races*, a piece composed by Stephen Foster, the famous musician and author of *Jannie with the Light Brown Hair* and so on.

The argument as to whether sailors devised it and Foster plagiarised it, or vice versa, is one, which I doubt at this late date can be proven one way or the other. I refer to the matter more lengthily in my first book on shanties. However, as to its popularity at sea, this cannot be gainsaid.

In their enthusiasm to disseminate rare 'finds', young folk singers (and older ones, too), always prefer, or so it would seem, to warble minor and uncommon variants of the run-o-the-mill shanties at the expense of the commoner ones. Now without wishing to disparage these enthusiastic young people in their efforts to offer something different (and the writer also, it must be pointed out, comes into this category), it must be emphasised that most of these unusual shanties were the property of Negro shantymen, and were rarely sung by white seamen – mainly because they were too difficult to sing. The seafaring types of Stepney, Wapping, Bootie, Butey Road and so on, were no Carusos! Also, many of such way-out shanties were the property of the timber and cotton-stowers and roustabouts of Quebec, Miramichi, Pensacola and Mobile, and, rarely, if ever, sung by the seafarers of Liverpool, the Tyne, the Bristol Channel ports, Limehouse and Rotherhithe.

The reason I'm adopting this attitude is the fact that many proper deep-sea shanties, once sung daily by British and American seamen, shanties such as *Shenandoah*, *Rolling Home*, *Paddy on the Railway*, *Rio Grande*, *Sacramento* and *Shallow Brown*, would appear to have been given the old heave-ho by club singers.

Whall in his earlier work took a similar, and yet, a reverse, attitude. He left out all shanties he considered to be of nigger minstrel or shore ancestry, although in later editions of his work, owing to public pressure, he did include what he called 'nigger shanties' and 'music-hall stuff', e.g. *Clear the Track Let the Bulgine Run*, *Whip Jamboree*, *Sacramento*, and *Paddy Works on the Railway*.

I now give a list of the hardy regulars sung at sea up to the latter days of sail:

Furling Sail: Paddy Doyle's Boots

Hauling Songs: Blow the Man Down, Tom's Gone to Hilo, Ranzo, Blow, Boys, Blow, Whiskey Johnny, Hanging Johnny, Haul Away Joe, Drunken Sailor, Johnny Bowker, Haul the Bowline

Heaving Songs: Ri*o Grande, Rolling Home, Blackball Line, Lowlands, Stormalong (the lay, ay, ay' version), Goodbye Fare-ye-well, A-rovin', Fire Down Below, Can't Ye Dance the Polka?, South Australia, Sally Brown, Leave Her Johnny, Hog-eye Man, Shallow Brown, Paddy on the Railway, We're all bound to go*

An average of 25 to 30 shanties would be known to each shantyman.

205

The Bosun's Locker Stan Hugill

On the other hand, although the latter-day shantyman limited his repertoire to the above shanties, he did not limit his text. New themes and different texts turned up in the mouths of different shantymen from ship to ship and port to port, and although I thought that even this angle was becoming a little threadbare, I can now report that, thanks to the work of my indefatigable researcher and correspondent Dr John Lyman, I have been the recipient of a collection of shanties (the common-or-garden ones) with texts, in most cases, such as I have never come across in all my extensive researches in both oral and literary fields.

This collection is dated San Francisco, Wednesday, June 23, 1909, and is found in the *'Coast Seamen's Journal, The Official Paper of the International Seamen's Union of America'*. As Dr Lyman points out, it's one that 'has escaped the attention of the bibliographers up to the present'.

This is a *'Journal of Seamen, by Seamen, for Seamen'*, and the collector, a sailing ship seaman, is Mr Fred H. Buryeson, who writes under the nom-de-plume of El Tuerto (Spanish for 'one-eyed').

It was through the good offices of friends in the San Francisco Maritime Museum that Dr Lyman obtained this interesting collection, a Xerox copy of which he kindly sent to me.

When I was putting together my series of Ratcliffe Highway songs and the following issue of similar sailor-chasing-girl songs in other ports beyond London, I remarked that I could find no more songs or shanties in this vein. Then an avid reader of the books of, and a personal friend of, James Joyce, wrote to me and asked me did I know a version of *Sacramento* in nautical *double entendre*, telling of a sailor chasing a flash packet through the purlieus of Sailortown. He said he had heard Joyce and some of his friends singing this bawdy song in a Dublin pub but he couldn't remember the words. I'm afraid I had to tell him that, although I did know a bawdy version to this shanty, the version he was referring to was unknown to me. However, now I do have it, or a slightly bowdlerised version of it, for it is one of the shanties in El Tuerto's collection. Here it is:

Blow for California

As I was a-walking one day up and down,
Chorus: To me hoodah. to me hoodah
I spied a gay damsel, she seemed outward bound
Chorus: To me hooday, hoodah day.

Blow, boys, blow for California etc. etc.

I fired my bow-chaser the signal she knew,
She backed her main topsail for me she hove to.

I hailed her in English, she answered me thus,
My name is Sally Gubbins, and I'm bound on a cruise.

Then I gave her my hawser and took her in tow,
And into an alehouse together we did go.

And drank ale and brandy till near break of day,
When I went a-rolling down home Tiger Bay.

She rifled my lockers while I filled my hold,
And aboard of my packet I had for to scull.

With a hookpot and pannikin I got under way,
Seven bells in the morning, the very next day.

And when I have finished a-singing my song,
I hope you'll excuse me if I have sung wrong.

She was a fine frigate you must understand,
But one of those cruisers who sail on dry land.

A regular old fire-ship rigged out in disguise,
To burn jolly sailors like me, damn her eyes.

Of course, these lines, slightly altered, have come from the Ratcliffe Highway fire-ship song *Rattle me Rigging*, and are much the same as the lyrics many shantymen fitted to the halyard song *Blow the Man Down*. In this collection, *Sally Brown* also has, to me, 'new' verses:

Sally wasn't tall or slender,
But her eyes were both blue and tender.

Sally's father kept a little tavern,
Just at the head of India basin.

Seven long years I courted Sally,
But Sally didn't want no coasting sailor.

And so I shipped on a China packet,
Just for to be a flying fish sailor.

Seven more years I did sail the seas, boys,
When, one day, I received a letter

Telling that Sally had married a tinker,
With nary a shilling – and seven small children.

So it's me for the life of a sailor,
And I'll spend no more money on Sally.

El Tuerto's *Santa Anna* has verses on the Mexican War not found elsewhere:

Santa Anna has gained the day,
From Vera Cruz to Manzanas Bay.

He marched his soldiers all over the land,
At Orizaba he took his stand.

He drove the gringos into the sea,
And hung the leader to a gallows tree.

I heard the skipper say yesterday,
We're going to Matamoros Bay.

So heave a pawl the wind is fair,
Likewise the donnas who live there.

After the incident in *A-rovin'* where the sailorman puts his arm around the waist of his new-found girlfriend, El Tuerto's version has, to me, this interesting stanza:

Then a great big Dutchman rammed my bow,
Chorus: Mark well what I do say
For a great big Dutchman rammed my bow,
And said, 'Young man, dis bin mein vrow.'
Chorus: I'll go no more a-roving, etc.

Followed by:

Then take a warning, boys, from me,
With other men's wives don't make too free.

For if you do you will surely rue,
Your act, and find my words come true.

His Stormalong has:

Stormalong was a good old man,
Chorus: Aye, aye, aye, Mister Stormalong
For he served his sailors grog by the can,
Chorus: To me 'way Stormalong
He gave us plenty of spud-hash, too,
And every Sunday we had black-ball stew.

With soups and bouilli and lots of duff,
Of soft-tack, also, we got enough.

Stormy never put us on our whack,
No pound and pint 'According to the Act'.

For Stormalong was a good old rip,
As good as ever sailed a ship.

The Bosun's Locker Stan Hugill

The version given of *Heave Away my Johnnies*, called here *Heave Away, Lads*, is a 'Tapscot' one with a difference.

> Then heave away, my bully boys, the wind is blowing fair,
> *Chorus:* Heave away, my bullies, heave away, lads
> Our ship will soon be rolling home to merry England's shores.
> *Chorus:* Heave away, my bully boys, we are all bound to go.
>
> Then break her out and square away, we are all bound to go
> Our course lies through those latitudes where the stormy winds do blow.
>
> When I was young and in my prime I sailed in the Black Ball Line,
> They were the finest ships e'er seen upon the ocean brine.
>
> One morning Bridget Donahue came down to the dock to see,
> Old Tapscot 'bout a steerage berth and presently said she.
>
> 'Good morning, Mr Tapscot, sir,' 'Good morning, ma'am,' says he,
> 'And have you got a packet ship to carry me over the sea?'
>
> 'Oh, yes I've got a packet ship to carry you over the sea,'
> 'And please ye, Mr Tapscot, sir, what may the fare then be?'
>
> 'It may be fifty pounds,' says he, 'and it may be sixty, too,'
> 'But eight pound ten we'll call enough, my pretty dear, for you.'
>
> 'And here's the money, sir,' says she, 'Step right aboard,' says he,
> 'The tide is up, the wind is fair, and soon we'll tow to sea.'

The verses of *The 'Dreadnought'* are much the same as usual, but the one about the Banks is different:

> It's now we're sailing' cross the Banks of Newfoundland,
> Where the lead shows sixty fathoms and bottom of sand,
> With icebergs all around and northwesters do blow,
> Bound away in the *'Dreadnought'* to the west'ard we'll go.

Its chorus is a repeat of the last two lines of each verse. In the case of *Tom's Gone To Ilo* the theme is most unusual:

Tom Is Gone To Ilo Set to the tune sung by The Spinners

Tom is gone and I'll go, too, Ch. A——way
I——lo   O Tom is gone and so may you,
Ch. Tom is gone to I——lo

For times are hard and wages low,
It's time for you an' me to go.

When I was young I served my time,
On board the coasting brig *'Sublime'*.

I had but sailed a voyage or two,

Haul Away, Joe, *Haul on the Bowline*, *Johnny Bowker* and *Ranzo* are much the same as expected with an occasional different line here and there, but *Boney* has a few new stanzas. After 'Moscow was a-burning' it runs:

There he lost a bunch of roses,
A bonny bunch of roses.

'Twas a token of disaster,
Bold Wellington was his master.

He tried to conquer all Europe,
But he couldn't conquer Old England.

The old favourite halyard song *Whiskey Johnny* also has a few verses not found elsewhere:-

Hard is our life and short is our day,
So I'll drink whiskey while I may.

It drove my sister on the street,
And sent my brother to the jail.

And whiskey made me leave my home,
In foreign countries for to roam.

For whiskey is what brought me here,
It surely is the devil's cheer.

And *Blow, Boys, Blow* has some 'new' uns:

And who d' ye think was the captain of her?
Why Bucko Brown, that damned old driver.

And what d' ye think they had for breakfast?
A chunk of salthorse and devilled lobscouse.

And who d' ye think was the chief mate of her?
'Twas Lily White the big Georgia nigger.

And as we passed by her to leeward,
Our skipper hailed that nigger chief mate.

'And how's things 'way down in Georgia?'
'Why, red-hot, sah, an' still a-heating.'

El Tuerto's *Shenandoah* has the normal 'river' verses, interpolated with stanzas more nautical in theme. *Goodbye Fare-ye-well* uses the 'Get up Jack, let John sit down' story, but his *Ten Thousand Miles Away* does not differ from the usual pattern. The only other 'shanty' he gives is *Dixie's Isle*. I've always doubted the yarn that this Civil War song was used as a capstan or windlass shanty. Harlow is the only other collector to give it. He writes, in his *'Chanteying Aboard American Ships'*, that a friend of his who made a voyage round the Horn in the American ship *'Young America'* declared that it was a very popular song aboard this ship when heaving at the capstan. But now that I have found it to be included in a regular sailor collection of 1909 I have to admit that it *was* a shipboard work song. I give it here in full.

Before I wind up this article I must say that El Tuerto does refer to timber shanties. He writes: 'As, however, they originated with, and were mostly sung by longshore timber stowers, I have not deemed it advisable to include them in the present collection. The most popular of the timber shanties were *Miss Rosa Lee*, *Somebody Told Me So*, and *Yankee John, Storm Along*. They are still sung by Negro timber stowers in the seaports of the south.' This would be in the early 1900s. With the exception of *Yankee John, Storm Along*, these shanties have, unfortunately, been lost to us.

The Bosun's Locker Stan Hugill

Dixie's Isle (capstan)

Oh, then Susie, lovely Susie —, I can no longer stay. For the bugle sounds the warning that calls me far away. It calls me down to New Orleans, the enemy for to rile, And to fight the Southern soldiers' way down on Dixie's Isle.

(The last line of each verse constitutes the chorus).

The owners they gave orders no women were to come,
The captain likewise ordered that none of them should come;
For their waists are much too slender and their figures not the style,
For to fight the Southern soldiers' way down on Dixie's Isle.

Oh, my curse attend those cruel wars and when first the began,
The robbed New York and Boston of many a noble young man;
They robbed us of our sweethearts, our wives and brothers while
We went fighting the Southern soldiers' way down on Dixie's Isle.

'To fight the Southern soldiers' way down on Dixie's Isle'

210

Vol. 9 No. 3
Fag ends

Long before the term 'fag-end' came to denote the remains of a Woodbine stuck to the lower lip of a joanna-player, it was used at sea to denote the very end of a piece of cordage; and the 'tying-up of fag-ends' indicated that after the ship had come through a hard blow, the watch was engaged in coiling up, on the belayin'-pins, the ends of buntlines, clew lines, braces and so on that had been swishing around the decks or were entangled in the bars of the wash-ports. This tying up of fag-ends (apropos shanties, their variants and origins) has been, in several previous 'SPIN's, to me a pleasant self-appointed task, and, without any apology to my readers, I am still at it.

One class of shanty-maker and singer I've overlooked in my works is the Sea Island Negro of the islands off the coast of Georgia, U.S.A. An odd song here and an odd reference there will be found in several American folk journals, but a full treatise on these happy watermen and their songs is apparently still lacking, although the Lomaxes, I believe, have recorded in this field. These people, being watermen and stevedores as well as fishermen, spent most of their lives either on or near the water, and work songs were naturally a part of their background. In regard to their versions of deepwater shanties, a lively variant of *Santiana*, with full chorus, has reached the folk song scene. Another is a variant of *Round the Bay of Mexico*, although one which more likely originated in the Gulf ports, and it's sung by, among others, Louis Killen, on disc. *Hanging Johnny* is another work song they are known to have used, but I suppose the most popular ditty produced in these islands is the now well-known, in fact world-famous, *Michael Row the Boat Ashore*, which originally was one of their boat-songs. Pete Seeger suggests that Michael (as well as being an Archangel) may have been the name of a local boatman. It was a rowing-song. Another of their work songs, which a few years ago reached the 'pop' stage, is *Pay Me the Money Down.* It is still used as a work song by coloured stevedores. Seeger seems to think that it is a remake of *Blow the Man Down*, but both Laura Smith and I have versions of a much older date, the theme of the song having been around since the 1880s and even earlier. White sailors sang:

> I wish I wuz Old Stormy's son,
> *Chorus:* Pay me the money down,
> I'd build a ship of a thousand tons,
> *Chorus:* Pay me the money down.

The Sea Island boatman sang:

> I wish I was Mr Howard's son,
> *Chorus:* Pay me the money down!
> Sit in the house and drink me rum,
> *Chorus:* Pay me the money down.

Negro shanties, as Whall writes 'were countless', and many hundreds must have been lost to us. L.G. Carr Laughton (*'The Mariner's Mirror'*, 1923) writes that, in the 1830s the loading of cotton on to the ships (in the Southern States) gave seamen many opportunities to listen to slave songs, the result being that white sailors picked up Negro work songs and took them to sea as shanties. From the West Indies (and in particular Barbados) many Negro work songs came, and were soon fitted to the hauling and heaving aboard the white man's

The Bosun's Locker Stan Hugill

deepwater ships. Harlow (*'Chanteying Aboard American Ships'*) gives three hauling songs from Barbados: *Lindy Lowe*, *John Crow* and *Sun Down*. He also gives a Barbadian version of *Shallow Brown* with unusual verses:

> Oh, Shallow Brown's a darkey,
> *Chorus:* Shallow, Shallow Brown
> She's neither slim nor stocky,
> *Chorus:* Shallow, Shallow Brown.
>
> Oh, Shallow Brown of New York,
> Her feet and legs just like a stork.
>
> Oh, Shallow Brown of Baltimoah,
> She's best li'l dancer on the floor.
>
> Oh, Shallow Brown of Washington,
> She's got us niggers on the run.
>
> Oh, Shallow Brown of Mobile Bay,
> She's picking cotton all de day.
>
> Oh, Shallow Brown of New Orleans,
> She's the blackest gal ob all de queens.
>
> Oh, Shallow Brown of Phila-ma-delf,
> She jumped in de ribba an' drown herself.

In the small volume *'Shanties'* by Marston and Allen there is a very rare and interesting shanty, which was sung to George Marston by Mr Hopkins, master mariner, who in turn had heard it performed by a Negro crew in his early days at sea.

> What did de blackbird say to the crow?
> Mahund how you sthwing yo' tail:
> If yo' don' get sunshine yo' sure to get snow,
> Mahund how yo' sthwing yo' tail
> Hilo below, hilo below,
> Mahund how yo' sthwing yo' tail,
> Mahund how yo' sthwing yo' tail.

But, although we have a few such work songs still with us, the greater portion has been lost. In many cases we have the titles only for both lost white and Negro shanties.

Several I have listed in my books but now I will endeavour to give a full list of these shanties which have disappeared – perhaps for ever.

From Dana's *'Two Years Before the Mast'* (1830s): *Jack Crosstree, Heave to the Girls Nancy O, Captain's Gone Ashore, Hurrah, Hurrah. My Hearty Fellows, Neptune's Raging Fury, Heave Round Hearty*

From Olmstead's *'Incidents of a Whaling Voyage'* (1839-40): *Oh, Hurrah. my Hearties O!*

From Haley N. Cole's *'Whale Hunt'* (1849-53): *High, Randy O!, Off She Goes, Off She Must Go!, Jigger in the Bumboat, Sally in our Alley*

From *'Coast Seaman's Journals'* San Francisco (1909): *Miss Rosa Lee, Somebody Told Me So*

From my own Shipmates: *My Aunt Sal is the Devil's Own Joker, Half a Fathom of Ribbon Over His Left Eye*

Of shanties of which we have the words only and no music the following come to mind:

From R. Hay's *'Landsman Hay'* (1811):
> Two sisters courted one man,
> *Chorus:* Oh, huro, my boys
> And they lived in the mountains
> *Chorus:* Oh, huro, boys. O!

and
> Grog time of day, boys,
> Grog time of day.
> *Chorus:* Huro, my jolly boys.
> Grog time of day.

212

From *'The Quid'* (1832):
> Oh, her love is a sailor,
> His name is Jemmy Taylor,
> He's gone in a whaler
> To the Greenland Sea.

and
> Oh, if I had her,
> Eh then if I had her,
> Oh, how I would love her
> Black though she be.

From Nordhoff's *'Nine Years a Sailor'* (1857):

> Oh, we work for a Yankee Dollar,
> *Chorus:* Hurrah, see-man-do
> Yankee dollar, bully dollar,
> *Chorus:* Hurrah, see-man-dollar.

and
> Lift him up and carry him along,
> *Chorus:* Fire, maringo, fire away
> Put him down where he belongs,
> *Chorus:* Fire maringo, fire away.

There is also, from the *'Journal of American Folklore'*, *Hi, Pretty Yaller Gal, Kickin' up Behind*, and *Ol' Joe,* the one verse of which I gave two issues ago.

This about completes the list, although one never knows when a rare item might crop up as the result of some voracious reader uncovering a hidden gem in the pages of some ancient tome.

Trying to find definite proof of shanties and shantying in the eighteenth century has been the aim of collectors and writers throughout the twentieth century; I'm afraid with very little result. However, thanks to my keen pen friend Dr John Lyman, I am able to offer a clue from that period but not in connection with Western seamen. I have at times remarked on Anglo-Indian shanties which were sung by Lascar crews aboard 'Jimmy' Nourse's fleet of sailing ships engaged in the 'triangular trade', i.e. out to India with 'general', to the West Indies and the Guianas with indentured coolies and then homeward with rum and sugar. Unfortunately we have none of such shanties today with the exception of one I collected some years ago:

> Ke, ke, ke, ke – Ekidumah!
> Ke, ke, ke, ke, Ekidumah!
> Somerset a-killa coolie man – Ekidumah!
> Somerset a-killa bosun's mate –
> Ekidumah!
> Somerset a-killa wire-fall – Ekidumah!
> Ke, ke, ke, ke – Ekidumah!

'Ekidumah' by the way, is a corruption of the Hindustani 'Ek dom' (one man).

There must have been hundreds of these shanties sung in a mixture of Hindustani and English and used, when hoisting tops'ls and weighing anchors, by the Lascar crews of ships in the Far Eastern trade. They might even have been sung, it is thought, in the great bluff-bowed, cargo-cum-passenger carrying ships of the old East India Company. However, until now, we have had no concrete evidence of such. Recently Dr John Lyman sent me a letter in which he tells me that on reading through a book called *'Hobson-Jobson'* (a Victorian compilation of Hindustani and other Asiatic words used in English) he came across a quotation from a book called *'Voyage to New Guinea'*, written in 1775, by a certain Mr Forrest, the ship obviously being an East 1ndiaman. The quotation reads: 'The Moors in what is called country ships in East India also have their cheering songs, at work in hoisting, or in their boats a rowing.'

'Country ships' (and probably this is the earliest literary reference to the term) were sailing ships built locally in India and Burma, owned mainly by natives, but at times by white men, and manned by both races, engaged in the coasting trades around Ceylon, Burma and Indian Ocean islands. The fact that such seamen called their shanties 'cheering songs' shows that English terms were heard aboard these ships. This must be the only reference we have to the actual use of shanties in the eighteenth century.

Of course, there are literary references to 'Moors' or rather Arabs, using shanties in more modern books. Alan Villiers, who voyaged in a Kuwaiti lateen-rigged *boom* the *'Triumph of Righteousness'*, in the 1930s, makes mention in his book *'Sons of Sinbad'*, of the brown-skinned children of Mahomet using heaving and hauling songs when setting sail and weighing anchor. He gives English translations of two such songs, the solos of which in true Moslem fashion, are well sandwiched with invocations to Allah for to help the True Believers fill their arduous chores.

Recently I came across an item, which may be of interest to folk dancers, in that ponderous tome, *'The Principal Navigations, Voyages, Traffiques and Discoveries of the English Nation'* by Richard Hakluyt (1598-1600). It is in the section devoted to the voyages of Sir Humphrey Gilbert. He had been given a small fleet of five ships to start colonising any area of the New World between Florida and Newf'n'land. Reference is made to agricultural workers and tradesmen taken aboard to start the colony. Also, for the 'solace of our people and the allurement of the savages he shipped aboard music in good variety; not omitting the least toys, as morris dancers, hobby horses and May-like conceits to delight the savage people, whom we intended to win by all fair means possible.' This was in the year of Our Lord 1583.

In the penultimate issue of *'SPIN'* I put forward a plea for the singing of more *Johnny Come Down to Hilo* type of shanty in the clubs, forgetting for a while the overworked *Blood Red Roses* and so on. Carrying on with this theme, I must point out the fact that many of the shanty forms of forebitters are also left to lie mouldering in the pages of the shanty books. Perhaps to some, the tunes of the shanty forms are not as dramatic or as interesting as those of the opposite numbers – the forebitters, but the choruses being shanties – are longer and usually more powerful.

When I first entered the 'club-singing' game I did sing such shanties, but finding the going tough and being merely human, I gave up singing the shanty forms and got in on the most popular forebitter versions. Examples I am thinking of, for instance, are *The Liverpool Packet*, *Go to Sea Once More* and *The Liverpool Judies*, all of which are to be found in both their forebitter and shanty forms in my *'Shanties from the Seven Seas'*. Other examples, too, will be found there, such as *Rolling Home* and *The Banks of Newf'n'land*. So, in order at least to clarify one example I will give *'SPIN'* readers the shanty version of *The Liverpool Packet*, which, incidentally, has other tunes, too (see Caedmon Records for an unusual Cornish version). It will be noted that the shanty version does not refer to the *'Dreadnought'* by name as is done in the forebitter.

The Liverpool Packet

At the Liverpool docks at the break o' the day, I saw a flash packet bound westard a-way, She was bound to the west'ard, where the wild waters flow, She's a Liverpool packet, oh, Lord let 'er go! Bound away-ay! Bound away-ay! Thro' the ice, sleet an' snow, She's a Liverpool packet, oh, Lord let her go!

The time of her sailing is now drawing nigh,
Stand by all ye lubbers we wish you goodbye;
A pair of clean heels to ye now we will show,
She's a Liverpool packet - Oh, Lord let her go!

Full Chorus
Bound away-ay! Bound away-ay!
Through the ice, sleet and snow,
She's a Liverpool packet - Oh, Lord let her go!

An' now we are leaving the sweet Salthouse dock,
The boys and the gals on the Pierhead do flock;
The boys and the gals are all shouting hurro
She's a Liverpool packet - Oh, Lord let her go!

Now the packet's a-lying in the River Mersey,
Awaiting the tugboat to tow her to sea;
Around the Rock Light where the salt tides do flow, She's a Liverpool packet - Oh, Lord let her go !

Sheet home yer big tops'ls - haul aft yer jibsheets,
Sheet home fore 'n aft boys, ye'll get no darn sleep;
Come aft, now, God darn yers, come aft, make a show,
She's a Liverpool packet - Oh, Lord let her go!

An' now we are sailing down the wild Irish Sea,
Our passengers are merry an' their hearts full o' glee;
Our sailors like tigers walk the decks to an' fro,
She's a Liverpool packet - Oh, Lord let her go!

An' now we are sailing the Atlantic so wide,
An' the hands are now ordered to scrub the ship's side;
Them holystones, boyos, the bosun do roar,
She's a Liverpool packet - Oh, Lord let her go!

An' now we are sailing the Banks o' Newf'n'land,
Where the bottom's all fishes and fine yeller sand;
An' the fishes they sing as they swim to 'n' fro,
She's a Liverpool packet - Oh, Lord let her go!

An' now we are sailing down the Long, Island shore,
Where the pilot's awaiting us as, he's waited before;
Then square away yer mainyard an' away we will go,
She's a Liverpool packet - Oh, Lord let her go!

An' now we've arrived in old New York town,
We're bound for the Bowery, oh, let sorrow drown;
With our gal and our beer boys, we'll let the song flow,
She's a Liverpool packet - Oh, Lord let her go!

The Bosun's Locker   Stan Hugill

Vol. 9 No. 4

Having more or less ransacked every book, magazine and journal which touches upon, however lightly, the subject of shanties and sailor songs and given to *'SPIN'* the results of my findings, I was astonished to come across a shanty form I had not previously seen. This find is on page 117 of *'The Clipper Ship Era'* by Captain Arthur H. Clark, and he stated it was to be sung, like *Cheerily Man*, when catting the anchor. Unfortunately no tune is given, but its words are reminiscent of *Blow, Boys Blow*:

> A Yankee sloop came down the river,
> Hah, hah, rolling John,
> Oh, what do you think that sloop had in her?
> Hah, hah, rolling John,
> Monkey's hide and bullock's liver,
> Hah, hah, rolling John.

On two pages earlier the writer gives a good description of setting single tops'ls aboard an outward-bound Californian clipper leaving the port of New York in the 1850s:

> "Sheet home the topsails."
> "Aye, aye, sir."
> "Boatswain, look out for those clewlines at the main; ease down handsomely as the sheets come home."
> "Foretop there, overhaul your buntlines, look lively!"
> "Belay your port maintopsail sheet; clap a watch tackle on the starboard sheet and rouse her home."
> "Maintop there, lay down on the mainyard and light the foot of that sail over the stay." "That's well, belay starboard."
> "Well the mizzentopsail sheets – belay."
> "Now then, my bullies, lead out your topsail halyards fore and aft and masthead her." "Aye, aye, sir."

By this time the mate has put some ginger into the crew and longshoremen, and they walk away with the three topsail halyards.

> Away, way, way, yar,
> We'll kill Paddy Doyle for his boots.

> "Now then, long pulls, my sons."
> "Here you chantyman, haul off your boots, jump on that maindeck capstan and strike a light – the best in your locker."
> "Aye, aye, sir."

And the three topsail yards go aloft with a rousing chanty that can be heard up in Beaver Street:

> Then up aloft that yard must go,
> Whiskey for my Johnny.

Ships with big crews rarely bothered with hauling songs; there being enough hands to stamp the sails up. Hence very little is heard about shanty-singing at tops'1setting and so on in the tea clippers with their big crews; in some cases, when racing they carried double

Were shanties ever sung aboard whalers?

This is a question, which has often been asked but has rarely been answered in any way conclusively.

The Bosun's Locker Stan Hugill

Stripping Ivory. (After a Sketch by R.E. Weir of the Whaling Barque 'Clara Bell' (1850s).

crews. Also, in sailing men-o'-war (another type of ship with a large crowd) there was no shantying, although in this case it was thought that shantying was bad for discipline and was likely to prevent the men hearing the commands of the officer in charge. This rather poor argument was also put forward in the Finn ships of the nineteen thirties, although these did have skeleton crews and, therefore, one would have thought, needed shantying.

However, although ships with big crews didn't need, or rarely used, hauling songs, when heaving up the anchor, songs for windlass and capstan were often sung even in ships with plenty of hands. And this was also the case with pumping songs. Whalers, of course, had large crews – officers, harpooners, flensers, coppers, carpenters, boat-steerers, seamen and boys – and therefore, in all probability, could have done without songs for hoisting sails and so on. But did they?

In regard to shanties sung aboard whalers, *Rueben Ranzo* is often cited as a whaler's shanty but although it is about a Latin green-horn joining a whaleship there is no *proof* that it was ever sung aboard such vessels.

When the writer first went to sea, believe it or not, there was the Moby Dick type of sailing whaler still in existence, hunting the seas for sperm and fighting a losing battle with the steam whaler. Actually, in the early 1920s, there were a dozen or so of the old-fashioned sort under sail employing the time-honoured boat and hand-harpoon methods. The last American sail whaler, the *'Wanderer'*, was lost on the island of Cuttyhunk, near New Bedford, in a gale in the month of August 1924. However, although the writer has been shipmates with men who had sailed in sailing whalers, he cannot remember any of them mentioning that a certain shanty was sung aboard a certain blubber-hunter in which they had shipped. So, orally, information, as far as the writer is concerned, is nil.

Turning to literature I find that a certain Francis Allyn Olmstead published a book in 1841 (New York) called *'Incidents of a Whaling Voyage'* (1839-40); (Scenery, Manners and Customs and Missionary Stations of the Sandwich and Society Islands.) The whaler concerned was called the *'New America'* and on page 115 there are a few paragraphs referring to shantying aboard this ship.

217

The Bosun's Locker Stan Hugill

The shantyman, whom Olmstead calls a 'choirister', is a certain Mr Freeman, who 'with many demisemiquavers strikes up the song, while all the rest join in the chorus.' He even gives, with music (probably, I believe, the first time any shanty with its music was ever put in print) two shanties: *Drunken Sailor* and *Nancy Fanana*. Here is a version of *Nancy Fanana* from my collection:

[musical notation: Nancy Fernaner she married a barber, Haul 'er a-way, oh, haul 'er a-way! Hoo raw, hooraw for Nancy Fernaner; Haul 'er a-way, oh, haul 'er a-way!]

He also mentions another shanty used for pulling out the lower jawbone with its teeth from the mouth of a sperm whale by means of a watch-tackle. He calls this song *Oh, Hurrah, My Hearties O!*

Carrying on with our search in literature I find, on page 116 of Keble Chatterton's *'Whalers and Whaling* (1925), the following:

> There is no question that the whalers had their own chanties, just like the other Merchant Sailormen. There were, for instance: *The Boston Come-All-Ye, There She Blows, Blow Ye Winds, Coast of Peru, Rolling Down to Old Maui* and *A Dead Whale and a Stove Boat*.

However, Chatterton was wrong in thinking *all* these to be shanties. The first item (a version of *South Australia*) and *Blow Ye Winds* (normally a forebitter but used at times at the capstan) can come into the shanty category, but not the others. *There She Blows* and *Coast of Peru* never were work songs; as for *Old Maui*, I will refer to this later. In regard to *A Dead Whale or a Stove Boat* I doubt if this was ever a shanty or even a forebitter. In fact it was a well-known whaleman's motto.

Chatterton quotes a little of Melville's *'Moby Dick'* to substantiate his theory that this was the title of a shanty or rowing song – something, clearly, Melville never intended his readers to read into the passage. Here is the quote:

> "What do ye when ye see a whale, men?"
> "Sing out for him" was the impulsive rejoinder from a score of clubbed voices.
>
> "Good!" cried Ahab, with a wild approval in his tones. . .
> "And what do ye next, men?"
> "Lower away, and after him."
> "And what tune is it ye pull to, men?"
> "A dead whale or a stove boat."

Later in the book Chatterton gives a couple of unusual stanzas from what is usually called in the folk clubs *The Greenland Whale*, but there are no 'brave boy' repeats. And he also, wrongly, calls it 'an old whaling chantey'.

> 'Tis well nigh sixty years ago
> On March the twentieth day,
> When we set sail from Yarmouth Roads,
> And bore due North away.
>
> Singing "aye, lads, give way lads"
> We're bound to the north countree,
> Where icebergs grow and whales do blow,
> And sunsets you never see.

He says it was used heaving at the capstan (windlass I should think) aboard Northern whalers when heaving up the 'blanket-piece' or long strip of blubber cut from the carcass of the whale alongside by means of cutting spades and flensing knives.

In *'Moby Dick'* there is a snatch of another interesting whaler's forebitter, one claimed more or less nowadays as the property of the old Scottish whalemen. In the clubs it is called The Bonnie Ship the *'Diamond'*. The Scottish version is thought to have been made a season or so before the *'Diamond'*, along with the whole whaling fleet, became embayed in ice in Melville Bay in the year 1830. (See notes by A.L. Lloyd on the cover of the Topic record *'Leviathan!'*).

The *'Diamond'*'s maiden voyage was made in 1825, so the song, in which no mention is made of this disaster, must date from about 1827. Melville sailed from New Bedford in his whaler the *'Acushnet'* (later to become the *'Pequod'*) in January 1841. He published his *'Moby Dick'* in 1851. He probably heard the song sung in the early 1840s. If it was 'invented' by a Scottish whaleman, it certainly moved fairly smartly (for those days) across the watery world, for the version given in *'Moby Dick'* is definitely a Yankee one, with no mention of the *'Diamond'* and with none of the Scottish accent heard in our folk clubs.

> Our captain stood upon the deck
> A spyglass in his hand,
> A viewing of those gallant whales
> That blow at every strand (span?)
> Oh, your tubs in your boats, my boys,
> And by your braces stand,
> And we'll have one of those fine whales,
> Hand, boys, over hand!
>
> So be cheery, my lads! May your hearts never fail!
> While the bold harpooneer is striking the whale!

The chorus of this American whaler's song is also given in a fine novel about Nantucket whalemen called *'The Manatee'* by Nancy Bruff.

In a previous issue of *'SPIN'* I mentioned that I had found the titles only of a few shanties now lost forever in an interesting book, the actual MS of a New Bedford whaleman of the 1850s, called *'Whale Hunt'*. The writer's name is Nelson Cole Haley and the Marine Historical Association of America is carrying out research into official documents and contemporary maritime reports and has established that his description of the 1849 voyage of the whaler *'Charles W. Morgan'* closely conforms to the actual facts. This book is probably the *only* book in which the singing of shanties aboard whalers is confirmed. But, here again, the jobs at which they were used were: (a) heaving up the anchor by means of the old-fashioned jiggity-jig windlass and (b) stripping off the blanket-pieces by means of the same windlass. At no other chore such as the setting of sail, were they apparently used. And the shanties he mentions, I don't think, with the exception of *Mobile Bay* (that is if it is the well-known one), were ever used in sailing merchantmen. Here they are: *High Randy O (or High, Randy, Dandy)*, *Oh, Off She Goes*, *Off She Must Go*, *Jigger in the Bumboat* (or words to that effect), and *Sally in our Alley* (not, do I think the Gracie Fields effort)

The only other reference to whalemen singing songs at work is to be found in Admiral W.H. Smyth's *'Sailor's Word-Book'* (1867). Here, under SONG, it reads: 'The whalers have an improvised song when cutting docks in the ice in Arctic Seas.'

Now let me give a little background to our present issue's song *Rolling Down to Old Maui*, a Yankee whaler's forebitter, which may have been used as a work song in some ships.

Maui, or as the oldtimers wrote it Mowee, is the Hawaiian island that was the

The Bosun's Locker Stan Hugill

Hoisting the Blanket-piece

headquarters of the Yankee whalemen who sailed to the Bering Straits, the Sea of Okhotsk and the Kamchatka Sea in search of Right and Bowhead whales. This was in the 1820s and 30s. The main port was Lahaina; in those days it was, in fact, the capital of the Sandwich Islands (as the Hawaiian Islands were then named). The King (Kamehameha) had the only brick building; all the other buildings were either grass huts or clinker-built wooden shacks. Grog-shops were set up here early by beachcombing whalemen and the native girls or 'wahines' were 'Oh So willing'. The sex-starved, booze-starved whalemen returning from the icy whaling grounds to the North, thought of the lovely bay of Lahaina as 'home'. Gangs of native girls – the Ship Girls – would swim out naked to the anchored blubber-butchers (there was a 'tapu' against women using canoes) and climbing up the bobstays and chain-plates would invade every ship in the harbour. Scenes of riotousness and licentiousness were to be seen both on board the ships in the bay, along the coconut groves either side the one and only street and in the sailor grog-shops along the beach. To quote from my book *'Sailortown'*: 'By the twenties many of the girls who swam out to the ships and danced the hula naked in the groggeries had acquired the sailor pox.' By 1846 as many as 395 whalers lay in the Lahaina roadstead.

The following fine song is probably the work of some Bowhead whaleman who had experienced the rigours of the Kamchatka Sea and warmth of the Ship Girls' welcome.

The Bosun's Locker Stan Hugill

Rolling Down To Old Maui

'Tis a damn tough life of toil and strife We whale-men un—der-go We don't give a damn when the gale is done How hard the winds do blow. We're homeward bound 'tis a damn fine sound, With a good ship taut and free We don't give a damn when we drink our rum With the girls of old Mau——ee.

CHORUS: Roll—ing down to old Mau——ee, me boys, Rolling down to old Mau——ee-ee. We're homeward bound from the Arc–tic ground Rolling down to old Mau-ee.

Once more we sail with a northerly gale through the ice and sleet and rain,
And them coconut fronds in them tropical lands, oh, we soon shall again;
Six hellish months have passed away in the cold Kamchatka Sea,
But now we're bound from the Artic Ground, rolling down to old Maui
Chorus: Rolling etc.

We'll heave the lead where old Diamond Head looms up on old Wahoo,
Our masts and yards are sheathed with ice, an' our decks are hid from view.
The horrid ice of the sea-cut tiles that deck the Artic Sea,
Are miles behind in the icy wind since we steered for old Maui

221

The Bosun's Locker Stan Hugill

How soft the breeze of the tropic seas now the ice is far astern,
And them native maids in them island glades are awaiting our return,
Their big black eyes even now look out, hoping some fine day to see,
Our baggy sails running fore the gales, rolling down to old Maui

And now we sail with a favourable gale towards our island home,
Our mainmastsprung, all whaling done, and we aint got far to roam;

Our stuns'l booms are carried away, what care we for that sound?
A living gale is arter us, thank God we're homeward bound.

And now we're achored in the Bay with the Kanakas all around,
With chants and soft aloha oes they greet us homeward bound;
And now ashore we'll have good fun and paint them beaches red,
Awaking in the arms of an island maid, with a big, fat achin' head.

Index

Advance Note	93	Grand Chorus	13	Pirates	102-104
				Press Gang	95
Barbarossa	102	Harpoon	134	Pumping Shanties	37
Barbary Coast	102	Hawaii, Folk Festival	89		
Barbary Pirates	102	Hawain Songs	89	Ratcliff Highway	142
Blackbeard	108	'Horn Book'	62	Rigging Plan	33
Bloody Forty	64, 181	Hornpipe	178	Ropemaking	42
Bosun's Locker	12	Humour At Sea	128	Rosemary Lane	150
'Brave Boys'	119				
Buccaneers	see Pirates	John Short	29	'Sailortown'	52
Bumboats	170			Sails & Rigging Plan	33
		Kidd, William	104	'Santiana'	16
Capstan	58			Saraband	179
Captain Samuels	64, 181	Lascar Shanties	212	Shanghaiing	92
Coastal Songs	48	Legman, Gershon	62	'Shanties and Sailor's	
Cock o' the Fo'csle	181	'Leviathan'	132	Songs'	140
Coffin Ships	63	'Limejuice Act'	190	Shipboard Music	177
Corsairs	102	Liverpool Place Names	69-71	Skylark	112
Cotton	202-203	Lyman, Dr. John	198	'Songs of the American	
Cotton Droghers	34			Sailormen'	67
Crimps	93	Mainhatch Songs (see Forebitters)		'Songs the Whalemen Sang'	61
Double Entendre	113	Mainwaring, Sir Henry	103	Tiger Bay	143
Downton Pump	37	Maui	219	Timber Shanties	82
Dutch Shanties	87	Merchant Shipping Act	189		
		Moir Collection	192	Wapping	142
'El Tuerto'	205-208			Ward, Captain	103
Enderby's Company	134	Negro Shanties	210	Welsh Shanties	172
		Nipper	58	Western Ocean Packet Law	181
Fag Ends	210			Whalers	147
'Farewell Nancy'	84	Packet Ships	63	Whaling Songs	132
Fiddles	178	'Packet Rats'	63, 117	Windlass	58
Fireship Songs	147-150	'Paint Chippers'	42	Women Sailors	123
Food at Sea	188	'Pidgin English' Songs	73	Wooden Walls	112
Forebitters	22	Pilot Verses	45		

The Bosun's Locker Stan Hugill

Songs

According To the Act	190	The Fancy Frigate	116	Oyster Girl	173
All Hands On Deck	53	The Fireship	154	Paddy Lay Back	80
The *'Balena'*	47	The Fishes	27	The *'Princess Royal'*	66
Blood Red Roses	187	Flash Girls of the Town	149	The Rambling Sailor	169
Blow Ye Winds In the Morning	135	The Flash Packet	162	The Rambling Sailor (2)	171
		'Flying Dutchman'	49	Ratcliffe Highway	56
Blow, Boys, Blow	122	Fourteenth of February	65	Rattled Me Rigging	165
Bold McCartney	182	The Girls Around Cape Horn	25	Rigs of Ratcliffe Highway	156
Bonnie Hieland Laddie-O	35	Go To Sea No More	139	Roll the Cotton Down	203
Bonnie Hieland Laddie-O (*American Version*)	36	The *'Golden Vanitee'*	111	Roll the Woodpile Down	83
		Handsome Cabin Boy	126	Rolling Down to Old Maui	220
Bound for South Australia	72	High Barbaree	106	Rolling Home	32
Can't Ye Dance the Polka	59	Home, Home, Home	153	Scramento	194
Chinee Bumboat Man	76	The Iron Man	88	Sailor's Grave	51
Clear the Track	91	Jack All Alone	174	Sampan Girl	75
Dixie's Isle	209	La Pique	116	Santiana	17
Down Ratcliffe Highway	158	Leave Her, Johnny, Leave Her	19	Shiny-O	200
Down Ratcliffe Highway (2)	163			Strike the Bell	38
Down Wapping	168	Let the Bulgine Run	91	Ten Thousand Miles Away	131
Dundee Whalers	47	Limejuice Ship	190	Tom is Gone to Ilo	207
The *'Ebeneezer'*	141	The Liverpool Packet	214	Wadham's Song	61
Eight bells	41	Lowlands Low	85	Way Down Low	200
		Maggie May	176		
		Married to a Mermai-ed	98		
		Me Have Got a Flowerboat	74		
		Missa Ramgoat	21		
		Nancy Dawson	20		
		Nancy Rhee	200		
		Old Moke Pickin' on a Banjo	180